Investigating psychology 2 – From cognitive to biological

Edited by Rose Capdevila, John Dixon and Gemma Briggs

This publication forms part of the Open University module DE200 Investigating psychology 2. Details of this and other Open University modules can be obtained from the Student Registration and Enquiry Service, The Open University, PO Box 197, Milton Keynes MK7 6BJ, United Kingdom (tel. +44 (0)845 300 60 90; email general-enquiries@open.ac.uk).

Alternatively, you may visit the Open University website at www.open.ac.uk where you can learn more about the wide range of modules and packs offered at all levels by The Open University. To purchase a selection of Open University materials visit www.ouw.co.uk, or contact Open University Worldwide, Walton Hall, Milton Keynes MK7 6AA, United Kingdom for a brochure (tel. +44 (0)1908 858793; fax +44 (0)1908 858787; email ouw-customer-services@open.ac.uk).

The Open University, Walton Hall, Milton Keynes MK7 6AA

First published 2015

Edited, designed and typeset by The Open University.

Printed in the United Kingdom by Page Bros, Norwich

ISBN 978 1 7800 7856 4

1.1

Contents

Chapter 1

Do you see what I see? The fundamentals of visual perception

Simon J. Davies

Contents

1   Introduction

For those with sight, experiencing the world through the sense of vision feels effortless. You wake in the morning, you open your eyes, and the world is present. This is the *perceptual consciousness* of yourself at a point in time as you become aware of your immediate surroundings. Although your visual perception of the world feels effortless, the process of seeing and perceiving is not so straightforward, nor is it necessarily as passive as it subjectively feels.

Here is a simple example. I am walking down a street at dusk with little street light. I scan the way ahead to avoid obstacles and to keep myself on course for home. In the distance I see a shape. As I approach, the shape and its movements feel familiar. It is Rupert, my ancient and adopted cat (Figure 1.1). As I move closer to the object of my perception a sudden gust of wind dissolves Rupert into a scattering of leaves, and I realise that my assumption about the state of the world has been mistaken.

Figure 1.1   Rupert the cat

This simple example highlights several things about the nature of visual perception. First, it must be based on the sensation achieved through the sense of sight, i.e. through seeing. The light structured by the environment that enters your eyes allows you to distinguish and recognise one object from another in most situations. Second, the realisation that Rupert is, in fact, a bunch of leaves leads to the conclusion that perceiving the world is not effortless or faultless. Third, the fact that I moved through the environment to get closer to Rupert and that the environment changed during that process indicates that perception and the environment are in many ways coupled; perception is an interaction between one's actions, one's personal interpretations of what is seen, and the light information as it is structured by the environment.

How perception is understood depends on the theoretical perspective one takes. This chapter explores two approaches. The first considers information from the environment provided by our actions as being most important, known as a bottom-up or data-driven perspective within the field of cognitive psychology. That is, the process of walking down the street changed the nature of the light (the data) reaching my eyes, and therefore transformed my perception. The second view considers that sensory input (photons of light in the case of vision) needs to be interpreted by reference to prior experience and what is expected; this is known as a top-down or conceptually driven perspective. In the example, my familiarity with the shape of Rupert and his habits allowed me to interpret the poor visual input (incorrectly) as a cat, and then subsequently as a scattering of leaves.

Bottom-up processing
Within the field of perception this view emphasises the importance and the role of information in the environment and its influence on our perceptual experience.

Top-down processing
Within the field of perception this view emphasises the importance and the role of internal representations and intentions upon our perceptual experience.

Definitions of visual perception normally reflect the example above. Perception is the process of acquiring knowledge from the environment by extracting the information emitted or reflected from objects or surfaces and making sense of these (Palmer, 1999). That is, *seeing* the world is necessary but not sufficient for perception. Perception requires one to interpret that input in a way that is personally meaningful, and this can include extracting information by exploring the environment through one's actions. *Perceiving* the world is therefore different from *seeing*. This distinction will be raised again in Chapter 3, which focuses on common and surprising failures of perception.

Multi-modal perception
Perceptual experiences that are derived from more than a single sensory modality.

This chapter starts with a biological account of the visual system and the processes and mechanisms of *seeing* because it is important to understand vision in order to understand visual perception. It then explores two theories of visual *perceiving*. Finally, it explores how one's experience changes when more than a single sense is involved. Most of our experiences are of **multi-modal perception** (i.e. derived from more than a single sensory modality), and these combined experiences can either enhance or hinder one's perception of the world. For example, if I had heard a sound as if Rupert was meowing, the additional confirmation of my experience would have made the sudden scattering of leaves much more surprising.

Learning outcomes

On completing this chapter you should:

- have an understanding of the anatomy and function of the visual system
- have an awareness of what visual illusions can tell us about the visual system as well as perception
- have an understanding of key psychological theories and research on visual perception.

---

2   How do you see?

Human vision is usually accepted as the most dominant of our multitude of senses. We can get a feeling for the importance of vision by looking at how much of the brain is dedicated to seeing. The largest sensory area of the brain is the **occipital cortex** at the back of the brain, which projects to many regions of the brain including to areas where connections are made with the other senses (known as association areas). Eyes and seeing also have special value to us as social animals. We can follow someone's gaze to share an event, or we can look at someone's eyes and understand their emotions. So seeing is not only a biological process, it is also a form of social awareness and social engagement. We have a plethora of figures of speech that demonstrate this importance, e.g. 'I can see what you're saying', 'to shed light on to a problem' (i.e. to make it visible), or 'I can see right through you.'

The traditional camera is an excellent analogy for the eye and vision (see Figure 1.2) because they have many similarities. They both invert the external source image on to a two-dimensional surface (the film plate in a camera, and the **retina** in the eye). They both have a variable aperture and a lens to control how the light is focused on to the internal surfaces. And ultimately, they both allow visual information to be indirectly stored for later inspection, as either a photograph or a memory.

Occipital cortex
The most posterior part of the brain whose role is to process visual information received from the retina. Information is analysed in terms of several features (e.g. colour, motion, orientation, etc.). Information is then relayed to higher centres via the dorsal and ventral streams.

Retina
The light-sensitive layer of cells at the back of the eye. Photoreceptors here convert light into neural responses to be passed to the brain via the optic nerve.

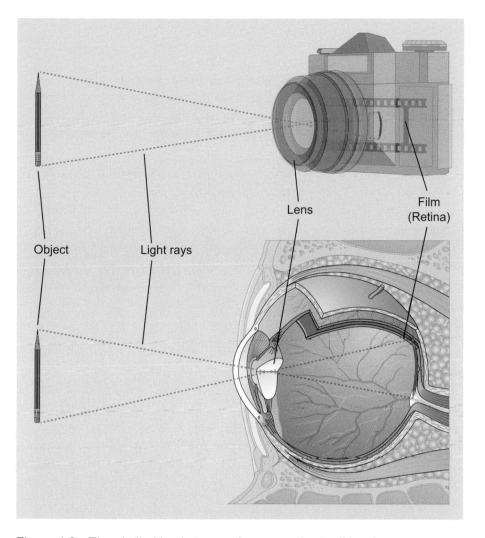

Figure 1.2 The similarities between the eye and a traditional camera

There are, however, some fundamental differences between the eye and a camera. The first is that we, as agents, can choose to direct our eyes to explore relevant features of the environment. The second is that we can extract meaning and experience from what we see; seeing is a way of knowing. The perceptual experience we have from what we see is also, in some circumstances, different from what we see (and therefore different from a camera), as it can change. A good example is the after-image we experience when we look at a bright light and then look away. Our perception is of a lingering dark patch, but this is not reflected in what the eye is currently seeing.

Pause for thought

Look at Figure 1.3 and think about how the experience you have of the inner circle's orientation is actually different from its true orientation (the central bars are actually vertical). Does the fact that you know that the inner bars are vertical change your perception?

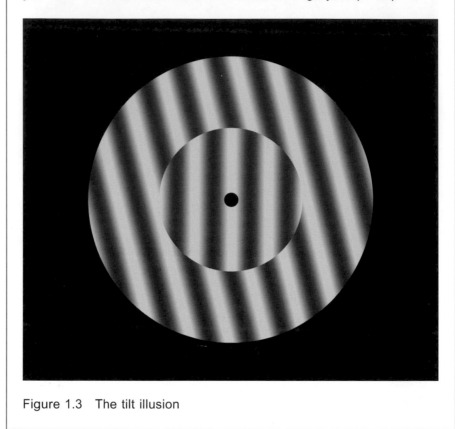

Figure 1.3   The tilt illusion

2.1   The eye

The main integrity and shape of the eye is created by the sclera: the white of the eye (see Figure 1.4). This thin and opaque globe is also continuous with the transparent cornea at the front of the eye, allowing light to pass into the eye. Below the cornea is the lens and the distinctive ring of colour of the iris that acts as a means of altering the amount of light entering the eye by constricting and changing its size and therefore the size of the pupil. The pupil is transparent but it appears black because most of the light entering the eye is absorbed and doesn't reflect back. (Camera flashes will occasionally show a 'red eye' effect when those photographed look directly at the camera in dim light conditions when the pupil is fully open.) All humans have a white sclera and a coloured iris, and this helps us to follow the gaze of another person. However, most animals do not have this ability because their sclera and iris are similarly coloured.

Focusing power
The ability of the cornea and lens of the eye to either diverge or converge incoming light to focus it on the retina.

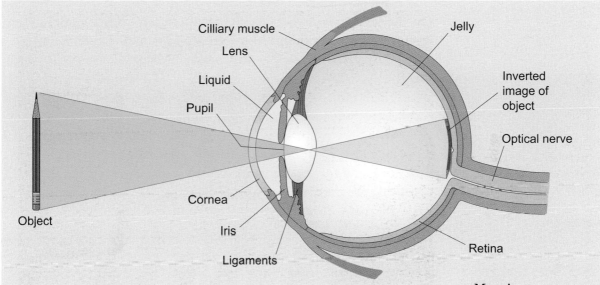

Figure 1.4   Cross-section of the human eye

Light is focused into the eye by the cornea and the lens. The main **focusing power** of the eye (about two-thirds) is from the cornea, but this spherical structure is immobile, so its focusing power is fixed. The lens, however, is a mobile structure that can alter its thickness, and therefore can alter the overall focusing power to bring objects at different distances into focus. There are frequently problems with the ability of the cornea and lens to refract light with the correct amount of power to give us focused vision. When there is too much focusing power, the image is formed in front of the retina, and this means that one has a condition called **myopia**, or short-sightedness (i.e. you can see objects very near to you in sharp focus). The opposite of this is where there is too little focusing power, and the image is formed behind the retina, in which case one has **hyperopia**, and therefore long-sightedness. You can, of course, have both of these conditions at the same time, in which case you are classed as having

Myopia
Or short-sightedness, where the image viewed is focused in front of the retina (rather than on it), meaning that you can see objects in the near distance, but not those far away.

Hyperopia
Or long-sightedness, where the image viewed is focused behind the retina (rather than on it), meaning that you can see objects in the far distance, but not those near to you.

Presbyopia
A condition that normally occurs with age where the lens stiffens, losing its elasticity, changing its focusing power and making near objects difficult to bring into focus.

Fixation
Brief or sustained pause in eye movements, normally to scrutinise an object or event and bring it into focus.

Saccade
A short and rapid eye movement which shifts one's fixation from one visual location to another.

Sensory adaptation
The process by which a neuron stops signalling a constant input when that input stops changing.

Troxler effect
A visual illusion where an unchanging stimulus that is stable on the retina fades from perceptual experience. The effect is largely thought to be due to the fact the most sensory neurons adapt to an unchanging

presbyopia. This occurs when the lens loses its facility to change shape and focus on near objects correctly, which usually comes with age.

Seeing obviously involves us moving our eyes, and this is achieved by a set of four muscles attached to the sclera. Our eyes can make movements that are parallel to one another (known as conjugate movements), or they can converge (known as vergence movements). When focusing on an object the eyes will converge when the object is closer. The most common form of eye movement is a brief ballistic change of **fixation** known as a **saccade**, and most of what is covered during the eye movement is not available for conscious awareness; that is, we are blind to information during an eye movement. Our eyes also move constantly between major eye movements, and these are thought to prevent the eye adapting to its visual input. **Sensory adaptation** is a process by which a sensory cell will stop responding if the stimulus doesn't change. In touch we aren't aware of our clothes once they are on, and with vision, if our eyes stop moving for long enough, the visual world fades (for an example, try Activity 1.1).

Activity 1.1: A disappearing ring

Look at the fixation point in the centre of the ring from reasonably close to the page (Figure 1.5). Avoid all eye and head movements or blinks. In a few seconds the experience you should have is of the ring disappearing. This is known as the **Troxler effect**.

Figure 1.5   A disappearing ring

2.2   The retina and the blind spot

At the back of the eye is a complex structure called the retina. This supports nerve cells that are sensitive to light, known as **photoreceptors**. These cells respond to light in different ways, giving rise to our ability to see colour and also to see under different levels of illumination (see Figure 1.6).

stimulus and cease sending a signal, known as sensory adaptation.

Photoreceptors
A class of sensory neuron that responds (i.e. is sensitive) to light. In the eye there are cone (colour-sensitive) and rod (contrast-sensitive) photoreceptive cells.

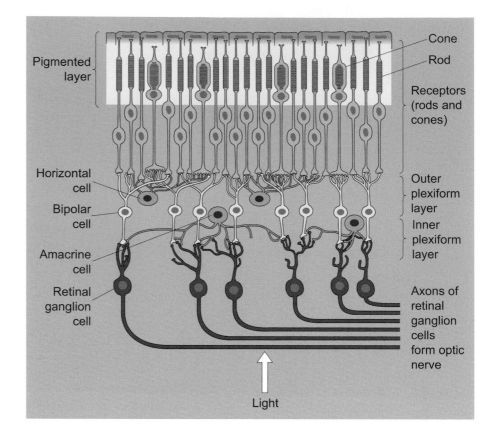

Figure 1.6   Cross-section of the retina

Light itself is confusingly understood to be both a photon (a packet of light) and a wave (an electromagnetic wave). When we talk about cells being light sensitive, we normally do so by saying that they are more sensitive to one specific wavelength than another. Human vision is sensitive to a range of wavelengths (see Figure 1.7(a)) between approximately 380–780 nm (a nanometre is one billionth of a metre). However, we can also talk about light-sensitive cells needing an amount of photons to stimulate the cell sufficiently to transmit a signal to the nervous system. Both of these are important to understand the different functions of different types of photoreceptors.

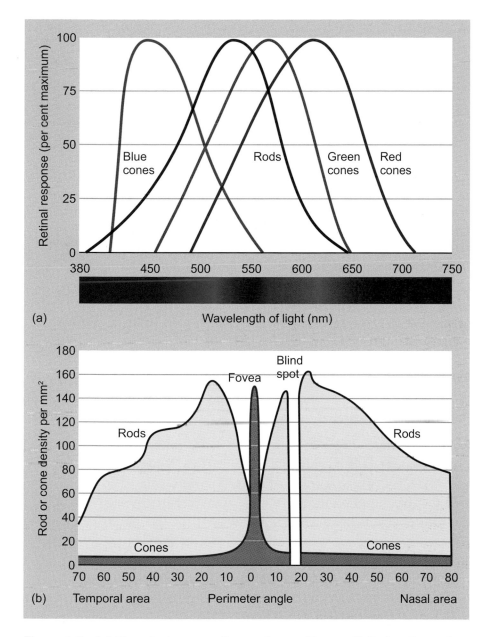

Figure 1.7 (a) The electromagnetic spectrum with sensitivity functions of cones and rods; (b) Distribution of rods and cones across the retina

The photoreceptive cells can be classified into two types, called **rods** and **cones** (named because of their distinctive shapes), and these are distributed across the retina in very different ways (see Figure 1.7(b)). Rods are by far the most abundant photoreceptive cell on the retina, numbering about 120 million. These are situated across the retina with the exception of the very central part of the retina, known as the

Rods
A class of photoreceptive cell that signals the luminance differences across the retina and does not code for colour.

Cones
A class of photoreceptive cell that is sensitive to colour. There are three types of cone cell, sensitive to long, medium and short wavelengths of light.

Fovea
A small area in the centre of the retina that provides high acuity and colour vision.

fovea. Rods are classed as being scotopic (i.e. good under dark conditions), as they respond better in dim light conditions, and therefore need fewer photons of light to instigate a signal. They also have a much lower level of acuity than cones; you can see this by looking at an object but at the same time trying to be aware of what is in the periphery of your vision.

It is only in the centre of our visual axis that we see detailed colour. This is achieved by three separate types of cone photoreceptor. These are situated mainly in the fovea, which takes up only 1 per cent of the surface of the retina. Vision here is of very high acuity and is sensitive to photopic conditions (i.e. high levels of direct illumination). There are about six million cones, and these are separated into cone types having peak sensitivities at long (560 nm), medium (530 nm) and short (420 nm) wavelengths (see Figure 1.7(b)). These correspond to red (long), green (medium) and blue (short) colours in the colour spectrum. You may be familiar with the acronym RGB, a system of mixing these three colours used in some colour television sets. By adding these three colours in different mixtures any colour can be produced, and the same sort of colour mixing is achieved in the retina by the various levels of stimulation of the different cones and how these are later integrated by the visual system.

One interesting feature of the retina is that it does not have photoreceptive cells covering its entire surface. Where the optic nerve is formed, and where it leaves the eye (known as the optic disc), is an area that has no photoreceptive cells, and therefore no signal to the brain. This area is known as the **blind spot** for this purpose. Interestingly, we are not normally aware of the blind spot, although its size in each eye is equivalent to the size of one's fist held at arm's length (see Activity 1.2 for an example of the blind spot). One explanation for not noticing it is that we have binocular vision, though if you cover one eye you will still not notice it!

Blind spot
An area on the retina in each eye where the optic nerve is formed and where there are no photoreceptive cells to signal information in the visual field.

Activity 1.2: Blind spot

Close your right eye and fixate on the cross on the right with your left eye (Figure 1.8). Move the image slowly towards and away from you. The cat on the left will disappear once it is in your blind spot.

Figure 1.8   Blind spot

2.3   From eye to visual brain

So how does light information about the world get to visual areas of the brain from our eyes? First, the optic nerve leaves the eye and is then divided into different tracts (at a point called the optic chiasm) to deliver signals to our two hemispheres. At this point something interesting happens. Rather than each eye projecting to just one hemisphere, or both eyes sending a complete signal to both hemispheres, the right half of each retina projects to the right hemisphere, and the same for the left half. Optically, this means the right side of visual space projects to the left hemisphere, and vice versa for the left side of visual space (see Figure 1.9). This might seem odd, but there are a number of advantages to this process. One important advantage is that it helps in calculating depth (called binocular stereopsis). As the eyes are separated by a short distance from one another, the slight difference in retinal stimulation for the same object in space can be used to determine how far it is from us. This is more easily and reliably achieved when both parts of visual space are processed by the same brain region (Howard and Rogers, 1995).

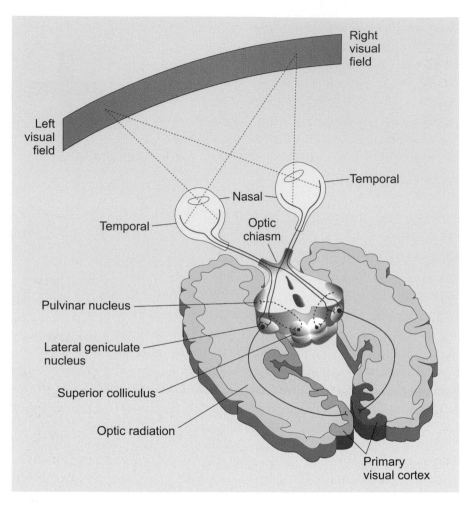

Figure 1.9   Pathways from the eyes to the primary visual cortex

Lateral geniculate nucleus
These thalamic structures are the main relay points between the retina and the occipital cortex.

Thalamus
The key relay station for incoming (i.e. afferent) sensory information to the cerebral cortex and also for outgoing (efferent) motor information to the body.

The optic tract connects to the primary vision-processing area of the brain (the occipital cortex) via a relay station known as the **lateral geniculate nucleus** (LGN) situated in the **thalamus** (a structure at the top of the brainstem that acts as the main relay for sensory and motor information to and from the cortex, and also between cortical areas). The LGN and its connections to the occipital cortex are responsible for giving us conscious visual awareness. However, there are many other connections to other sub-cortical structures from our eyes, and these are involved in a whole range of functions, including changing the size of our pupils in different lighting conditions, as well as a role in regulating our internal body clock, and making sure that our eyes stay on target irrespective of head movements.

Once at the **primary visual cortex**, also known as area V1 (areas of the brain are labelled according to convention), the signal is mapped on to the cortex in a way that retains its retinal location and an overall picture of what the retina is experiencing. This is known as retinotopic coding, and is not confined to vision. The retinal map is not only organised in terms of space, but also based on visual acuity. As the fovea is the most sensitive area of the retina, it gets scaled up to match its sensitivity (known as retinal scaling or **cortical magnification**). Thus, the fovea takes up a disproportionate amount of V1 in terms of its actual size, in much the same way as other sensitive areas of the body are magnified, such as the tongue and hands, on their respective brain maps.

Processing of the retinal image continues beyond V1. Here other aspects of the scene are analysed, leading to more and more complex representations of the world, until there are representations of the spatial layout of the world, the objects that are in the world, their colour, motion and also their meaning. Area V5/MT, for example, is largely dedicated to the detection of motion within the visual field. Damage to V5 can lead to a condition known as motion blindness, and Zihl et al. (1983) report an interesting case study of a patient with damage to this area whose perception of motion was a series of still images rather than the experience of fluid motion most of us enjoy.

As you should now be aware, seeing is a complex activity that involves a series of stages and a considerable amount of processing. Damage to any of these stages can lead to individual differences in how we see, and therefore how we perceive the world. Box 1.1 expands on this further with a demonstration of what happens when two different images are viewed by each eye. Section 3 will take seeing further, and will develop an account not only of how we see, but of how we perceive and how our perceptions can be different from the account of seeing laid down so far.

Primary visual cortex
Also called V1, the most posterior part of the occipital cortex, where inputs from the lateral geniculate nucleus first arrive. Further processing is then carried out within the occipital cortex before being transferred to the dorsal and ventral streams.

Cortical magnification
The process by which some parts of the visual field (e.g. the fovea) take up a disproportionate amount of the occipital cortex to reflect the density of cells in that area and to maintain a high degree of sensitivity.

Box 1.1 Crossing boundaries: binocular rivalry and the Cheshire cat illusion

As mentioned, binocular vision permits the perception of depth by fusing the slightly different viewpoints experienced by each eye. Each eye also projects a nearly full view of visual space to each hemisphere of the brain. Under normal viewing conditions, this anatomical setup allows for clear and reliable vision. An interesting

---

question is: What would happen if totally different images were viewed by each eye? Seeing two images in the same retinal location would imply a strong contradiction to normal perceptual consciousness. In some manner this contradiction needs to be dealt with. In this situation one might think there would be a rivalry between the eyes, with one eye being more dominant, and therefore the dominant image would be experienced. An alternative is that each image would exist for a short period to be replaced by the other image, or even that the images would be in some way combined to form a hybrid of the two. In fact, all three alternatives can occur depending upon a range of factors to do with the nature of the images (Blake et al., 1980).

Binocular rivalry
The perceptual experience that arises when completely different images are seen by the left and right eye. Rivalry can produce a range of unusual perceptual experiences, including seeing part of the right eye's image and part of the left eye's image.

A fascinating demonstration of **binocular rivalry** and its effect on perception is the Cheshire Cat illusion (Crick and Koch, 1992). Using a very simple setup you can experience all three of the above possibilities (and you don't need a cat!). The important thing is that each eye is seeing something completely different. To achieve this, hold a small mirror between your eyes with your left hand, but have the reflecting side angled slightly towards your right eye and with the mirror facing a white wall (see Figure 1.10). Now look at an object straight ahead of you against a white background. At the same time wave your right hand so it can be seen in the mirror in the same retinal position as the object you are viewing with the other eye. Your experience should be of the object, the hand, or an odd mixture of the two, with the object fading into and out of awareness, either partially or wholly.

Figure 1.10   The Cheshire Cat illusion
(Source: Crick and Koch, 1992)

Visual field
Also known as the field of view, this is all the light in the environment currently available directly to the eye.

Binocular rivalry is thus highly informative about both the biology of vision and the perceptual experiences that can arise when there are unusual conflicts within the **visual field**,. This area of research crosses the fields of biological psychology, cognitive psychology and the philosophy of consciousness. Many of the demonstrations you will encounter (including this one) in this chapter and in

Chapter 3 are currently being utilised in the study and philosophy of consciousness. As you will see in the following sections, philosophy is becoming an important ally for the development of psychological theories.

2.4 Summary

In this section you have discovered that seeing involves a complex series of mechanisms and stages from the optical structures of the eye to the occipital cortex where basic features of the visual input are analysed and gradually built up to represent the world. You also saw that although the eye is similar to a traditional camera in some ways, in other ways a camera lacks the agency humans have to explore the environment, and sometimes what we perceive is not what is seen. A good example of this is the activity on the blind spot, where you found that *perceiving* the world can be different from *seeing* the world in that we do not normally perceive the blind spots in our visual field. You also learned that the eye and its structures (e.g. the retina) help to explain how seeing is possible, but this is sometimes called into question by the perceptual experiences we have; for example, when binocular rivalry occurs as in the Cheshire Cat Illusion. So, the biology of seeing is not the complete story of perceptual experience.

3   Why do we perceive?

3.1   What is visual perception for? The perception–action model

The biological account in the previous sections outlined the basics of vision and seeing. This section will start by developing this account a little further before moving on to look at how perception can be understood according to the emphasis one places upon it in terms of its function.

Let us start by asking: 'What is perception for?' Well, one of its functions is certainly to recognise objects in the world. In the example at the start of the chapter, I was able to recognise my adopted cat Rupert. This was because I had encountered Rupert in the past, and had laid down a memory (i.e. a stored representation of Rupert). But vision is also for knowing things about the world. I know that Rupert has a name; that he likes cat treats; and also that he is 21 years old. So vision is also about the meaning of things, that is, their semantics. Vision is also about allowing us to act reliably in the world, and to know where we are with reference to the objects that surround us.

It will be no surprise then to learn that there are two streams. or pathways, of connections in our brain that are dedicated to these two different functions for visual perception. Ungerleider and Mishkin (1982) (see also Mishkin et al., 1983) were the first to clearly demonstrate this distinction biologically. They showed that one of the streams of processing ascends from V1 to parietal areas. The **parietal cortex** is just above the visual cortex and is involved in mapping near and far space as well as integrating information from different senses. For reasons of neurological labelling, this became known as the **dorsal stream**, or the 'where' stream, owing to its role in understanding the spatial properties of objects and ourselves in space. The second pathway descends from V1 and ends in the inferior temporal area (IT), and is known as the **ventral stream** (or 'what' stream). The **temporal cortex** is at the side of the head and anterior to V1 and is responsible for a range of functions, including face and object recognition (see Figure 1.11).

Parietal cortex
This area of the brain, just above the occipital cortex, has a major role in integrating information from different senses and also in spatial mapping and bodily sensation.

Dorsal stream
Also known as the dorsal pathway, this stream of processing ascends from the occipital cortex to the parietal cortex and is involved in spatial awareness and action. It is often referred to as the 'where' or 'how' pathway because of its functions.

Ventral stream
Also known as the ventral pathway, this stream of processing descends from the occipital cortex to the inferior temporal cortex and is involved in objects recognition. It is often referred to as the 'what' pathway owing to its primary function.

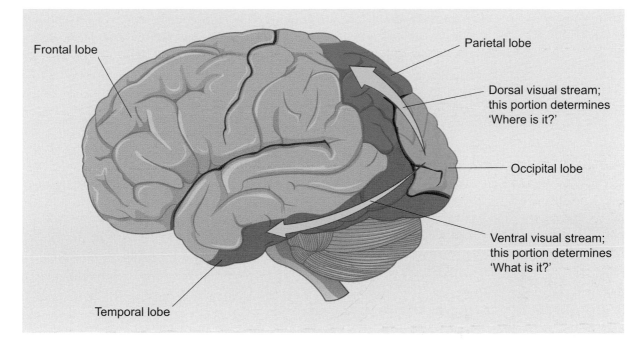

Frontal lobe

Parietal lobe

Dorsal visual stream; this portion determines 'Where is it?'

Occipital lobe

Ventral visual stream; this portion determines 'What is it?'

Temporal lobe

Figure 1.11   The dorsal and ventral streams mapped on to the human brain

This simple but elegant model was updated more recently by Milner and Goodale (Milner and Goodale, 1995; Goodale and Milner, 1992; see also Milner and Goodale, 2008) to emphasise the functions of the two streams rather than simply what elements of the environment they seem specialised for. In their **perception–action model** they view the dorsal stream as vision-for-action and the ventral stream as vision-for-perception. Their model heavily emphasises what the *goals* of perception are for. For this reason, some now refer to the dorsal stream as the 'how' stream, rather than the 'where' stream because the dorsal stream is seen as the system that guides action.

Earlier in the chapter the distinction between bottom-up processing and top-down processing was made. In the perception–action model the ventral stream is seen as being involved in higher-level, abstract representations and understanding of the world that will influence behaviour (i.e. top-down processing). The dorsal stream, in contrast, is driven by the environmental data, so that once an object is perceived, one can act upon it *directly* and effortlessly, without the need to have actions directed in a top-down manner. That is, many actions are highly automatic and unconscious, wired either through learning or through our evolutionary past. This suggests dissociation between perception and action. However, the degree of dissociation is currently

Temporal cortex
A complex structure situated at the side of the brain and responsible for object recognition, face processing, emotion, memory and language comprehension.

Perception–action model
A theoretical and biological model that views the dorsal and ventral streams as having defined and independent roles in action and perception respectively.

being debated in the literature as more evidence comes to light about the degree of inter-stream communication (see Schenk and McIntosh, 2010; and also Goodale and Milner, 2010). Table 1.1 shows the characteristics of each pathway.

Table 1.1   Characteristics of the perception–action model

	Ventral stream	**Dorsal stream**
Behavioural function	Vision for perception	Vision for action
Spatial properties	Allocentric coding/relative metrics	Egocentric coding/absolute metrics
Temporal properties	Sustained representations	Transient representations
Visual awareness	Critically linked to awareness	Independent of awareness

Source: Schenk and McIntosh, 2010

3.2   Evidence for the perception–action model

So what evidence is there for two routes that serve different functions for perception? One way to answer this question is to look at neurological cases where there has been specific damage to either of the two streams.

If the primary visual cortex was damaged, one would imagine that all visual experience would be lost. Such a person would be functionally blind. Lawrence Weiskrantz and colleagues (Weiskrantz et al., 1974; see also Weiskrantz, 2009) reported the case of D.B., a man who had suffered from headaches and visual distortions for many years and subsequently had an operation to remove the majority of his right primary visual cortex. The consequence of this, despite a relief in the occurrence of headaches, was functional blindness in his left visual field. (Remember how the visual field maps on to the two cerebral hemispheres.) When a light was shone in his left visual field, however, D.B. was able to guess where the light was projected, and even to discriminate between some basic shapes. This is despite his subjective experience of blindness to that region of space. Weiskrantz et al. (1974) referred to this ability as **blindsight**.

So how was D.B. able to achieve this apparent ability to see, despite being functionally blind? Subsequent research has shown that not all

Blindsight
The neurological phenomenon of having damage to areas of the brain that give rise to conscious visual experience. In blindsight patients can still locate features of the environment using a non-conscious visual route in the brain.

cells from the eyes project solely to the lateral geniculate nucleus and then to V1. Some cells project to an area of the thalamus called the superior colliculus, and then onwards to the parietal cortex (Cowey and Stoerig, 1991). So, D.B. had an intact system for vision-for-action, and used this to locate a stimulus in space, despite not consciously experiencing it. The next logical question would be to ask what would happen if part of the dorsal stream was damaged, say the posterior parietal cortex? What would be the consequences for perception and action?

Well, as the ventral stream is intact, people with damage to the parietal cortex would still be able to recognise objects and report a full visual experience. However, as the dorsal stream is damaged, they might have difficulty performing visually guided actions. In fact, patients with such defined brain damage have exactly that problem; the condition is known as optic ataxia. Perenin and Vighetto (1988) asked a patient with parietal damage to post a letter through a slit in a piece of wood. The patient was able to say what orientation the slit was at, but was unable to reliably guide their hand to post the letter. In this case, then, their patient had an intact vision-for-perception route, but a damaged vision-for-action route.

Brain damage can be somewhat unreliable owing to damage not being consistent across patients, but also because damage to parts of systems can have unexpected and unpredicted effects. Another way of exploring the two-streams hypothesis (i.e. the perception–action model) would be to use healthy undamaged brains. One way this has been achieved historically is by asking a participant to make two judgements about a visual illusion; one that is based on action, and one that is based on perception.

A classic study in this field used the Ebbinghaus/Titchener illusion (see Figure 1.12(a)). Aglioti et al. (1995) asked participants to look at the illusion and make a judgement about which of the two central discs appeared larger. (They are both the same size, but the one on the left looks larger.) They also asked them to reach out and grasp one or other of the discs. What they found was that although participants' visual perception was fooled and they saw the left disc as being larger, their hand grasped both inner circles in the same way, suggesting that the vision-for-action system was not fooled. More recent evidence, however, contradicts this finding. For example, Hoffman and Sebald (2007) asked participants to look at a hollow mask and to focus their eyes on its nose. This famous illusion (the hollow mask illusion; see

Figure 1.12(b)) works by rotating a mask through 360 degrees and asking participants to report what they perceive. What people experience is that regardless of whether one is currently looking at the convex or concave side of the mask, one always experiences the mask as though it is convex, i.e. it always appears to be pointing out towards you. By looking at the convergence of the participants' eye movements (by using a form of eye-tracking), Hoffman and Sebald found that the eyes were focused at a point in space consistent with the illusory nose rather than the real location of the nose when the mask was facing away from them. This seems to imply that one's actions (i.e. eye convergence) and one's perception (how the mask is perceived as convex when it is concave) are conjoined and therefore not dissociated (for further coverage of this debate see Franz and Gegenfurtner, 2008; and also Schenk and McIntosh, 2010).

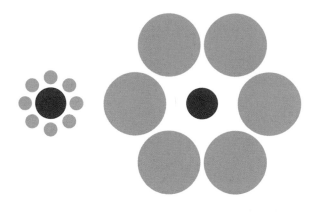

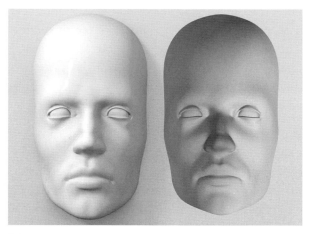

(a)   (b)

Figure 1.12   (a) The Ebbinghaus/Titchener illusion; (b) The hollow face illusion

Pause for thought

Looking at Figure 1.12(b), which face do you think is convex, and which is concave? What factors do you think make you experience the reverse of the mask as convex rather than concave?

Having read a considerable amount about psychology at this point, you should not be too disconcerted to find there are frequently empirical findings that contradict one another. This is certainly the case for the perception–action debate and the results used to support the systems as being functionally separate, or functionally more closely connected (Schenk and McIntosh, 2010; Goodale and Milner, 2010). However, one can take a utilitarian perspective and accept that there is evidence for two systems that support the ability to perceive and act in the world. You will now look at two influential theories of perception that map on to (more or less) these two streams. Keep in mind that these theories were first developed before the perception–action model was conceived by Milner and Goodale (1992). The first theory, that of Richard Gregory, emphasises vision-for-perception, while the second, that of James Gibson, emphasises vision-for-action.

3.3   Do we construct our own reality?

Do we in some way construct our own perceptual experience? This question is really asking whether perceptual experience is a direct reflection of the sensation we experience at any moment, or whether it is in some way different. One of the first people to think about this, and come to the conclusion that perception is more than sensation, was Hermann Helmholtz (1821–1894), a German scientist who worked in a range of disciplines, including psychology.

Helmholtz's breakthrough came about when he realised that the perceptual experience he had of looking at a piece of paper was changed according to the surrounding environment it was placed in. For example, if he placed a grey piece of paper against a red background it appeared to be tinged with green (red's complementary colour). Despite what is now known about the physiological explanation for this experience of colour (in this case simultaneous colour contrast), Helmholtz reasoned that his perception was driven by the knowledge that green was the complement of red. That is, his experience of the world was affected by what he knew. If the outside world and inner experience are different and not identical, then there must be an intermediary process responsible for the resulting experience. Visual perception of the world is therefore *indirect*.

Helmholtz also realised he was not consciously aware of this intermediary constructive process. It therefore appeared as though the processes employed were unconscious. Furthermore, the processes appeared to be inferential (i.e. they were looking to draw conclusions based on the data they received and the knowledge they stored).

Unconscious inferences
The idea that some conclusions about our experience of the world can be made without us necessarily being aware of them.

Indirect perception
The idea that perception is not a direct mapping of experience to the information in the environment, but rather that additional cognitive processes influence our perception.

Hypothesis theory
Richard Gregory's development of the idea of indirect perception, which emphasises the role that hypotheses play in the perceptual experience we end up having. In many ways this is a more detailed version of the idea of unconscious inferences.

Reasonably, Helmholtz named these processes **unconscious inferences**. Such inferences could explain perceptual phenomena such as size constancy (the experience that an object appears the same perceptual size, despite it being at different distances) by in some way compensating for the different retinal sizes with a knowledge of the size–distance relationship.

Subsequent to Helmholtz, a whole host of psychologists demonstrated that our perceptual experience can be different from the information we receive, and this extended to one's prior experience (i.e. memory) and also one's motivation and recent experience. For example, Sanford (1936) showed children images of ambiguous scenes and asked them what they saw. When the children were asked to do this before mealtimes they responded with many more food-related items than at other times of the day, showing an influence of our current needs on perception. Chapter 3 will show that what we attend to in the world can be similarly biased by our current state, or goal, as well as prior experience.

3.4 Richard Gregory: perception as hypotheses

Richard Gregory (1923–2010) (Figure 1.13), the British psychologist, developed the constructivist account of perception throughout a long and esteemed career (Gregory, 1970). His main contribution to the idea of **indirect perception** was the development of Helmholtz's notion of unconscious inferences. In Gregory's **hypothesis theory** he suggests that we actively develop predictions, or hypotheses, about the most likely cause of our sensations. Developing hypotheses in a top-down, or conceptually driven, manner has an array of benefits for human behaviour. For example, we can anticipate what is about to happen, we can make sense of ambiguous or cluttered scenes, and we can also act towards objects whose features are mainly obscured or are currently being viewed from an odd angle, all of which require us to use prior knowledge to either predict the world or to reliably perceive it. However, our predictions can also be mistaken, as when I mistook a pile of leaves for Rupert the cat.

Figure 1.13   Richard Gregory

Pause for thought

Gregory argues that perception is partly directed by developing hypotheses about what is experienced. Importantly, these hypotheses can be incorrect, highlighted dramatically through the use of illusions. In everyday life it is also possible to incorrectly perceive the world. I have given you an example of how this has occurred to me; can you think of times when you have made perceptual mistakes? This does not have to be a visual experience; it can involve any sense.

Sideways rules
An important part of Gregory's hypothesis theory, which apply basic forms of organisation and order to the raw input received through the eyes.

Gregory's theory conceives of perception as a complex interplay of sensory stimulation, top-down knowledge, a hypothesis generator and what he refers to as '**sideways rules**' that are applied to the sensory inputs in order to organise them (see Figure 1.14; Gregory, 1997). Importantly, Gregory sees relationships between the elements of his model that allow us to learn. When the world is perceived incorrectly, then a new attempt is made to draw a correct inference by taking into account the knowledge learned from the error. Hypothesis generation and testing is therefore an active means of closing the distance between errors in what is seen and the truth in the world.

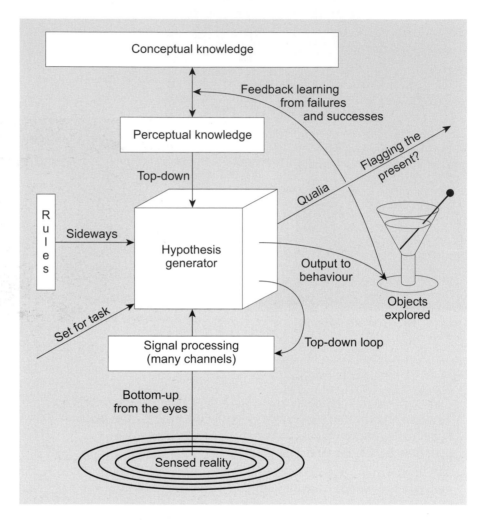

Figure 1.14 Gregory's hypothesis generator model of perception
(Source: Gregory, 1997)

Perceptual demonstrations are frequently employed as evidence for Gregory's hypothesis theory. One class of demonstration that is particularly informative are images that are bi-stable or multi-stable. These images can be perceived in more than one way. If seeing was veridical (i.e. always true) then we should have a single percept rather than the ability to perceive the image in different ways. The classic example put forward is the Necker cube (see Figure 1.15(a)). When viewing this two-dimensional 'cube' one normally sees a three-dimensional shape quite easily. First, we have taken a simple arrangement of lines and angles and arrived at the percept of a cube. More interestingly, the Necker cube is bi-stable in that there are two alternative interpretations of the image. If you stare at the cube you will find that your percept shifts between the two alternatives, something that should not occur if perception was not an inferential process.

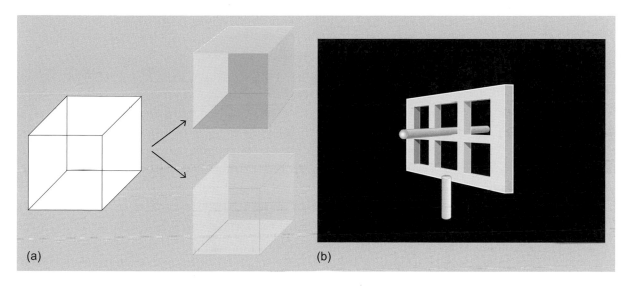

(a)   (b)

Figure 1.15   (a) Necker cube; (b) Ames's window

Gregory argues that illusions, or mistaken perceptions, are highly informative of the way in which we generate hypotheses about what we are experiencing. Illusions can occur because we make incorrect inferences about what we are sensing. (For a taxonomy of illusions and their causes, see Gregory, 2009.) A classic example is the Ames's window illusion (see Figure 1.15(b)). The window itself is constructed so that perspective is built into it. When viewed face on, one sees the window to be trapezoidal in shape with shading as though light were coming from the side. If the window is now rotated through its axis you will experience the window flipping and changing directions as your knowledge and expectation of light, depth and movement are contradicted. If you then put a pencil through the centre of the window (i.e. at right angles to the window) and rotate the window again, you will have an even more bizarre experience. The pencil rotates consistently in the direction of rotation, but the cues you perceive from the window are still contradicting the direction of motion, and therefore flipping direction at each half rotation. The resulting perception is now that the pencil performs an impossible act; it appears to pass through the window. One explanation for this experience is that the only way to 'make sense' of the conflicting information is to infer an impossible event. Perception can be paradoxical.

Another interesting problem for perception is dealing with incomplete information in the world. For example, from any vantage point some aspects of objects will be hidden from view. From where I am sitting I can see a pen partly hidden by a mug of tea. My experience, though, due to my experience of pens in the past, is that I perceptually complete the object and experience a whole pen. If I moved the mug and saw two pen parts, I would be surprised. The process of perceptual completion feels effortless, but there are 'sideways' rules that constrain whether we see a completion as being possible (Kellman and Shipley, 1991). There are two forms of completing objects, known as modal and amodal completion. **Amodal completion** is the example I just mentioned, where I infer object parts that are not visible (see Figure 1.16(a)). **Modal completion** is where we actually 'see' properties of an object that do not exist, but which can be inferred by the elements that are visible. In Figure 1.16(b) a triangle can be perceived (known as a Kanisza triangle), induced by the arrangement of the three Pacman shapes. It might surprise you to know that the boundaries you see, and the brighter surface of the triangle, are both illusory; inferred by our knowledge of objects and surfaces.

Amodal completion
The perceptual experience of a whole object, despite parts of the object being hidden from view.

Modal completion
The sensory–perceptual experience of parts of an object that do not exist, yet can be inferred from parts that are visibly present.

(a)   (b)

Figure 1.16   (a) An amodally completed cat; (b) A Kanizsa triangle

One controversial form of filling in is that which happens across the blind spot. Activity 1.2 is continued in Activity 1.3. Following the instructions for the activity you should notice that when the blind spot falls over the gap between the two lines of Activity 1.3, the gap is filled in and you experience a solid gapless line. How this is achieved, and whether there is a neural representation of the filled-in area, is hotly debated among both psychologists and philosophers (Dennett, 1991; O'Regan and Noe, 2001; Pessoa et al., 1998; Ramachandran, 1992). What cannot be disputed is that the perceptual experience is of filled space. What is interesting is that the gaps are filled in with what might best be *inferred* from the surrounding space.

Activity 1.3: Perceptual filling in of the blind spot

Close your right eye and fixate on the cross on the right with your left eye (Figure 1.17). Move the image slowly towards and away from you. When the gap in the line is within your blind spot, your perceptual experience should be that the gap disappears and the line is experienced as complete.

Figure 1.17   The blind spot

From Table 1.1 it is evident that indirect theories of perception map on to the characteristics of the ventral stream. Representations are sustained for the duration of an experience, they are conscious, and they serve the ability to perceive the world reliably. More recent work echoing the constructive and inferential nature of perception views the brain as a 'predictive machine' (Clark, 2013). This view sees a tight coupling between action and perception, but importantly establishes a central role for perception as a predictive process, drawing conclusions about incoming information by the degree to which they match stored representations and expectations.

3.5   James Gibson: perception as an evolved activity

> Perceiving is an achievement of the individual, not an appearance in the theater (sic) of his consciousness.
>
> (Gibson, 1979, p. 239)

James Gibson (1904–1979; see Figure 1.18), an American psychologist, developed a highly influential account of perception that argues that perception (in most cases) does not need to be mediated by internal representations, but rather the information necessary for perception is 'picked up' directly from our interactions with the environment. In contrast to the indirect and traditional approach that sees perception as a means of receiving information that is conveyed by the world, Gibson's theory sees perception as an activity that 'obtains stimulation in order to extract the information' (Gibson, 1979, p. 243). Gibson's theory then is about the relationship an animal has with its environment, and specifically how the animal has evolved to act in ways that allow it to extract meaningful information from the world.

Figure 1.18 James Gibson

So, in what ways can information be picked up from the world directly? Gibson's modern work started by exploring just this question when he worked for the US military, selecting and testing pilots. An important part of flying is being able to accurately perceive and judge motion in terms of direction, elevation and speed. Due to a lack of research on motion perception in three dimensions, Gibson set out to conduct his own research on how motion in real-world settings is perceived and obtained (Gibson, 1950; 1957). The result was an impressive understanding of what he called the **optic array**, the light structured by the environment that enters the eye, and the nature of how the structure of light changes in predictable ways. The change in features of the environment caused by movement he termed **optic flow** (Figure 1.19), and the direction we are heading in is the point from which all motion equally expands, the *focus of expansion*. Gibson would argue that mobile animals such as humans, with intact visual systems, can directly pick up information from movement about speed, distance and direction.

Optic array
The light experienced by the eyes as it is structured by the surfaces and textures in the environment.

Optic flow
The ordered change in patterns of light which results from movement within an environment.

Figure 1.19   Optic flow
(*Source: Gibson, 1950*)

Gibson was particularly emphatic about the need to experiment in real environments, and it is a point he often used against those with a constructive take on perception. Gibson starts his 1979 book *The Ecological Approach to Visual Perception* with a short critique of some of the more standard ways of researching visual perception in the laboratory using two-dimensional pictures. In this critique he identifies various ways in which seeing is dependent upon the situation you are in. He refers to typical perceptual experiments as employing *snapshot vision*, where the participant is asked to look at a fixation point and a stimulus is very briefly displayed. An improvement on this is where the image remains for several seconds and the participant can explore the image with several successive eye movements, what he refers to as *aperture vision*. In more realistic settings (i.e. in settings of improved ecological validity) where the participant can move around, one has *ambulatory vision*. While Gibson considers each of these as valid ways of seeing, the latter form of vision he considers as being the type of vision that we have evolved to use, where the animal and the environment are conjoined in the experience of perception, and the additional ability to move through the environment allows one to extract information that is not available to either *snapshot* or *aperture vision*.

The idea that the animal's perception of the world is driven by the environment it evolved in is part of Gibson's argument for what he refers to as *ecological optics* (Gibson, 1961), or the **ecological theory of perception** (Gibson, 1979). Classic accounts of optics that we see in typical ray diagrams, and classic pictorial stimuli in perceptual experiments, fail to account for the experience of optic flow and exactly what information is present within it (see Figure 1.20). Gibson argues that there is sufficient information for perception to be accurate without the need to impose an intervening level of representation, as is the case for indirect theorists such as Gregory.

Ecological theory of perception
Gibson's theory of perception which emphasises the direct and important link between actions and perception, with a strong emphasis on information revealed by optic flow.

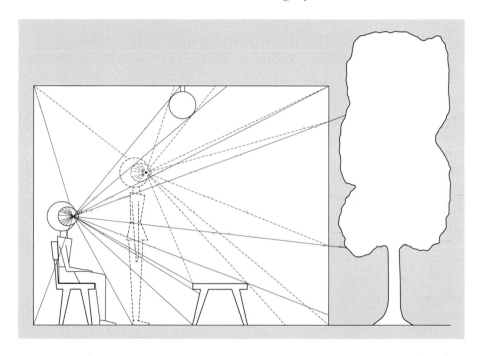

Figure 1.20   An example of how optical information is transformed through movement
(Source: Gibson, 1979)

An obvious question is how it is that we can perceive directly without in some way transforming the retinal stimulation to make sense of it? How does one make sense of the optic flow? The world is an apparently chaotic and ambiguous place of overlapping objects, a multitude of light sources and reflections, and a place in which objects can be viewed in a whole range of ways that make them appear very different depending upon one's perspective. Gibson answered these problems with a series of principles, including the principles of invariants and affordance. This discussion is restricted to invariants because of their central importance for Gibson's theory.

To understand these ideas you need to appreciate that Gibson argued that the light we experience in the environment is structured in such a way that it contains a specification of that environment (Michaels and Carello, 1981). Light is structured by the surfaces it reflects off, and it is structured in a predictable way, which Gibson referred to as a **structural invariant**. Given that the world is a place of change and movement, some of the received information changes as the viewer moves or as objects move, but these too are predictable in how they transform; Gibson referred to this as a *transformational invariant*. Importantly, as one moves in the world, some patterns remain invariant. The perception of these invariants gives rise to knowledge of the environment, especially in direct response to actions and movements. So, although the world appears to change, some aspects of it are predictable and remain constant. Gibson argues that sensory systems have evolved in response to the relationships between action and perception.

Structural invariant
A central principle of ~~Gregory~~'s theory which emphasises the lawful (i.e. invariant) relationships that occur between our actions (including movement) and the resulting changes in our perceptual experience.

Gibson

A classic example of an invariant is how an object's texture changes according the viewer's proximity to the object, or their movement towards or away from it. So, although as they move towards it the features of an object increase in size, and as they move away its features decrease in size, and therefore change, the relationship between size and movement is invariant and therefore informative. This can be extended to more complex forms of perception, such as human movement. In a series of experiments that Gibson might have questioned in terms of their ecological validity, Johansson (1973) demonstrated that human viewers are near perfect at identifying movement consistent with the pattern of another human walking, even when only a few points of light are visible (see Figure 1.21 for a point-light display featuring a cat, rather than a human). Johansson showed viewers images of humans walking that consisted of between five to ten points of light per display. These point-light displays only reveal the reflecting points that are attached to the major joints of the human body. If the point-light displays show a random but equivalent amount of motion, then biological motion is not picked up by the invariant properties of human motion by the perceiver. Therefore, there is something special and invariant about biological motion that we are able to 'pick up'. However, biological motion is not restricted to humans viewing human movement; the same holds for humans viewing other animals, such as the cat point-light displays in Figure 1.21.

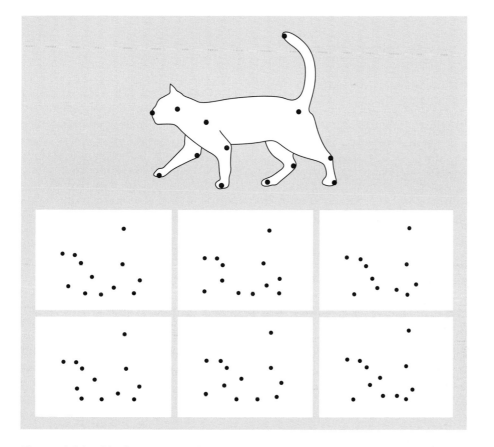

Figure 1.21   Six frames showing point-light motion for a cat
(Source: Vallortigara et al., 2005)

Gibson's theory is not included here merely as a historical account of the literature on perception. There is ongoing research and development of his controversial ideas. They are controversial in the sense that they call into question the majority view that perception is mediated by internal representations. The modern development is referred to as 'enactive perception', or the 'sensorimotor account of perception' (Noe, 2004; O'Regan and Noe, 2001). One of its key assumptions is that perception is not in the brain, but rather is an activity of the whole animal and that 'seeing is a way of acting' (O'Regan and Noe, 2001, p. 939). Just like touch, when the eyes move they explore the environment to extract information based on those actions. The actions of vision, such as eye movements and blinking, and indeed changes on the retina induced by bodily movement, highlight a direct relationship between actions and consequences. This relationship is seen to be predictable and informative. In many ways, these newer views are extensions of Gibson's notion of invariants.

3.6 Summary

In this section you have learned that there are two main visual streams of information processing in the brain, one that emphasises where things are (the dorsal stream), and one that emphasises what things are (the ventral stream). The approaches to understanding perception that were introduced centre on the distinction between perception-for-recognition and perception-for-action, most recently by Milner and Goodale's (1995) perception–action model, which focuses on the functions of these two streams. The two main approaches to understanding perception centre on these two streams. In the first the notion of unconscious inferences introduced by Helmholtz was subsequently developed by Gregory into his hypothesis model of perception, which is closer to a perception-for-recognition model. The second approach we covered was Gibson's ecological theory of perception that emphasises a direct relationship between the environment and perception, unmediated by cognitive processes, which is closer to a perception-for-action model.

4 Perceiving with more than a single sense: multisensory perception

Our day-to-day experience of the world around us and the events in it are normally registered by more than a single sense. For example, when you drink a cup of tea you are probably aware of its colour (vision), its smell, the weight and feel of the cup (touch), the warmth of the tea in your mouth (temperature), its flavour (a mixture of taste and smell), and possibly the sound as you drink. Your experience is thus multisensory. The question is, to what extent is your primary perception of flavour influenced by the other senses: how does perception change when more than a single sense is involved? This final section will broaden the chapter to explore two related areas that seek to understand perception in a more applied manner.

Pause for thought

If you were blindfolded, do you think that the experience of what you taste would change in any way? Does the flavour of your favourite drink change when you taste it in different cups? Would peas dyed blue taste the same as green peas? Compare your answers with the material below.

4.1 Multisensory perception

Most perception research has focused on single senses, such as vision and hearing. However, most experiences are multisensory. When more than a single sense responds to the same event, does this in some way make the perception sharper, more accurate or have greater clarity? Is one sense more dominant than the other? We have already met the idea that our brains can be thought of as predictive machines (Clark, 2013), so one reason why we have multisensory experiences could be that they reduce the amount of error in our perception. That is, having more than one piece of evidence for an event can help to confirm the validity of the event. However, it might be the case that not all evidence is treated equally.

A simple example of the influence of one sense upon another, and one sense dominating, is the experience we have each time we go to the cinema. The experience we normally have is that the words spoken by the cast are emanating directly from their mouths rather than from the speakers at either side of the screen. The illusion is also used to great effect by ventriloquist performers. When a ventriloquist mimes words that are articulated by the ventriloquist's dummy, the experience is very much that the sound is coming from the dummy's mouth (known as the ventriloquist effect; Driver, 1996). This is a good example of vision dominating the perception of sound. In this case the cues are still congruent in the sense that the sound and the lip movements are synchronised. What might happen if they were out of sync?

McGurk effect

A multisensory distortion of reality when what one hears is incongruent with the lip movements one sees. The resulting perception is often a fusion of what is heard and seen.

One way to test what happens when signals are combined from more than one sense is to explore the potential conflict between what is heard and what is seen. McGurk and MacDonald (1976) did just this. In what has become known as the **McGurk effect** (or, to be fair, the McGurk–MacDonald effect), they paired different sounds (phonemes) with a video of someone making silent lip movements. When sound and lip movements were compatible, people correctly identify the sound. However, when the sound and the lip movements were incompatible (e.g. the sound is 'ba-ba', and the lip movements are saying 'ga-ga') then something rather odd occurs. The viewer now has an experience of hearing a fusion of what is heard and what is seen. In this case, the perception is of the sound 'da-da'. What has happened here is that perception is driven more by what is seen than what is heard, resulting in a fusion of the senses as the best estimate of the experience.

Although vision is usually thought to be the dominant sense, and hence its influence on the fusion experience generated by the McGurk effect, the reverse can also occur. Sound can affect the visual perception of an event. In an intriguing experiment, Shams et al. (2000) presented participants with a variable number of audible beeps accompanied by a variable number of visual flashes. Their results showed that participants perceived more flashes than were presented when the number of beeps was greater than the number of flashes. In this case at least, what is visually experienced is partly determined by what is heard.

One of the more bizarre examples of multisensory perception is the rubber hand illusion (Botvinick and Cohen, 1998). The setup for the illusion involves a false arm being placed in view of the participant but emerging from their own clothing or a towel covering their real arm. Their own hand is placed out of sight at a slightly different location from the rubber hand. The experimenter then strokes both the rubber hand and the real hand at the same time, while the participant watches. After a while the participant senses that the rubber hand has become their own, due to the correspondence between the sensation of being stroked and the visual experience that the sensation is coming from the rubber hand. This is measured by asking them to point with their opposite hand to the location of their hidden hand. They reliably misalign where their real hand is. Their perception of limb location has been affected by vision. Recently, the illusion has been extended to the whole body. Petkova et al. (2011) used a head-mounted display so that what the participant saw was the view from a camera mounted on to a mannequin. When touch was simultaneously applied to the mannequin and their own body, their experience was that their body had swapped with the mannequin (see Figure 1.22).

Figure 1.22   The body swap illusion
(*Source: Petkova et al., 2011*)

An applied extension of the rubber hand illusion has been used for the treatment of phantom limb pain. The majority of amputees experience pain in their amputated limb. This pain can be very difficult to treat and the experience can be chronic and even lifelong. One method of treating the pain is to induce in the amputee the visual experience that the limb still exists. This can be achieved by using a mirror box (see Figure 1.23) whereby the amputee can view their missing limb as a reflection of their existing limb. Therapeutic manipulation of the existing limb during viewing sessions has shown to have dramatic improvements in reported pain (Chan et al., 2007). In this case the visual perception of the amputated limb as being the real limb appears to alter how the nervous system deals with the pain signals.

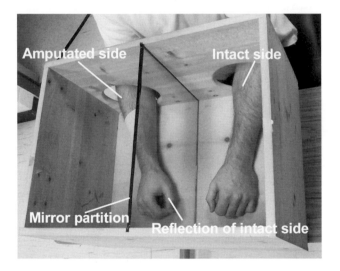

Figure 1.23   An example of a mirror box for treating phantom limb pain

Much is now known about the biological basis of multisensory perception and integration. It is known that specific multimodal centres in the brain respond more when signals are coincident from more than one sense, highlighting the fact that the different sensory signals are related to the same event, and these can be specific to certain combinations of senses (e.g. audiovisual). There is also evidence that multimodal sites can have downward connections to unimodal sensory sites, effectively enhancing or inhibiting the other sensory input to improve perception (Driver and Noesselt, 2008). A reasonable conclusion is that the influence of multiple senses can enhance our experience of the world and it almost certainly helps us to establish the correct interpretation of our visual perception, despite one or two of the multisensory illusions highlighted above.

4.2   Cross-modal correspondences: is a glass of white wine high-pitched or low-pitched?

In the previous section you learned that most experiences are influenced by more than a single sensory modality. However, in the absence of a second sensory input, there are still some relationships between senses such that an experience in one sense normally corresponds to a perception in another sense. These associations can be useful in helping us to have richer perceptions of the world. An example would be that some sounds, on their own, will elicit an experience of speed. Hearing a screech near you doesn't require you to see the speeding vehicle; the high-pitched sound *on its own* corresponds with high speed. Activity 1.4 demonstrates this concept.

Activity 1.4: Cross-modal questions

Answer the following questions as quickly as possible (i.e. intuitively) by selecting one of the two alternatives provided:

Is a glass of white wine high-pitched or low-pitched?

Which is a large object, 'mal' or 'mil'?

In Figure 1.24 the shapes are Bouba and Kiki. Which one is Kiki?

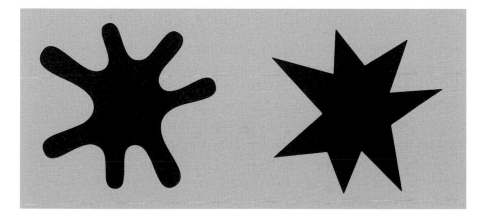

Figure 1.24   Kiki and Bouba

You have now seen that perception is not only determined by vision; it can also be influenced by other perceptual experiences arising from the same event (e.g. sound). This final section will explore a closely related phenomenon whereby perceptual experience in one modality can *induce*, or give rise to, a perceptual experience in another. This relationship between perceptual experiences is normally predictable and common to most people. The experiences themselves can be said to range along dimensions, so that an extreme experience in one modality will correspond to a more extreme experience in the other modality (Spence, 2011).

A good example to start with is the common correspondences for a high-pitched sound. When we hear a high-pitched sound and are given alternatives, we typically say that the sound is related to things that are high in terms of elevation, things that are sharp, thin, quick, small, bright, and light in weight. When we hear a low-pitched sound we are likely to experience correspondences that are low in elevation, dull, heavy, slow, blunt and thick (Walker and Smith, 1984). The answer to the first question in Activity 1.4 is that a glass of white wine in normally perceived as high-pitched. It also corresponds with the cluster of correspondences listed above for a high-pitched sound.

Some of the earliest research into cross-modal correspondences examined the symbolism certain sounds have (Sapir, 1929). The suggestion is that we use certain words (or have created them) because their sounds symbolise their meaning. Sapir uses the example that 'teeny' not only means smaller than 'tiny' but it also *sounds* smaller that tiny. In a series of experiments Sapir shows a very distinct correspondence between 'i' and things that are small, and 'a' and things that are large. If you said the answer to the second question of Activity 1.4 was 'mal' then you have just demonstrated a common correspondence between a sound and its symbolism. Sapir's participants mostly said the word 'mal' was a large object, while the word 'mil' was a small object. Such symbolism extends to correspondences between sound and abstract shape. Ramachandran and Hubbard (2003) showed participants the shapes you see in Figure 1.24. When asked which one was named 'Kiki' almost everyone chose the angular form on the right. It seems that the jaggedness of the shape corresponds with the word Kiki, and similarly, the roundness of the second shape corresponds with the smoothness of the word Bouba.

If correspondences between the senses exist, then they should have some effect on behaviour. Many studies use an experimental design called a speeded classification task to reveal cross-modal correspondences. The task is rather easy in the sense that it doesn't require much learning. All the participant needs to do is identify which class an item (the target) belongs to, e.g. is the stimulus bright or dark? At exactly the same time they are presented with another stimulus that is irrelevant to the task (the distractor). If correspondence exists, then what we should see is that when the target and distractor correspond, the time to make a response should reduce (i.e. the participant gets quicker). The opposite should be true if the distractor does not correspond (i.e. is incompatible). Marks (1987) used this task to look at the correspondence between brightness (dark/light) and pitch (low/high). He found that participants were faster for corresponding pairs (dark/low: light/high) than for non-corresponding pairs (dark/high: light/low). This same task has been used to demonstrate a whole range of perceptual correspondences we mostly all share.

An interesting question is whether cross-modal correspondences are learned or innate. There is some evidence that young children show sensitivity to some of the same correspondences that adults are sensitive to. For example, Roffler and Butler (1968) assessed whether there is a correspondence between pitch and height. They presented tones varying in pitch from behind a screen and asked participants where they perceived the sound to originate. They found that the higher the pitch then the higher up the screen participants pointed. The groups they tested ranged from young children (aged 4–5 years), adults and those born without vision. All exhibited the same correspondence for height–pitch. A more recent study by Walker et al. (2010) showed that preverbal infants display a similar correspondence for shape (angular or rounded) and height. It does appear that some correspondences are innate.

Spence (2011) puts forward the view that *some* correspondences are likely to be an innate evolved capacity (e.g. loudness–brightness). Others he suggests are likely to be learned through semantic associations once language develops; a good fit for the indirect theory of perception, and the idea that experiences can be associated and relationships inferred. Another possibility for some correspondences is that they are learned from the regularities of experience in the environment. This latter point matches well with the Gibsonian principle of invariants in the environment, and the way in which our perceptions are contingent upon regular patterns in the world revealed by our actions.

The world is full of fun and interesting cross-modal correspondences of which we are normally unaware. The colour of the wine you drink, the shape of the glass you drink it from, the noise that surrounds you while you drink, all have a degree of cross-modal correspondence, whether learned or otherwise.

4.3   Summary

In this section you have learned that most perceptual experiences involve more than a single sense. These are called multisensory experiences and can help to improve the accuracy of perception. A variety of effects can be observed when senses agree or conflict with one another. Perceptual demonstrations, such as the McGurk effect, reveal the difficulty of interpretation when different senses conflict. In this case, the fusion of two sensory inputs gives rise to a new perceptual experience that is different from the two original inputs. In everyday experience perception is not only driven by more than a single sense, but also by learned and innate relationships across sensory modalities, called cross-sensory correspondences. These can affect our perceptual experience in different ways; in particular, they can heighten or deepen our experience in the absence of a secondary sensory input, simply by the correspondences or associations that already exist.

5   Concluding thoughts

This chapter started with the experience of visual perception being effortless: waking in the morning and opening one's eyes to experience the world. Hopefully you now understand that this subjectively simple process is far more complex than it feels. This chapter has drawn a distinction between the biology of vision (*seeing*) and the cognitive processes and mechanisms of visual experience (*perceiving*). These are not separate, but they do offer different levels of explanation for the perceptual consciousness we enjoy. They complement one another to provide a more complete understanding of perception.

In places the chapter has also touched upon the philosophy of sensation and perception, a much older arena of debate for these topics, and how this is influencing current research within the field. Although this chapter has focused primarily upon the sense of sight, the arguments, debates and theories covered are also relevant to the other senses. In the following two chapters you will be introduced to topics that are closely related to what has been covered here, in particular how the focus of our experience (i.e. what we attend to) determines whether we perceive something or not. So, it is not whether I misperceive Rupert the cat as a pile of leaves; the question will become: 'Is there any likelihood that I will notice him at all?'

Further reading

- Although not the most recent book on vision science, this is still the most comprehensive account for those interested in vision. The book covers a wide range of material, from the biological structures supporting vision through theories on visual perception, to the psychophysical methods used to measure vision. Whether you are interested in the neuropsychological abnormalities of visual perception, the perception of colour, or how we visually attend to the world, then the answers are all here:

Palmer, S. (1999) *Vision Science; From Photons to Phenomenology*, Cambridge, Mass., The MIT Press.

- For those of you who find illusions fascinating, this is one of the few attempts to organise illusions into a taxonomy. Throughout the book Gregory explains each illusion and how it relates to other illusions of a similar type. The book also explains Gregory's hypothesis theory and how this relates to visual illusions and their causes. More generally, Gregory also reminds the reader of the difference between bottom-up and top-down influences on visual perception:

Gregory, R. (2009) *Seeing Through Illusions*, Oxford, Oxford University Press.

- This is one of the most influential papers on visual consciousness and perception written this century. It ties in well with what you have learned of Gibson's theory of perception, but also about visual consciousness more generally. This allows you to see the degree of debate around some of these ideas. The article is followed by several replies by other academics working in the same field, some supporting their ideas, but some critiquing them. This article also relates to some of the central ideas you will encounter in Chapter 3:

O'Regan, J.K. and Noë, A. (2001) 'A sensorimotor account of vision and visual consciousness', *Behavorial and Brain Sciences*, vol. 24, pp. 939–1031.

- In the final section of the chapter we looked at the fascinating associations that exist between different perceptual dimensions (e.g. perception of height and auditory pitch). Spence's article reviews the development, methods, evidence and possible explanations for this area of perception research:

Spence, C. (2011) 'Cross-modal correspondence: A tutorial review', *Attention, Perception and Psychophysics*, vol. 73, pp. 971–95.

References

Aglioti, S., DeSouza, J.F.X. and Goodale, M.A. (1995) 'Size-contrast illusions deceive the eye but not the hand', *Current Biology*, vol. 5, pp. 679–85.

Blake, R., Westendorf, D.H. and Overton, R. (1980) 'What is suppressed during binocular rivalry?', *Perception*, vol. 9, pp. 223–31.

Botvinick, M. and Cohen, J. (1998) 'Rubber hands "feel" touch that eyes see', *Nature* , vol. 391, p. 756.

Chan, B.L., Witt, R., Charrow, A.P., Magee, A., Howard, R., Pasquina, P.F., Reed, W., Hellman, K.M. and Tsao, J.W. (2007) 'Mirror therapy for phantom limb pain', *New England Journal of Medicine*, vol. 357, pp. 2206–07.

Clark, A. (2013) 'Whatever next? Predictive brains, situated agents, and the future of cognitive science', *Behavioral and Brain Sciences*, vol. 36, pp. 181–204.

Cowey, A. and Stoerig, P. (1991) 'The neurobiology of blindsight', *Trends in Neurosciences*, vol. 14, pp. 140–5.

Crick, F.C. and Koch, C. (1992) 'The problem of consciousness', *Scientific American*, vol. 267, pp. 152–9.

Dennett, D.C. (1991) *Consciousness Explained*, Cambridge, MA, MIT Press.

Driver, J. (1996) 'Enhancement of selective listening by illusory mislocation of speech sounds due to lip-reading', *Nature*, vol. 38, pp. 66–8.

Driver, J. and Noesselt, T. (2008) 'Multisensory interplay reveals cross-modal influences on "sensory specific" brain regions, neural responses, and judgments', *Neuron*, vol. 57, pp. 11–23.

Franz, V.H. and Gegenfurtner, K.R. (2008) 'Grasping visual illusions: consistent data and no dissociation', *Cognitive Neuropsychology*, vol. 25, pp. 920–50.

Gibson, J.J. (1950) *The Perception of the Visual World*, Boston, MA, Houghton Mifflin Co.

Gibson, J.J. (1957) 'Optical motions and transformations as stimuli for visual perception', *Psychological Review*, vol. 64, pp. 288–95.

Gibson, J.J. (1961) 'Ecological optics', *Vision Research*, vol. 1, pp. 252–62.

Gibson, J.J. (1979) *The Ecological Approach to Visual Perception*, Boston, MA, Houghton Mifflin Co.

Goodale, M.A. and Milner A.D. (1992) 'Separate pathways for perception and action', *Trends in Neuroscience*, vol. 15, no. 1, pp. 20–5.

Goodale, M.A. and Milner, A.D. (2010) 'Two visual streams: interconnections do not imply duplication of function', *Cognitive Neuroscience*, vol. 1, pp. 65–8.

Gregory, R. (1970) *The Intelligent Eye*, London, Weidenfeld & Nicolson.

Gregory, R. (1997) 'Knowledge in perception and illusion', *Philosophical Transactions of the Royal Society*, vol. 352, pp. 1121–8.

Gregory, R. (2009) *Seeing Through Illusions*, Oxford, Oxford University Press.

Hoffman, J. and Sebald, A. (2007) 'Eye vergence is susceptible to the hollow-face illusion', *Perception*, vol. 36, pp. 461–70.

Howard, I.P. and Rogers, B.J. (1995) *Binocular Vision and Stereopsis*, Oxford, Oxford University Press.

Johansson, G. (1973) 'Visual perception of biological motion and a model for its analysis', *Perception and Psychophysics*, vol. 14, pp. 201–11.

Kellman, P.J. and Shipley, T.F. (1991) 'A theory of visual interpolation in object perception', *Cognitive Psychology*, vol. 24, pp. 141–221.

Marks, L.E. (1987) 'On cross-modal similarity: audio-visual interactions in speeded discrimination', *Journal of Experimental Psychology: Human Perception and Performance*, vol. 13, pp. 384–94.

McGurk, H. and MacDonald, J. (1976) 'Hearing lips and seeing voices', *Nature*, vol. 264, no. 5588, pp. 746–8.

Michaels, C.F. and Carello, C. (1981) *Direct Perception*, Upper Saddle River, NJ, Prentice-Hall.

Milner, A.D. and Goodale, M.A. (1995) *The Visual Brain in Action*, Oxford, Oxford University Press.

Milner, A.D. and Goodale, M.A. (2008) 'Two visual systems re-viewed', *Neuropsychologia*, vol. 46, pp. 774–85.

Mishkin, M., Ungerleider, L. and Macko, K. (1983) 'Object vision and spatial vision: two central pathways', *Trends in Neuroscience*, vol. 6, pp. 414–7.

Noe, A. (2004) *Action in Perception*, Cambridge, MA, MIT Press.

O'Regan, J.K. and Noe, A. (2001) 'A sensorimotor account of vision and visual consciousness', *Behavioral and Brain Sciences*, vol. 24, pp. 939–1031.

Palmer, S. (1999) *Vision Science: From Photons to Phenomenology*, Cambridge, MA, MIT Press.

Perenin, M-T. and Vighetto, A. (1988) 'Optic ataxia: a specific disruption in visuomotor mechanisms. 1: Different aspects of the deficit in reaching for objects', *Brain*, vol. 111, pp. 643–74.

Pessoa, L., Thompson, E. and Noe, A. (1998) 'Finding out about filling in: a guide to perceptual completion for visual science and the philosophy of perception', *Behavioral and Brain Sciences*, vol. 21, pp. 723–802.

Petkova, V.I., Khoshnevis, M. and Ehrsson, H.H. (2011) 'The perspective matters. Multisensory integration in ego-centric reference frames determines full body ownership', *Frontiers in Psychology*, vol. 2, no. 35, pp. 1–7.

Ramachandran, V.S. (1992) 'Filling in gaps in perception: Part 1', *Current Directions in Psychological Science*, vol. 1, pp. 199–205.

Ramachandran, V.S. and Hubbard, E.M. (2003) 'Hearing colors, tasting shapes', *Scientific American*, vol. 288, pp. 52–9.

Roffler, S.K. and Butler, R.A. (1968) 'Factors that influence the localization of sound in the vertical plane', *Journal of the Acoustical Society of America*, vol. 43, pp. 1255–9.

Sanford, R.H. (1936) 'The effects of abstinence from food upon imaginal processes: a preliminary experiment', *Journal of Psychology*, vol. 2, pp. 129–36.

Sapir, E. (1929) 'A study in phonetic symbolism', *Journal of Experimental Psychology*, vol. 12, pp. 225–39.

Schenk, T. and McIntosh, R.D. (2010) 'Do we have independent visual streams for perception and action?', *Cognitive Neuroscience*, vol. 1, pp. 52–78.

Shams, L., Kamitani, Y. and Shimojo, S. (2000) 'What you see is what you hear', *Nature*, vol. 408, p. 788.

Spence, C. (2011) 'Cross-modal correspondences: A tutorial review', *Attention, Perception and Psychophysics*, vol. 73, pp. 971–95.

Ungerleider, L.G. and Mishkin, M. (1982) 'Two cortical visual streams', in Ingle, D.G., Goodale, M.A. and Mansfield, R.J.Q. (eds) *Analysis of Visual Behavior*, Cambridge, MA, MIT Press, pp. 549–86.

Vallortigara, G., Regolin, L. and Marconato, F. (2005) 'Visually inexperienced chicks exhibit spontaneous preference for biological motion patterns', *PLoS Biology* [online], DOI: 10.1371/journal.pbio.0030208 (Accessed 27 April 2015).

Walker, P. and Smith, S. (1984) 'Stroop interference based on the synaesthetic qualities of auditory pitch', *Perception*, vol. 13, pp. 75–81.

Walker, P., Bremner, J.G., Mason, U., Spring, J., Mattock, K., Slater, A. and Johnson, S.P. (2010) 'Preverbal infants' sensitivity to synesthetic cross-modality correspondences', *Psychological Science*, vol. 21, pp. 21–5.

Weiskrantz, L. (2009) *Blindsight: A Case Study Spanning 35 Years and New Developments*, Oxford, Oxford University Press.

Weiskrantz, L., Sanders, M.D. and Marshall, J. (1974) 'Visual capacity in the hemianopic field following a restricted cortical ablation', *Brain*, vol. 97, pp. 709–28.

Zihl, J., von Cramon, D. and Mai, N. (1983) 'Selective disturbance of movement vision after bilateral brain damage', *Brain*, vol. 106, no. 2, pp. 313–40.

Chapter 2

Can I do two things at once? Attention and dual-tasking ability

Gemma Briggs and Graham Hole

Contents

1 Introduction

In our everyday activities we take for granted our ability to pay attention and respond appropriately to different things. How do we know what to attend to and what to ignore? How can we cope with all of the sensory information that bombards us? And what happens when we want to perform two tasks at once? This chapter will explore some basic models of attention and executive control, providing you with an understanding of the approach cognitive psychologists take to understanding and investigating our capabilities and failures. It will then apply these models to a very topical issue: how safe is it to combine driving with talking on a mobile phone? By examining this issue you will gain an understanding of the methods used in experimental research as well as how models of attention help psychologists to devise specific hypotheses.

Learning outcomes

On completing this chapter you should:

- have an understanding of what attention is and how psychologists measure it

- have an understanding of key psychological theories, models and research on attention

- have an awareness of the importance and application of research on attention.

---

2   What is attention and why is it important?

Attention is a set of processes that enable us to selectively enhance the processing of some information, and inhibit the processing of other information. It is vitally important for efficient functioning, and its evolutionary advantages are obvious. At times we need to maintain focus on a task to the exclusion of everything else (e.g. 'keep rubbing these two sticks together to make fire'). However, it is also essential that we can be distracted by important events in the environment (e.g. 'watch out for sabre-tooth tigers'). We need to strike a fine and constantly shifting balance between focus and distraction, as tasks, goals and environmental circumstances change.

2.1   What do we mean by 'doing two things at once'?

At first sight this question seems very straightforward. However, as with many issues in psychology, a closer look at the question reveals it is surprisingly complex.

The first thing to consider is what is meant by 'two things'? Tasks vary in the demands they make upon us. There's plenty of evidence that we can combine a highly practised physical activity with a task that requires some mental (cognitive) effort. According to Madame August Boissier, the composer and virtuoso pianist Franz Liszt practised for up to 14 hours a day, reading books while he played (Mach, 1975). (Boissier didn't say how Liszt managed to turn the pages of the book!) This was practice of scales and arpeggios, so the muscular actions involved in producing long sequences of notes became over-learned and executable without conscious effort. A modern-day pianist, Charles Rosen, claims he too combines practising with reading. Interestingly, his account suggests that reading and practising are not wholly independent activities because he finds that reading poetry interferes with practising more than if he reads sociology, literary criticism or detective novels! He thinks this may be due to the rhythmic nature of poetry (Rosen, 2004).

Activity 2.1: Doing two things at the same time

Try doing two tasks at the same time. As you read the first few lines of the next paragraph, tap your right index finger on the table for each syllable you read.

Eastbourne, at first sight a pleasant seaside town on the south coast, is populated by two distinct sets of inhabitants. By day, it is crowded with elderly people. They amble along the seafront, admiring the attractive flower displays, basking in the sun on one of the many benches along the promenade, or perhaps indulging in some greasy chips or a half-melted ice-cream from one of the eating places near the pier or bandstand. By dusk, these people are no longer to be seen: they vanish into the safety of the seafront hotels. Then, the second set of inhabitants emerge: young hard-faced men prowl the streets in their Vauxhall Corsas, with spoilers, loud exhausts and stereo systems that guarantee their owners will be visiting NHS Audiology departments before they are 40. Woe betide any pensioner caught trying to cross the road after 7 pm: pedestrian-controlled lights mean nothing to these drivers, and the road-crossing senior is unlikely to get more than half-way across before their fate is sealed.

Activity 2.1 asked you to combine a physical activity with a cognitive one. You probably found that you were able to complete both tasks, but that your reading was slower than normal as you tried to read the words at the same time as detecting the individual syllables. All of the above examples suggest we can combine a physical activity with a cognitive one – at least if the physical activity is already practised to the extent that it can be performed fairly automatically. The issues of 'practice' and '**automaticity**' will be returned to later in the chapter.

Can we combine two activities that both make *cognitive* demands on us? Activity 2.2 is an example of this.

Automaticity
A mode of information processing in which processing of incoming stimuli and selection of an appropriate response seem to occur in the absence of conscious awareness.

Activity 2.2: Reading while counting

As you read the first few lines of the next paragraph, try counting backwards in 3s, beginning at 30 (e.g. 30, 27, 24 ...).

Lewes, county town of East Sussex, is another town of two cultures that exist in parallel worlds. The most visible inhabitants of this delightful medieval town spanning the river Cuckmere are very middle class. They

Information-processing systems
The cognitive systems responsible for manipulating information in all its aspects, i.e. receiving, selecting, storing, integrating and using information. Psychologists produce models of these systems that are based on behavioural and neuroanatomical/ neurophysiological data. Information-processing models often rely heavily on analogies to computer information-processing systems.

Neuron
A type of cell that is specialised for the transmission and processing of information within the nervous system.

Attention
A cognitive process involving the selection of information for further processing, such as the extraction of meaning.

Executive function
Our ability to plan, organise and coordinate our activities in a coherent and adaptable way.

generally have a gite in France, shop in Waitrose and send their children to violin lessons as a matter of course. But there are also the Bonfire People. They wear stripy jumpers (the colour of which denotes their affiliation to a Bonfire Society) and spend much of their time burning or blowing up things, or planning how to do so. Lewes Bonfire Night is renowned for its crowds and its spectacular processions and firework displays, and these are the people who make that happen.

This question has been investigated by psychologists for over a century. The short answer seems to be that it depends on the complexity of the two tasks and the similarities between them. In most cases, trying to perform two simultaneous cognitive tasks leads to some deterioration in performance on one or both of them. You probably found it very challenging to complete both the tasks in Activity 2.2 at once. Perhaps you found yourself switching between tasks, rather than completing them at the same time.

By investigating how people cope with trying to perform two cognitive tasks like this at once, we can find out a lot about how we process information, and the limits of our **information-processing systems**. We can use this knowledge to construct 'models' of these systems. These models, in turn, can be used to make testable predictions about what we should be able to do.

2.2   What's the point of attention?

The brain is a massively parallel computer, with billions of **neurons** carrying out millions of computations at the same time. Why, then, do we experience any difficulties in performing more than one task at a time? Although it's true that the brain can perform many operations simultaneously, it still has its limitations: there is a vast amount of information in our environment, and not all of it can be processed at any given moment. Also, because we can only perform a limited number of physical actions at the same time, activities need to be selected and prioritised.

The concept of '**attention**' (our ability to focus selectively on one task and ignore distractions) is closely bound up with the notion of '**executive function**' (our ability to plan, organise and coordinate our activities in a coherent and adaptable way). To function effectively, we need to set goals and organise our behaviour towards achieving them. In order to do this, we need to attend selectively to some environmental information (information that's relevant to the goal) while largely ignoring irrelevant information. The importance of **selective attention** is shown by neuropsychological studies of people who have lost this ability due to brain damage (primarily to the frontal lobes, which are heavily involved in executive control). These individuals become incapable of organising even the simplest aspects of their daily lives, such as shopping or preparing a meal (e.g. Shallice and Burgess, 1991).

Given the importance of these processes, Posner and Petersen (1990) suggest that the main functions of attention are to enable us to orient to sensory stimuli, engage in executive control and remain in an alert state. Stuss et al. (1995) further suggest that attention has seven functions:

- *sustaining* attention over time

- *concentrating*

- *suppressing* irrelevant information

- *switching* between tasks

- *sharing* resources with other tasks

- *setting* task goals

- *preparing* to respond.

When considering failures in attention and executive control, it's helpful to think about where the limitations in processing might occur. In theory, there are three stages in information processing: input, central processing and output. Restrictions could occur at any or all of these stages.

2.3   When do we decide what's important? Filter models of attention

In *Investigating psychology 1* you were introduced to **filter models of attention**. These considered limitations on information processing that were primarily at the *input* stage. It is worth briefly recapping these models because they are very relevant to understanding what happens

Selective attention
Focusing on specific elements of a stimulus or task. Looking for your friend at a railway station, ignoring all other faces, would be an example of selective attention.

Filter models of attention
Theoretical models that propose we actively select only a limited amount of information to attend to, either at an early or a late stage in the sequence of information processing.

when a person tries to perform two cognitive tasks simultaneously. Can we attend to more than one sensory input at the same time?

Early models of attention focused on how information was selected for processing in the first place. These models were based heavily on data from a particular experimental technique, **the dichotic listening task** (Cherry, 1953). Separate messages were fed into each ear by means of headphones and the participant had to selectively 'shadow' (repeat) one of the messages and ignore the other. The properties of the two messages were manipulated systematically to see how this affected shadowing performance (see Figure 2.1).

Dichotic listening task
An experimental procedure in which two different messages are presented simultaneously, one to each ear. Normally the participant is asked to show that they are attending to one of them by repeating ('shadowing') it.

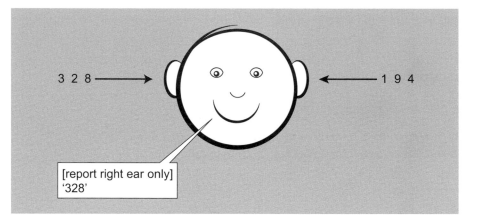

Figure 2.1   The dichotic listening task

Early research focused on two issues:

- What differences between two messages are needed for us to be able to distinguish one message from another?

- What happens to the information in the unattended channel? How much of it is actually processed?

2.3.1   Broadbent's 'early selection' filter model

Initial research seemed to show that for efficient shadowing, there had to be a clear physical difference between the two messages (e.g. in pitch, such as one message being spoken by a man and the other by a woman). Participants were apparently largely unaware of the content of the unattended message except for its simple physical properties (such as if a loud tone occurred or it contained a sudden change in pitch). Broadbent (1958) therefore proposed an '**early selection**' model, containing two successive stages of processing. The first 'pre-attentive'

Early selection
Stimuli are selected early on for processing, at the expense of competing stimuli, which receive little further processing.

stage extracted low-level 'physical' properties from incoming sensory inputs. A second 'attentive' stage was much more limited in capacity, and it extracted more complex psychological properties (such as meaning) from the inputs passed to it by the first stage. Broadbent suggested that this second stage operated in a serial fashion (i.e. processing one piece of information at a time), and thus produced a **bottleneck in processing**.

Broadbent's theory would suggest that we selectively attend to one voice by filtering out other voices on the basis of their physical characteristics. The cost of doing so is that we do not process the other voices at anything beyond a rudimentary analysis of their physical characteristics.

2.3.2 Deutsch and Deutsch's 'late selection' model

In a dichotic listening experiment, people cannot consciously report much about the information in the unattended ear; however, just because they don't remember it at the end of the trial doesn't mean they weren't processing it at a high level *at the time it was presented*. They may simply have forgotten the unattended information by the time they are tested on it. Subsequent research therefore used more indirect measures to assess the extent to which the unattended information is processed. These showed, for example, that words in the unattended message could bias the interpretation of ambiguous sentences in the attended stream (e.g. Mackay, 1973). Corteen and Dunn (1974) paired words with electric shock, so that a **galvanic skin response** (GSR) was evoked by each word. When these words were presented in the unattended channel, they still produced a GSR, even though participants generally reported no awareness of hearing them.

Moray (1959) showed that participants sometimes detected their own name when it was presented in the unattended ear. Treisman (1960) performed a study in which a message would suddenly shift from being presented in the attended ear to being presented in the unattended ear. Under these conditions, participants would sometimes switch to shadowing the unattended ear, implying they must have been processing information in the unattended ear to some extent.

Findings such as these led Deutsch and Deutsch (1963) to propose a **'late selection'** model of attention. They suggested that the initial parallel and unlimited-capacity stage included all perceptual processing,

Bottleneck in processing
A restriction in the speed or amount of information that can be processed, arising from a limitation in the capacity of our information-processing systems.

Galvanic skin response (GSR)
A measure of the change in electrical resistance of the skin, often used as a measure of autonomic reaction and arousal.

Late selection
Stimuli are selected for full attention after some processing of competing stimuli has occurred.

up to quite a high level, and that the second limited-capacity stage involved selection for awareness, memory and making a response.

2.3.3   Treisman's attenuation theory

Instead of abandoning Broadbent's model altogether, Treisman suggested a modification to it. She proposed that unattended stimuli were *attenuated*, or weakened, rather than being completely filtered out. The second stage received some input from unattended stimuli as well as attended ones, but the inputs from unattended stimuli were usually so weak they could not support the extraction of high-level properties, such as the meaning of words. However, in special circumstances (such as hearing your own name being spoken, or hearing Corteen and Woods' shock-paired words) the threshold for identification might be so low that the weak input was enough to trigger identification.

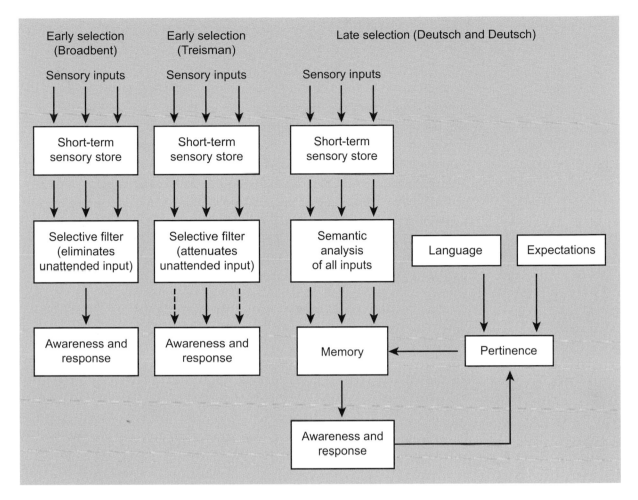

Figure 2.2 Early- and late-selection models of selective attention

Much of the evidence that apparently supports 'late selection' models can be accounted for by Treisman's modification to Broadbent's original theory (Treisman, 1960, 1969). A further twist comes from Lachter et al. (2004), who argue that Broadbent may have been right all along: they suggest that many studies claiming to show high-level processing of unattended information (including Treisman's 1960 demonstration) actually failed to ensure these stimuli were truly unattended. Lachter et al. performed a series of experiments in which there was very tight control over where attention was located; under these conditions, there was no evidence that unattended stimuli could be identified. Figure 2.2 summarises the above models.

2.3.4   Early and late selection combined: Lavie's 'perceptual load theory'

After 30 years of research following Broadbent's original work, there seemed to be as many studies favouring an early selection account of attention as there were supporting late selection! Lavie (1995, 2001, 2005) then came up with a theory that seems to explain these inconsistencies. She looked at the effects of **'perceptual load'**. This is operationally defined in terms of the number of distractor items simultaneously accompanying a target; the amount of variety among them; or the amount of perceptual operations that are required by a target (for example, looking for combinations of features in a visual display, such as a square of a particular colour, imposes a higher perceptual load than merely looking for a single feature, such as *any* shape of a particular colour; see Figure 2.3).

Perceptual load
The amount of perceptual operations required by a target: the greater the number of items in a visual display, the higher the perceptual load.

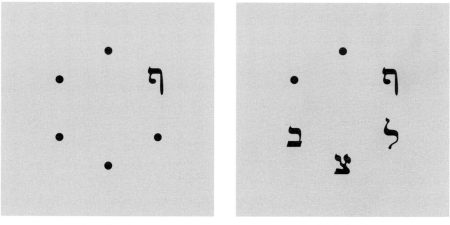

Low load   High load

Figure 2.3   Examples of high and low perceptual load

Lavie and Tsal (1994) reviewed previous research on the early versus late selection debate. They noted that results that apparently supported late selection had been obtained under conditions of low perceptual load, for example with a single target and single distractor, and a relatively undemanding primary task. In contrast, apparent support for early selection tended to come from experiments involving a high perceptual load, e.g. where there were more stimuli and/or a demanding primary task.

Lavie's (1995) explanation combines elements of both early- and late-selection theories. She suggests that perceptual processing is largely automatically evoked by stimuli; it is not wholly under the participant's conscious control. It is also limited in capacity. Whether or not information from distractors is deeply processed depends on whether the demands of the primary task exceed this limited capacity. If the primary task is undemanding, spare perceptual capacity will automatically be used on other aspects of the scene, and distractors will get processed. As a result, distractors will have more of an effect on primary task performance. If the primary task is higher in load, it may completely take up all available perceptual capacity, leaving no spare capacity for processing distractors. Performance on the primary task will then be less affected by distractors.

Another factor that affects selective attention is the load on a person's **working memory**: placing heavy demands on working memory makes it harder to keep focused on a task and to ignore irrelevant stimuli (Lavie et al., 2004; Lavie and De Fockert, 2005; Burnham et al., 2014). Lavie suggests that working memory is part of a second system of attentional control, used actively to maintain current processing priorities, thus ensuring that low-priority stimuli do not take control of behaviour (Lavie et al., 2004).

Working memory has a number of components. Two are involved in the short-term storage and manipulation of information acquired via a particular sensory modality. The 'phonological loop' deals with auditory-verbal information (such as speech), and the 'visuospatial scratchpad' handles visual/spatial information. A third component, the 'Central Executive', is not tied to any particular modality: it controls and coordinates the modality-specific systems. On the strength of experiments in which working memory was loaded with different types of information (visual, spatial or verbal) Burnham et al. (2014) concluded that secondary tasks interfere with selective attention most when the primary and secondary tasks both require the same working memory component. Performance on a visual search task was impaired more by trying to simultaneously remember the colour or location of a set of squares (visual and spatial tasks respectively) than by trying to remember vowel sounds (a task involving phonological working memory).

2.4   Summary

Completing two cognitive tasks appears to be very challenging owing to competing demands on our attentional resources. Filter models provide insight into the issue of whether we can *attend* to more than

Working memory
A flexible memory system comprising three components: a supervisory system (the central executive) and two temporary memory systems, the phonological loop and the visuospatial sketchpad. These are specialised for retaining verbal material and visual/spatial material respectively.

one thing at once. When task demands increase, a bottleneck in processing is reached, slowing down performance. Whether the bottleneck appears early or late in processing, all theories would agree that we are severely limited in our ability to pay attention to more than one thing at a time, and that we have finite resources available to us. Early- and late-selection theorists disagree about why this is the case.

3 Are there limits to our attentional capacity?

What about *performing* tasks, including those for which conscious attention seems not to be required? The remainder of this chapter will focus on models that postulate the existence of limitations largely at the stage of *central* processing, and which provide insight into our abilities to execute more than one action at a time.

Kahneman (1973) suggested there was a central limited pool of resources available for dealing with tasks. We cannot do everything all at once, so we have to prioritise some activities at the expense of others. Looking at Figure 2.4 shows how this might be achieved.

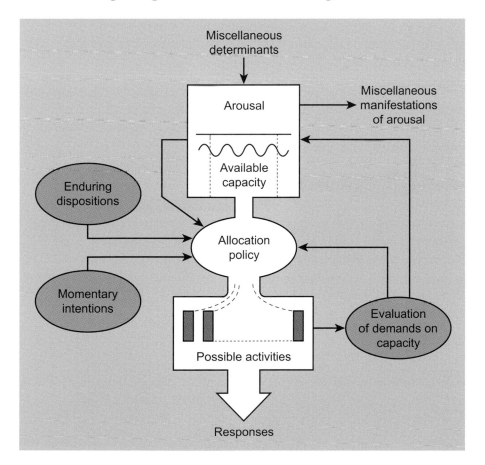

Figure 2.4   Kahneman's capacity model of attention

First, the amount of resources we have available for any tasks depends on our level of arousal. 'Arousal' is a fairly nebulous concept in psychology, but in this context it can roughly be equated with 'alertness': how awake we are. The more alert we are, the more spare capacity we might have for dealing with tasks.

Second, how we decide which tasks to perform is determined by an 'allocation policy'. This is affected by lots of different factors. One set is 'enduring dispositions', factors such as our personality (for example extroverts typically need more external stimulation than introverts), interests and needs. The allocation policy might also be affected by more short-term factors, as indicated by the 'momentary intentions' bubble in Figure 2.4. Once the allocation policy has determined which activities will actually be performed, its success at performing them is continually monitored and evaluated. If the demands on capacity are deemed to be too great, or performance of the activities is unsatisfactory, then the allocation policy will be reviewed and the tasks being executed will be revised accordingly.

Kahneman's model draws attention to some of the influences over how we allocate resources to activities, and it places greater emphasis on the way in which we actively and adaptively allocate resources. However, it doesn't provide much detail about the 'allocation policy' component of the model. Around the same time as Kahneman produced his model, Shiffrin and Schneider (1977) made an important distinction between two modes of processing: 'controlled' and 'automatic', roughly corresponding to conscious and unconscious processing. Controlled processing is a limited-capacity system that requires focused attention. Automatic processing has much greater capacity, and requires no attention, but it is less flexible than the controlled processing system.

3.1   How do we balance automatic and controlled processing?

Norman and Shallice's model (1986) (Figure 2.5) incorporates a similar dichotomy to Schneider and Shiffrin's, between controlled and automatic processing. Information enters from the senses and activates 'triggers' within a database. These triggers in turn activate schemas: these are well-rehearsed frameworks for actions. At any given moment, there are probably lots of different, and often competing, schemas to choose between. An unconscious 'contention scheduling' system selects which schema to perform, in a fairly automatic way.

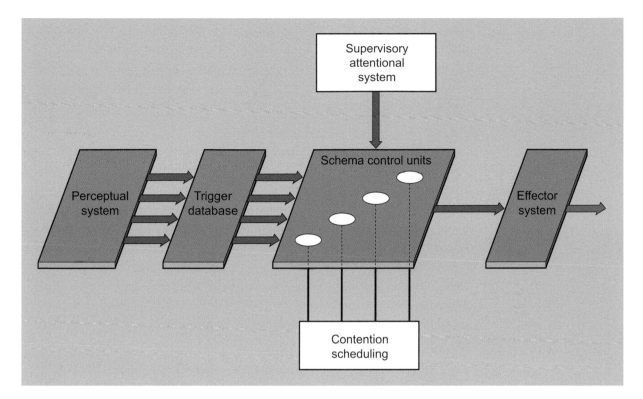

Figure 2.5   Norman and Shallice's model of executive function (1986)

Much of the time, this system works well; however it will fail if the person encounters a novel situation for which they don't have any existing schemas, or if the schema is disrupted for any reason. In those situations, a more conscious system, the 'supervisory attentional system', intervenes and takes control of behaviour, albeit at the expense of more mental effort and more conscious, deliberative processing.

This model accounts nicely for many everyday experiences. In fact a good example occurred to Graham Hole, one of the authors of this chapter, during the writing process. His partner is an inveterate tea drinker, and so his schema for making cups of tea is extremely well developed. During a break from writing, he asked his partner if she wanted a cup of tea. She did, but unusually she wanted liquorice tea for a change. While concentrating on the finer points of research on attention, he boiled the kettle, got a cup from the kitchen cupboard, put a tea-bag into it ... and then watched himself pour milk into the cup. (For the non-tea drinkers among you, liquorice tea is not taken with milk.) Up to that point, Graham's extensively rehearsed schema for making tea had run quite automatically. Starting with boiling the kettle, each action had triggered the next part of the schema without him having to pay any attention to what he was doing. Now, realising his mistake, his supervisory attentional system sprang into action and took control of the situation, pouring away the tea, washing the cup and starting the process all over again – this time, without the milk.

3.2   Dual-tasking models: are resources discrete or shared?

Both Kahneman's and Norman and Shallice's models conceive of there being a single pool of resources that can be allocated to different tasks. However, they fail to account for why some tasks interfere with each other more than others: for example, two verbal tasks interfere with each other much more than a verbal task interferes with a spatial task (Brooks, 1968). More recent models have therefore proposed there are multiple 'pools' of resources, rather than just one.

Wickens' multiple resource theory (Wickens, 1984, 2002, 2008) suggests that all tasks have three stages: input, cognition and response. The extent to which two tasks will interfere with each other is determined by three factors:

- The *modality* by which information is acquired. Two tasks will compete for resources if they are both visual tasks or both auditory tasks, but not so much if one is an auditory task and the other a visual task.

- The way in which the information is *coded*. Information can be coded spatially or verbally. Again, two tasks that require the same kind of coding will interfere with each other more than two tasks that employ different kinds of coding.

- The type of *response* that is required. Tasks may compete for response systems. Two responses will interfere with each other less if they use different response systems, for example if one task requires a vocal response and the other a manual response. Wickens therefore suggests cognitive resources are separated into distinct 'pools' that are accessed according to the task in hand. The basic premise of his theory is that dual tasking should be possible if each task demands separate resources from different pools (see Figure 2.6).

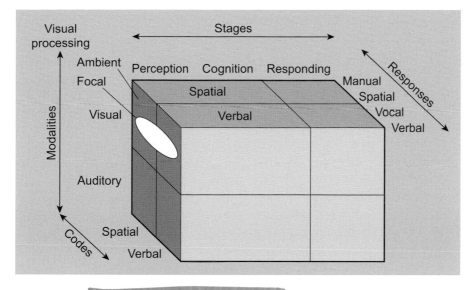

Figure 2.6 Wickens' multiple resource theory
(Source: Wickens, 2002)

Wickens (2002) later added a fourth dimension to his model: the visual channel used to process information. This can be either focal vision, which uses information presented in our central (foveal) visual field and is specialised for high acuity tasks, such as object recognition and reading; or ambient vision, which includes peripheral vision and is specialised for the detection of movement and orientation. A task requiring focal vision, such as reading a book, will require different resources and processing from those involved in a task requiring ambient vision, such as maintaining a vehicle's lane position.

Activity 2.3: Applying Wickens' model

Now that you have examined Wickens' model, try to identify the modality, code, response and visual channel for two tasks:

- driving *visual spatial manual spatial*

- having a phone conversation. *Audiverbal, vocal verbal*

You will come back to this example later in the chapter.

Box 2.1   Crossing boundaries: the neurophysiological underpinnings of multiple resource theory

Wickens claims his theory is supported by neurophysiological research using brain scans. He considers it important that the four dimensions have *neurophysiological plausibility* – meaning that the different 'routes' outlined in the model have parallels in brain anatomy. For example, perceptual–cognitive tasks show activity in posterior cortical areas, whereas motor and action-oriented tasks show activity in anterior (frontal) areas. Information processing is lateralised, with most individuals showing right hemisphere activity for processing spatial information and left hemisphere activity for processing verbal information. Auditory and visual processes activate different cortical areas (auditory and visual cortex respectively). The distinction between focal and ambient vision is supported by the existence of different visual pathways: focal vision makes use of a ventral processing stream, whereas ambient vision uses a dorsal stream.

You will return to Wickens' model later in the chapter because it has been very influential on dual-tasking research in relation to driving. However, note here that there is evidence that tasks interfere with one another even when they do not overlap in either sensory input or output modality. This implies there is a more central source of interference during dual-tasking that is not modality-specific (Marois and Ivanoff, 2005; Pashler, 1994). Wickens' model suggests that different modalities have quite discrete processing resources. However, more recent research has suggested that significant amounts of cross-modal integration occur, which means that the visual and auditory modalities probably compete for shared resources to a much greater extent than was previously envisaged (see Ho and Spence, 2008).

3.3   Does applying more control enable dual tasking?

Hockey's (1997) compensatory control model is based on the premise that performing any task involves a fine balance between behaviour and motivation. This balance can change at any point. He argues that humans are distinct from machines in their vulnerability to stress and emotion, both of which can interfere with completion of a given task.

For this reason, although Hockey supports Kahneman's suggestion that we have a limited capacity for information processing, he also argues that we cannot ignore the impact of affective state on our control of attention. However, rather than simply suggesting that performance in a primary task may decrease with the introduction of a secondary task, this model proposes that we are able to consciously apply greater effort in dual task situations in order to maintain performance, or at least keep the number of errors made in a task at a manageable level.

Hockey shares the view that attention is the result of a combination of automatic and controlled processing. He claims that behaviour is goal-directed, and that these goals can be either externally imposed (as is the case when a participant completes a psychological experiment) or internally driven (e.g. from emotional or biological needs). Hockey points out that psychologists tend to assume that when they ask a participant to complete a task, the participant makes that task their primary goal and, therefore, focuses their attention fully on that task. However, due to ongoing internalised goals, it could be the case that there is some competition between concurrent goals. Hockey argues that individuals can self-regulate the control of goal states; that is, task prioritisation, and applied effort, may change. So, someone in a dual task experiment may choose to maintain primary task performance by consciously applying more effort to that task, thus exerting greater control over their attention. However, this will carry a cost in the form of greater perceived strain or stress. Alternatively, they may choose to accept a reduction in primary task performance, and therefore not apply any greater effort or control over attention, meaning there is no cost to them. In this latter case, although performance may be worse, subjective experience may be better and internally driven goals may be more easily achieved.

The model proposes two levels of processing (see Figure 2.7). Loop A, the lower level, is responsible for more routine or automatic regulation of resources. Individuals are largely unaware of processing at this level. Loop B is the higher level, responsible for effort-based regulation of resources, when tasks are more demanding. Individuals have a subjective awareness of this increased effort. At the lower level, well-practised and rehearsed skills and performance goals are processed with little conscious awareness or effort, whereas at the higher level the application of increased effort enables an individual to control attention and task performance. An individual's goal for a given task helps to determine the behaviour they display (e.g. how fast the task is completed, what order tasks are completed in, etc.). However, this goal can change, depending on alternative goals (such as the introduction of a secondary task), and the perceived costs and benefits to altering behaviour to accommodate additional goals. As such, this is a negative feedback system: change in one goal affects the effort and control applied to another goal.

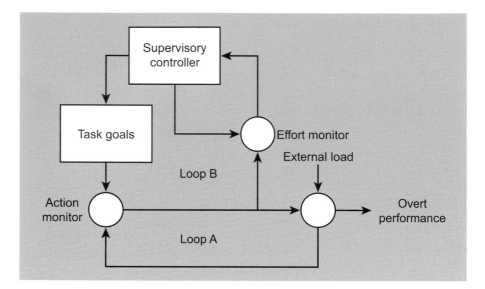

Figure 2.7   Hockey's compensatory control model

To monitor these changing goals and states, the action monitor compares the current behaviour with the target output behaviour, while the effort monitor tracks increased need for control, in Loop A. The system adjusts for any discrepancy between these two behaviours, either by increasing the amount of effort and control applied in order to maintain performance, or by adjusting the primary task goal to allow for some manageable error in that task. The process is managed by the supervisory controller. Importantly, in contrast to other models, increased effort is not automatically applied when the effort monitor detects demands that exceed capacity; instead control is shifted to the supervisory controller, where a conscious decision can be made about task demands and application of effort. This means that the higher-order processes can compensate for difficulties at the lower level, allowing performance to be maintained and preventing top-down processing of the primary task from being distracted by bottom-up processing of an attention-capturing secondary task.

3.4 Summary

There seems to be a balance between automatic and controlled processing of information. This may enable us to dual task, to some extent. While Wickens suggests two tasks requiring different attentional resources shouldn't interfere with each other, Hockey claims that when demands on attention increase, applying extra effort, or control, can enable us to dual task.

Different components of the models outlined can help to explain why we make errors in dual task situations.

4   Can we learn to multitask?

At the start of the chapter, it was noted that research suggests that trying to perform two tasks simultaneously generally results in performance deteriorating in one or both tasks. However, there is evidence that sometimes, with extensive practice, people can learn to combine two tasks quite well, performing them almost as well as either task alone.

Shaffer (1975) studied skilled typists. He found their ability to type visually presented text was essentially unimpaired when they additionally shadowed a message played through headphones. Spelke et al. (1976) trained two participants, Diane and John, to read short stories while they wrote down lists of random words that were dictated to them. By the end of the study (17 weeks and 85 sessions later!), they were able to combine the two tasks quite effectively. Memory for the dictated words was initially very poor, but by the end of the study Diane and John were able to categorise the words according to their meaning, while reading at normal speed and with near-normal comprehension. Spelke et al. claimed their participants had achieved a true division of attention between the two tasks. How did they do this? Spelke et al. considered three possible mechanisms:

- 'Task switching': participants could engage in rapid alternation of attention between the two tasks, making use of redundancy in the texts that were being read.

- 'Automatisation' of one of the tasks, so that it could be performed with minimal conscious intervention. Spelke et al. discussed various definitions of 'automaticity'. They concluded that a process was 'automatic' if it did not involve higher-order attentional skills in order to extract meaning from the world. By this definition, they suggested that writing to dictation was initially automatic, because Diane and John seemed not to process anything related to the meaning of the words they were writing. However, by the end of the study, writing to dictation had ceased to be 'automatic' in this sense: Diane and John showed evidence of understanding both the text they were reading and the words they were copying.

- Reorganisation of task components: instead of performing two separate tasks, participants might reorganise them so that in effect they perform a single, new task that was qualitatively different from what they were doing originally.

Hirst et al. (1980) performed two studies to test the 'redundancy' and 'automaticity' explanations of Spelke et al.'s results. The basic task was the same: to read while writing to dictation. Reducing the degree of redundancy in the text seemed not to impair performance, although Hirst et al. conceded that time sharing of attention between the two tasks did seem more frequent at the start of the training. The 'automaticity' explanation was tested by dictating sentences to the participants that varied in their degree of relatedness. This affected the participants' recall, even though the participants remained explicitly unaware of the relations between the sentences. This implies that the participants were sensitive to the structure and meaning of the sentences they copied, in the absence of explicit awareness of these attributes.

In an attempt to separate experience of a task from expertise, Allen et al. (2004) devised a multiple target tracking experiment comparing the performance of professional radar operators and novices. Participants saw a screen containing 12 crosses. After participants fixated on a white square at the centre of the screen, some of the crosses (up to six) began flashing, indicating that these were the crosses the participant must track (the 'target acquisition' stage, see Figure 2.8). The crosses then began moving around the screen (the 'target tracking' stage). Participants were asked to press a button whenever one of their target crosses turned into a white square.

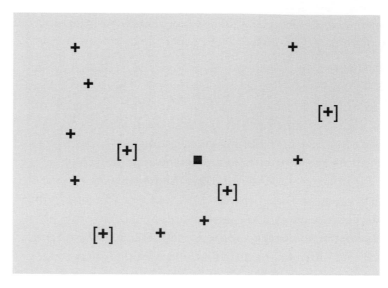

Figure 2.8 An example of Allen et al.'s (2004) procedure. Brackets indicate flashing targets

After completing one trial, a secondary task was introduced requiring participants to detect a number that was flashed on to the screen and say aloud 'low' if it was between 1 and 4 and 'high' if it was between 6 and 9. This secondary task either began before or after the target acquisition stage.

Regardless of expertise, detection accuracy decreased when there were more targets to track. However, the experts could keep track of more targets than the novices in both the single- and dual-task conditions, and were seemingly unaffected by the point at which the secondary task began. Novices demonstrated worse performance when the secondary task began before the target acquisition phase, but experts did not. Allen et al. suggest this is because the novices needed more attentional resources at the target acquisition phase than the experts did: the latter's experience in tracking multiple targets made this phase more automatic for them. Nevertheless, experts' performance was still degraded with the introduction of a secondary task, demonstrating that expertise does not insure against distraction, and that attentional capacity remains limited.

The studies by Shaffer, Spelke et al. and others are impressive demonstrations of how 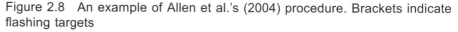practice can improve dual-task performance. However, the measures of performance in these studies are quite coarse and may not have detected any fine-grain differences between single- and dual-task conditions. Pashler (1998) argues that complex, continuous tasks, like those used by Shaffer and Spelke et al., do not convincingly rule out the possibility that participants perform the tasks by task switching. He suggests that you would obtain results that looked like Spelke et al.'s if the two tasks did interfere with each other, but participants learned an effective way of scheduling each task's demands on limited central resources.

More recent research has focused on more artificial tasks, with greater control over the precise timing of stimuli and responses. It has investigated a phenomenon called the **psychological refractory period (PRP)** (Telford, 1931; Welford, 1952; review in Pashler, 1994): if a participant performs two tasks, each of which requires a fast response to an individual stimulus, it takes longer to respond to the second stimulus when the interval between the stimuli is very short (typically, up to about half a second). The PRP effect persists even if one response is made verbally and the other manually (i.e. it is not a problem with moving the fingers) and if the stimuli are presented in different modalities.

Psychological refractory period (PRP)
The delay in responding to the second of two stimuli presented very close together in time, assumed to occur because information-processing systems are still preoccupied with processing the first stimulus.

Pause for thought

Given what you know about filter models of attention, how can we explain this PRP?

One explanation is that the PRP reflects a bottleneck in central processing (perhaps including response selection): processing of the first stimulus has to be completed before the second stimulus can be processed. Tasks effectively 'queue' for access to central processing resources. The PRP can be reduced with practice (probably by reducing the processing time for the first stimulus so that it acts as less of a bottleneck). However, there is no evidence that the PRP can be eliminated altogether, even after extensive practice (Pashler, 1988; Ruthruff et al., 2001; see Figure 2.9).

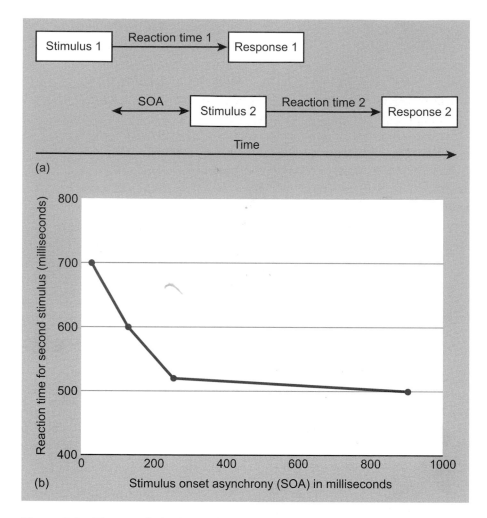

(a)

(b)

Figure 2.9   The psychological refractory period (redrawn from Pashler, 1998) (a) The PRP paradigm: two stimuli are presented sequentially, separated in time by a variable interval (the 'stimulus onset asynchrony' or 'SOA'); (b) Typical effect of varying the SOA, on reaction time to the second stimulus: as the SOA becomes shorter (left side of graph) RT becomes longer

Box 2.2   Crossing boundaries: neuropsychological studies of dual tasking

Neuroimaging studies can also throw some light on what happens during dual tasking. Deprez et al. (2013) used fMRI to record brain activity while participants performed one, two or three tasks at the same time. Behaviourally, performance was slower and less accurate in the dual- and multitask conditions than when only a single task was performed. fMRI showed that in the single-task conditions, there was increased activity in the relevant sensory **cortex** (i.e. increased activity in visual cortex during a visual task and increased activity in auditory cortex during an auditory task). Dual tasking produced no more activity in sensory areas, but instead produced increased activation in predominantly right-sided frontal and parietal areas of the cortex (including areas of dorso-lateral prefrontal cortex, well known to be involved in executive function) and in the **cerebellum**. Adding the third task (a memory task) produced additional activity in corresponding left-hemisphere pre frontal regions. Thus, as multitasking demands increase, there is progressively greater involvement of brain regions involved in executive control, top-down control of attention processes, and working memory. Multitasking involves both task-specific brain regions (related to holding the visual and auditory stimuli in memory) plus regions involved in more domain-general activities (trying to coordinate the different tasks, allocate attention appropriately, etc.).

Dux et al. (2009) scanned participants on three occasions while they learned to perform two tasks simultaneously (an auditory–vocal task and a visual–manual task). They then looked specifically for evidence of any changes in activity in areas known to be involved in multitasking and sensorimotor training. One area was particularly interesting, the left inferior frontal junction (IFJ), located between the prefrontal and premotor cortex. Before training, this area showed increased activity in dual-task trials compared with single-task trials. As training progressed, this difference decreased, as did processing time in the IFJ. Dux et al. found no evidence that any brain regions were recruited anew or more extensively with training, as would be required if improvements in multitasking performance were based on reorganisation of existing areas or the recruitment of new ones.

Dux et al.'s interpretation is that multitasking interference results from the funnelling of information from distinct sensorimotor tasks

Neuroimaging

A generic term referring to techniques for visualising brain activity ('functional' imaging, e.g. PET, SPECT, MEG and fMRI) or brain structure ('structural' imaging, e.g. CT and MRI).

Cortex

('Bark' in Latin.) In psychology and neuropsychology, usually shorthand for 'cerebral cortex', the outer layer of the cerebral hemispheres of the brain. It consists of 'grey matter' (principally neurons, q. v.).

Cerebellum

('Little brain' in Latin.) Two small hemispheres located beneath the cortical hemispheres, at the back of the head; the cerebellum plays an important role in directing movements and balance. Recent research shows it is also implicated in executive control, spatial cognition and emotional processing.

into overlapping groups of neurons in the prefrontal cortex. This produces a bottleneck of information processing at the central stage of decision making/response selection. Training speeds up information processing through this prefrontal bottleneck, thereby reducing the overlap in time of the sensorimotor tasks in this brain region. Dux et al. suggest that the efficiency of information processing in the prefrontal cortex is thus the limiting factor in our ability to multitask – a conclusion that is broadly in line with the interpretation of the PRP described earlier.

4.1   Summary

So, can we learn to dual task? The overall conclusion is that we can learn to perform two tasks simultaneously to the point where, on a superficial level at least, performance seems almost as good as when each task is performed separately. A closer investigation of how this is done suggests that participants may learn to more efficiently time-share limited central resources between the tasks.

5   Applying the research: attention and driving

Now several models of attention have been examined, let's consider their relevance to a familiar everyday activity: driving a vehicle. The ability to drive is something that an experienced driver takes for granted, but it is a more complex and attention-demanding task than it initially appears.

[handwritten margin notes: Visual Space, Auditory, Attention, Coordination]

> ## Pause for thought
>
> What types of cognitive resources are needed for driving? Does driving require controlled attention all of the time?

[handwritten notes: ✓ / NO.]

Let's examine the components of driving. Routinely, while driving, you must monitor several views, make decisions about speed and braking distances, ensure you stay in lane, track the movements of other vehicles and road users (and react appropriately), as well as make plans for route choice. At any moment, a driver's plans and behaviour may have to alter, based on the movements of other road users or unexpected events. Driving therefore involves numerous cognitive processes: visual and auditory perception, spatial awareness, coordination, attention, the motor system and decision-making skills. Given the necessity to combine so many skills in order to drive safely, it appears that driving isn't a simple, unitary, task. Why, then, do experienced drivers often claim that driving feels 'automatic' and undemanding to them?

The models of attention described earlier would suggest that experienced drivers perhaps have a lower cognitive load and greater central executive control over their attention due to increased practice. However, given that any driving environment is, by nature, dynamic and constantly changing, can any part of the driving task be processed automatically?

5.1   Can driving be performed automatically?

For a novice driver, operating all of the driving controls at once is challenging and tiring. With greater practice and experience, most feel that the task becomes less taxing and perhaps more 'automatic' in nature. As you have seen, research suggests that increased practice results in faster processing and less subjective effort. Indeed, many drivers report having experienced so-called 'highway hypnosis' – the realisation that you have driven somewhere seemingly on auto-pilot, without consciously having applied your attention. While this phenomenon could be seen to support the suggestion that driving can become automatic, Wertheim (1991) suggests an alternative explanation: when driving along familiar or uneventful routes, an individual's arousal level drops, resulting in less alertness to the visual environment. When arousal declines a driver perceives the visual scene as fixed and non-changing, leading them to alter their driving style to one that appears more automatic.

However, there may be a simpler explanation for why many drivers claim the task becomes automatic: experienced drivers do not need to make such a *concerted* effort to attend to the environment, maintain control of their vehicle and drive safely. From this standpoint, Groeger (2000) argues that driving feels automatic because experienced drivers have little recollection of individual elements of the task (e.g. changing gear, steering, etc.) and can also complete other non-interactive tasks, such as listening to the radio, apparently without driving performance being affected. Therefore, after mastering the skills of driving, it seems as if fewer of these control demands are placed on the driver.

Given this argument, some contend that certain aspects of driving, such as changing gear, do indeed become automatic (Anderson, 1995; Duncan et al., 1991) However, in an experiment comparing experienced and novice drivers' performance in manual and automatic transmission cars, Shinar et al. (1998) showed that experienced drivers detected significantly more road signs when driving the automatic vehicle. This suggests that changing gear carries a 'cognitive cost' and therefore cannot be considered automatic.

Perhaps then, rather than driving *actually* becoming automatic, our subjective experience *suggests* this is the case. This subjective experience of automaticity may lead drivers to feel that, because driving requires little conscious effort, attention can be safely applied to other tasks, such as talking on the phone. Pashler (1998) points out that driving is largely a 'non-paced' activity, in the sense that – unlike many laboratory experiments – the driver can choose to perform actions as and when they feel they need to. Although, in theory, a driver should be continuously monitoring their environment, in practice the process is forgiving of brief lapses. Likewise a driver does not have to continuously steer the car: course corrections can be intermittent. Pashler speculates that as a driver becomes more experienced, the processes involved in driving take up progressively shorter amounts of central processing time, so there is ample opportunity for drivers to switch constantly between the tasks of driving and whatever else they choose to do in the car. Driving has not become automatic: it has merely become so efficient in its use of central processing resources that task switching occurs so rapidly the driver is unaware it is taking place.

5.2   Can I dual task while driving?

Given what we have learned about models of attention, and our ability to divide and switch our attention between tasks, it could be argued that dual tasking behind the wheel is possible. Many people engage in phone conversations while driving, and report no negative effects on their driving performance. This, paired with a driver's subjective experience of automaticity, could suggest that drivers have 'spare' attentional resources they can apply to other tasks. Some researchers have claimed that during 'routine' driving, around 40 per cent of a driver's attention could be allocated to non-driving tasks (Green and Shah, 2004). If an individual's **cognitive workload** (that is, the amount of information being processed at any one time) is low then perhaps this argument holds true, but what if something unexpected happens in the driving environment while we are completing a secondary task? Do we have enough attentional resources to maintain performance in both tasks, or does one task suffer (and which one)? These questions will be addressed by looking at the example of phone use while driving in relation to cognitive models of dual tasking.

Cognitive workload
The amount of mental activity or effort that is required at a given time.

5.3   Behavioural effects of dual tasking ✗

In the UK it is legal to converse on a hands-free phone while driving. This implies that the main problems with dual tasking when driving are physical ones: holding the phone, dialling a number or typing a text message. However, although these actions do represent a significant distraction to drivers, research has unequivocally demonstrated that hands-free phone use can be equally distracting because of the attentional resources required by the secondary task.

Research into phone use and driving has revealed that drivers using mobile phones demonstrate longer reaction times for hazards; poor decision-making abilities; poor lane discipline; a failure to detect other road users and road signs; alterations in speed choice; questionable headway and gap judgements; reduced use of mirrors; and a greater likelihood of being involved in an accident than undistracted drivers (reviews in Hole, 2007; Strayer et al., 2011) (Figure 2.10). What is it about talking on the phone that is so distracting to a driver?

Figure 2.10   Risky behaviour: a dual-tasking driver

5.4   Dual-tasking research findings: do we shift or divide our attention?

Brown et al. (1969) were among the first to investigate the behavioural effects of dual tasking while driving. Participants had to drive around a test track and judge whether or not certain gaps were large enough for their car to pass through. At the same time, they had a hands-free phone conversation with an experimenter, which involved solving verbal reasoning tasks. Brown et al. found that when participants were dual tasking there was little to no negative effect on vehicle control (i.e. steering, changing gear, etc.), tasks that they termed to be 'overlearned', but that perceptual, decision-making abilities, such as those measured in the gap judgement task, were negatively affected. Brown et al. concluded that while phone use does not necessarily have much effect on vehicle control, it does impose greater demands on a driver in terms of increased cognitive workload, which in turn could then affect driving performance.

This view was supported by the classic study of Alm and Nilsson (1994). They manipulated the complexity of the driving task to see whether higher task demands engender higher cognitive load and subsequent poorer driving performance. Participants drove along either an 'easy' (flat and straight) or a 'hard' (winding and hilly) route in a driving simulator, while holding a phone conversation. It was predicted that the harder the driving route, the higher an individual's cognitive workload would be, so that driving performance (as measured by reaction times, lane discipline and headway distance) would be worse than when completing an easier route. Cognitive workload did indeed increase in line with the introduction of the phone task (and braking times were greater and speed was reduced). However, contrary to predictions, driving performance was worse in the 'easy' condition than in the 'hard' and control conditions. Rather than simply dividing attention between the two tasks, drivers in the 'easy' condition may have shifted their attention predominantly towards the phone task, as the driving task was uneventful and predictable. However, drivers in the 'hard' condition tended to divide their attention between the two tasks – demonstrating some degree of deteriorated driving performance, but not to the level shown by those in the 'easy' condition. Alm and Nilsson therefore concluded that, based on the complexity of the driving situation, dual-tasking drivers either shift or divide their attention between the two tasks.

Redelmeier and Tibshirani (1997) analysed accident statistics of individuals who had been involved in a road traffic collision. These statistics were then cross-referenced with the drivers' phone records, to determine whether a phone was actually in use before or during the accident. Individuals who spoke on the phone while driving, or who had recently finished an in-car phone conversation (i.e. within five minutes), were around four times more likely to be involved in an accident than those who did not use a phone. These findings clearly demonstrate that introducing a secondary, attention-demanding task impairs driving performance. Moreover, the distracting effects persisted after the conversation had ended. This suggests that attentional resources necessary for 'safe' driving may be required not just for processing the conversation while it happens, but also for thinking about the contents of the conversation after it has ended. This is supported by the results of a laboratory study by Savage et al. (2013), demonstrating that hazard perception is impaired by thinking about the contents of an earlier conversation.

According to the models of attention addressed earlier, a dual-tasking driver may exceed their maximum cognitive workload, meaning they reach a bottleneck in their attentional abilities. If so, they need to decrease this cognitive workload by reducing task demands (in line with Hockey's 'compensatory control' model). Ideally, this would take the form of ending the phone conversation, but dual-tasking drivers may often choose to maintain the conversation and alter the driving task instead. A driver may dispense with seemingly less important aspects of driving, such as use of mirrors or indicators. They may also move to a slow lane and reduce their speed. All of these actions, though undesirable in terms of safe driving, may reduce the rate of information-processing demands placed on the driver, decreasing overall cognitive workload and enabling some level of performance in both tasks. Alternatively, a driver may pause in their conversation while they navigate the driving situation before returning their attention to the call when the perceived danger is reduced.

It seems apparent, then, that a dual-tasking driver may demonstrate a combination of shifting *and* dividing their attention between tasks. This appears to depend on the task demands at any one moment, along with the perceived importance of the secondary task to the driver.

5.5   Can I safely talk to a passenger in my car?

McEvoy et al. (2007) compared accident risk in drivers talking on the phone and those talking to passengers. In support of Redelmeier and Tibshiriani's findings, they found that, compared with driving without any distraction, participation in a hands-free phone conversation resulted in a four-fold increase in the risk of being involved in an accident, whereas in-car conversations doubled accident risk. These findings suggest that while any type of conversation increases accident risk, phone conversations may be more distracting than conversations with passengers.

Crundall et al. (2005) suggest that one reason why a mobile phone conversation is more distracting for a driver is because, unlike a passenger, the remote converser is unaware of any variations in the cognitive demands being placed on the driver, and hence is unable to adjust their conversation to suit. Crundall et al. compared drivers' performance while they conversed with a sighted passenger, a blindfolded passenger, and while engaged in a hands-free phone conversation. Passengers who could see what was happening suppressed conversation when driving demands increased; but blindfolded and phone conversation partners did not, and were consequently more distracting to drivers.

5.6 Multiple resource theory and driving

Wickens' (1984) multiple resource theory would seem ideally suited to explaining what might happen if a driver tried to use a mobile phone while driving. Remember that the model suggests there are separate pools for resources for each sensory modality, for central processing and for output. Look back at your response to Activity 2.3 now. The model seems to predict that driving and conversing on a mobile phone should be compatible activities. If driving involves visual input (focal vision for hazard detection and ambient vision for lane maintenance), spatial coding of information and manual responses (steering, braking, etc.), it should be using separate pools of resources from those involved in conversing on a phone (auditory input, verbal coding and vocal responses).

In practice, a wealth of empirical research shows this is emphatically not the case: phone conversations do affect driving performance. The reasons for the discrepancy between the model's prediction and the real-world data may arise from a misconception of what talking on a mobile phone actually involves. Many phone calls involve visual imagery, and hence have a spatial component that probably competes with driving for resources (Briggs et al., in preparation).

A potential limitation of multiple resource theory as an explanation of dual tasking in drivers is that in the laboratory, an experimenter instructs a participant on what their primary and secondary tasks are, and it is assumed that the participant allocates their attention accordingly. In the real world, however, individuals make their own decisions on how to allocate their attention, and these choices may change from moment to moment. Individuals often fail to prioritise the driving task over a secondary conversation task, even when cognitive workload is already increased due to the challenges of the driving task (Nowakowski et al., 2001).

5.7   Compensatory control and driving

How does Hockey's (1997) compensatory control model apply to phone use while driving? Refer back to Figure 2.7. A driver has the primary goal of travelling from destination A to destination B (controlled by lower-level Loop A processing). However, if the phone rings and the driver engages in a conversation, additional effort and control will need to be applied to the driving task in order to maintain performance. If the action monitor and effort monitor detect demands beyond the capacity of lower-level processing, the supervisory controller will take charge, enabling higher-level Loop B processing. To compensate for increased attentional demands, and to reduce the cognitive cost to themselves, the driver may also decrease their speed or dispense with seemingly less crucial aspects of the driving task, such as checking mirrors and indicating, while applying more conscious effort overall to performing the two concurrent tasks.

Endogenous factors
Factors within the body or mind, rather than external factors. For example, lost and thirsty in a desert, our internal state would direct our attention towards any potential sources of water.

Hockey points out that although such behaviour may enable competent dual tasking up to a certain point, consistent performance at the upper level of processing drains attentional resources, leads to increased strain and cognitive workload, and subsequently could result in the selection of a 'coping strategy' that no longer protects the primary task from the distracting effects of a secondary task, leading to overall decreased task performance.

Exogenous factors
External factors or events in our environment, rather than internal thoughts or feelings. For example, a sudden loud noise is an exogenous factor that automatically grabs our attention.

Hockey's model provides a plausible explanation for how drivers cope with short-term dual tasking by applying control and compensating for increases in cognitive workload by altering primary task goals. However, although the model takes into account both **endogenous** and **exogenous factors** (in the form of internal and external goals), it still tends to assume that the primary task is viewed as the most important task to be completed, even in the face of secondary tasks. It does not consider the possibility that the secondary task may be assessed as being more important, leading to a shift in attention (e.g. a driver may consider a phone conversation to be more important than the seemingly simple task of driving). Furthermore, the model does not take into account the possibility that different tasks may use different attentional resources, leading to either competition for shared resources or alterations in attention allocation strategies. Nevertheless, the compensatory strategies demonstrated in a great deal of driving research (e.g. reducing speed, reduced use of mirrors, etc.) offer support for Hockey's model, at least in general terms.

5.8   Can I learn to dual task while driving?

Is it possible to learn to control our attention and therefore competently dual task while driving? Evidence on this issue is mixed. Using a driving simulator, Shinar et al. (2005) considered the effects of the driving situation, the type of conversation and the effect of practice on cognitive workload and dual-task performance. Participants completed five trials of simulated driving while holding a phone conversation. While driving initially deteriorated when dual tasking, by the fifth trial no such detriments were apparent, suggesting that individuals could learn to divide attention successfully. Shinar et al. claim this is because participants learned to pace both the conversation and their driving speed in order to reduce the rate of information input, meaning they had a lower level of cognitive workload at any one time.

Contradictory findings come from a study by Cooper and Strayer (2008). Also using a simulator, they showed that mobile phone use impaired driving performance just as much in drivers who used their phone regularly as it did in drivers who never used a phone. This might seem at odds with research showing that with extensive practice, people can learn to combine tasks; however Cooper and Strayer suggest that practice only improves dual tasking when the secondary task is highly consistent so that it can become automatised: driving is just too variable for this to happen. Given the inconsistent findings on this important topic, more research is clearly warranted.

5.9   Summary

Research on the effects of mobile phone use during driving, using a variety of methods, all points to one conclusion: contrary to their subjective impressions, drivers cannot safely combine the two tasks, because conversing on a mobile phone diverts attention away from driving. Psychological theories of attention can account for why this is so. Once it is appreciated that conversing on a phone has visual–spatial elements as well as verbal ones, Wickens' multiple resource theory can explain why the two tasks are so incompatible: they compete for the same limited attentional resources. Hockey's compensatory control theory explains how drivers attempt to dual task. They try to reduce the demands of the driving task, by driving more slowly and using the mirrors and indicators less, but this may not be enough to compensate for the impairments produced by dual tasking. Norman and Shallice's theory of controlled and automatic processing explains why drivers might think they can combine the two tasks: by relying on their experience and expectations about the driving environment, a great deal of driving can probably be performed by the contention scheduling system's responses to environmental triggers. This gives drivers the false impression that driving is an 'automatic' activity. Unfortunately, sometimes situations arise that require the urgent intervention of the supervisory attentional system: by the time this has taken control of behaviour, it may be too late to avert an accident.

6 Individual differences in dual-tasking ability

The preceding discussion has considered whether extensive practice of tasks might facilitate dual-tasking performance. There has been surprisingly little research on other potential sources of individual differences in the ability to do two things at once. A few studies have investigated whether there are any gender or age differences in dual-tasking ability.

6.1 Are women better at multitasking than men?

The popular belief that women can multitask better than men actually has no scientific basis: Hambrick et al. (2010) searched the literature and couldn't find a single study to support this claim. Mäntylä (2013) compared men and women on multitasking with 'gender-fair' component tasks (i.e. tasks that neither gender had practised before). In two experiments, men outperformed women. Mäntylä points out that individual differences in multitasking could come from two sources: how well a person can perform each specific task and how well they can coordinate and monitor different activities. He suggests this coordination involves working memory abilities (maintaining and updating multiple task goals) and spatial abilities (ability to coordinate spatial relations).

The latter might seem surprising, but Mäntylä suggests that multitasking involves time processing, and one strategy for doing that is to think of time in spatial terms (e.g. using a spatial 'timeline'). Mäntylä believes that his observed gender differences in multitasking were really attributable to gender differences in spatial ability. However he concedes he has only looked at multitasking in a very limited domain (when coordination in time was important), and that in other contexts, other factors might come into play: in short, he points out that rather than there being gender differences in 'multitasking' in general, the pattern of gender differences (if any) is highly likely to depend on the nature of the tasks being coordinated.

In the context of driving, Watson and Strayer (2010) found no gender differences in dual-tasking ability: men and women were equally impaired when using a mobile phone while driving.

6.2   Does age predict dual-tasking ability?

There is some evidence that older adults find multitasking harder than younger adults (review in Kramer and Madden, 2008). One theory is that attentional resources diminish with age, leaving older adults with fewer total resources to distribute across tasks and greater dual-task costs. There's also considerable evidence that walking and balance require increasing cognitive control with age. In the elderly, dual tasking is associated with an increased risk of falling, although training can ameliorate these effects (review in Wollesen and Voelcker-Rehage, 2014).

Neider et al. (2011) performed an interesting study on age differences in dual tasking. They constructed a virtual street-crossing task, using video displays and a treadmill. The task was to safely cross the 'road', avoiding collisions with oncoming 'traffic'. Participants crossed while undistracted, while listening to music on an iPod, or while using a mobile phone. Under difficult crossing conditions (heavy 'traffic'), older adults (aged 59 to 81) were more impaired than younger participants, chiefly because they took longer to initiate their crossings. Impairment was worsened by phone use, suggesting disruption to planning processes during multitasking. As has been found in research on driving, using a mobile phone affected performance much more than listening to music.

6.3   Summary

The effects of age and gender on dual-tasking ability are relatively under-researched: while there are some indications that multitasking might show some decline with age, there is certainly little support for the popular notion that women are naturally good multitaskers.

7   Concluding thoughts

The theories and findings discussed in this chapter suggest that attention is a more complex process than might be imagined, based on our own introspections. Overall, it seems we can perform two tasks at once, but there are definite limits on our capacity to do so. If an individual practises or has specialist training on a task, certain aspects of that task may become 'automatic' in the sense that fewer attentional resources may be required. However, experience and expertise do not remove the possibility of distraction, especially in dynamic tasks such as driving. While we can learn to dual task to some extent, the limits to our processing capacity are still evident even after extensive practice and experience.

Further reading

- For those who are interested in further research on the psychology of driving, this is an interesting and accessible review of relevant research:

Hole, G.J. (2007) *The Psychology of Driving*, Hove, Erlbaum.

- This paper provides an interesting application of Lavie's theory of perceptual load to the question of whether there are age differences in selective visual attention:

Maylor, E. A., and Lavie, N. (1998) 'The influence of perceptual load on age differences in selective attention', *Psychology and aging*, vol. 13, no. 4, pp. 563–73.

- This paper explores so-called 'supertaskers' – individuals who seem to be capable of dual tasking without any detriment to performance in either task. It provides interesting insight into how we can understand and develop further models of attention:

Watson, J. M. and Strayer, D. L. (2010) 'Supertaskers: profiles in extraordinary multitasking ability', *Psychonomic Bulletin & Review*, vol. 17, no. 4, pp 479–85.

- Pashler's contribution to the study of attention has been clearly shown in this chapter. In this, now classic, paper he discusses early research relating to attentional bottlenecks and questions if we can really do two things at the same time:

Pashler, H. (1993) 'Doing two things at the same time', *American Scientist*, vol. 81, no. 1, pp. 48–55.

References

Allen, R., McGeorge, P., Pearson, D. and Milne, A.B. (2004) 'Attention and expertise in multiple target tracking', *Applied Cognitive Psychology*, vol. 18, pp. 337–47.

Alm, H. and Nilsson, L. (1994) 'Changes in driver behaviour as a function of hands free mobile phones: a simulator study', *Accident Analysis and Prevention*, vol. 26, no. 4, pp. 441–51.

Anderson, J.R. (1995) *Learning and Memory: An Integrated Approach*, New York, Wiley.

Briggs, G.F., Hole, G.J. and Land, M.F. (in preparation) 'Imagery-inducing distraction leads to cognitive tunnelling and deteriorated driving performance'.

Broadbent, D.E. (1958) *Perception and Communication*, Oxford, Oxford University Press.

Brooks, L.R. (1968) 'Spatial and verbal components of the act of recall', *Canadian Journal of Psychology*, vol. 22, pp. 349–68.

Brown, I.D., Tickner, A.H. and Simmonds, D.C.V. (1969) 'Interference between concurrent tasks of driving and telephoning', *Journal of Applied Psychology*, vol. 53, pp. 419–24.

Burnham, B.R., Sabia, M. and Langan, C. (2014) 'Components of working memory and visual selective attention', *Journal of Experimental Psychology: Human Perception and Performance*, vol. 40, no. 1, pp. 391–403.

Cherry, E.C. (1953) 'Some experiments on the recognition of speech with one and with two ears', *Journal of the Acoustical Society of America*, vol. 25, pp. 975–9.

Cooper, J.M. and Strayer, D.L. (2008) 'Effects of simulator practiced and real-world experience on cell-phone related driver distraction', *Human Factors*, vol. 50, pp. 893–902.

Corteen, R.S. and Dunn, D. (1974) 'Shock-associated words in a non-attended message: a test for momentary awareness', *Journal of Experimental Psychology*, vol. 102, pp. 1143–4.

Crundall, D., Bains, M., Chapman, P. and Underwood, G. (2005) 'Regulating conversation during driving: a problem for mobile telephones?', *Transportation Research Part F: Traffic Psychology and Behaviour*, vol. 8, no. 3, pp. 197–211.

Deprez, S., Vandenbulcke, M., Peeters, R., Emsell, L., Amant, F. and Sunaert, S. (2013) 'The functional neuroanatomy of multitasking: combining dual tasking with a short term memory task', *Neuropsychologia*, vol. 51, pp. 2251–60.

Deutsch, J.A., and Deutsch, D. (1963) 'Attention: some theoretical considerations', *Psychological Review*, vol. 87, pp. 272–300.

Duncan, J., Williams, P. and Brown, I. (1991) 'Components of driving skill: experience does not mean expertise', *Ergonomics*, vol. 34, pp. 919–37.

Dux, P.E., Tombu, M.N., Harrison, S., Rogers, B.P., Tong, F. and Marois, R. (2009) 'Training improves multitasking performance by increasing the speed of information processing in human prefrontal cortex', *Neuron*, vol. 63, pp. 127–38.

Green, P. and Shah, R. (2004) 'Task times and glance measures of the use of telematics: a tabular summary of the literature. A report on safety vehicles using the adaptive interface technology (SAVE-IT, Task 6)', Ann Arbour, MI, University of Michigan Transportation Research Institute.

Groeger, J.A. (2000) *Understanding Driving*, Hove, Psychology Press.

Hambrick, D.Z., Oswald, F.L., Darowski, E.S., Rench, T.A. and Brou, R. (2010) 'Predictors of multitasking performance in a synthetic work paradigm', *Applied Cognitive Psychology*, vol. 24, pp. 1149–67.

Hirst, W., Spelke, E.S., Reaves, C.C., Caharack, G. and Neisser, U. (1980) 'Dividing attention without alternation or automaticity', *Journal of Experimental Psychology: General*, vol. 109, no. 1, pp. 98–117.

Ho, C. and Spence, C. (2008) *The Multisensory Driver: Implications for Ergonomic Car Interface Design (Human Factors in Road and Rail Transport)*, Aldershot, Ashgate.

Hockey, G.R.J. (1997) 'Compensatory control in the regulation of human performance under stress and high workload: a cognitive-energetical framework', *Biological Psychology*, vol. 45, pp. 73–93.

Hole, G.J. (2007) *The Psychology of Driving*, Hove, Erlbaum.

Kahneman, D. (1973) *Attention and Effort*, Englewood Cliffs, NJ, Prentice Hall.

Kramer, A. F. and Madden, D. (2008) 'Attention', in Craik, F.I.M. and Salthouse, T.A. (eds) *The Handbook of Aging and Cognition*, 3rd edn, New York, Psychology Press.

Lachter, J., Forster, K.L. and Ruthruff, E. (2004) 'Forty-five years after Broadbent (1958): still no identification without attention', *Psychological Review*, vol. 111, no. 4, pp. 880–913.

Lavie, N. (1995) 'Perceptual load as a necessary condition for selective attention', *Journal of Experimental Psychology: Human Perception and Performance,* vol. 21, pp. 451–68.

Lavie, N. (2001) 'The role of capacity limits in selective attention: behavioral evidence and implications for neural activity', in Braun, J. and Koch, C. (eds) *Visual Attention and Cortical Circuits*, Cambridge, MA, MIT Press.

Lavie, N. (2005) 'Distracted and confused?: Selective attention under load', *Trends in Cognitive Sciences,* vol. 9, pp. 75–82.

Lavie, N. and De Fockert, J. (2005) 'The role of working memory in attentional capture', *Psychonomic Bulletin and Review*, vol. 12, issue 4, pp. 669–74.

Lavie, N., and Tsal, Y. (1994) 'Perceptual load as a major determinant of the locus of selection in visual attention', *Perception and Psychophysics*, vol. 56, pp. 183–97.

Lavie, N., Hirst A., Jan W. de Fockert, J.W. and Viding, E. (2004) 'Load theory of selective attention and cognitive control', *Journal of Experimental Psychology: General*, vol. 133, no. 3, pp. 339–54.

Mach, E. (1975) 'Recollections of the young Liszt as teacher', *Piano Quarterly*, vol. 23/89 (Spring), pp. 12–16.

Mackay, D. (1973) 'Aspects of the theory of comprehension, memory and attention', *Quarterly Journal of Experimental Psychology*, vol. 25, pp. 22–40.

Mäntylä, T. (2013) 'Gender differences in multitasking reflect spatial ability', *Psychological Science*, vol. 24, no. 4, pp. 514–20.

Marois, R., and Ivanoff, J. (2005) 'Capacity limits of information processing in the brain', *Trends in Cognitive Science*, vol. 9, pp. 296–305.

McEvoy, S.P., Stevenson, M.R. and Woodward, M. (2007) 'The contribution of passengers versus mobile phone use to motor vehicle crashes resulting in hospital attendance by the driver', *Accident Analysis and Prevention*, vol. 39, no. 6, pp. 1170–6.

Moray, N. (1959) 'Attention in dichotic listening: affective cues and the influence instructions', *Quarterly Journal of Experimental Psychology*, vol. 11, pp. 56–60.

Neider, M.B., Gaspar, J.G., McCarley, J.S., Crowell, J.A., Kaczmarski, H. and Kramer, A.F. (2011) 'Walking and talking: dual-task effects on street crossing behavior in older adults', *Psychology and Aging*, vol. 26, no. 2, pp. 260–8.

Norman, D.A. and Shallice, T. (1986) 'Attention to action: willed and automatic control of behaviour', in Davidson, R.J., Schwartz, G.E. and Shapiro, D. (eds) *Consciousness and Self Regulation: Advances in Research, Vol. IV*, New York, Plenum, pp. 1–18.

Nowakowski, C., Friedman, D. and Green, P. (2001) 'Cell phone ring suppression and HUD Caller ID: effectiveness in reducing momentary driver distraction under varying workload levels', *Technical Reports for The University of Michigan Transportation Research Institute* (Report No. UMTRI-2001–29).

Pashler, H. (1994) 'Dual-task interference in simple tasks: data and theory', *Psychological Bulletin*, vol. 116, pp. 220–44.

Pashler, H.E. (1998) *The Psychology of Attention*, Cambridge, MA, MIT Press.

Posner, M.I. and Petersen, S.E. (1990) 'The attention system of the human brain', *Annual Review of Neuroscience*, vol. 13, pp. 25–42.

Redelmeier, D.A. and Tibshirani, R.J. (1997) 'Association between cellular-telephone calls and motor vehicle collisions', *New England Journal of Medicine*, vol. 336, pp. 453–502.

Rosen, C. (2004) *Piano Notes: The Hidden World of the Pianist*, London, Penguin.

Ruthruff, E., Johnston, J.C. and Van Selst, M. (2001) 'Why practice reduces dual-task interference', *Journal of Experimental Psychology: Human Perception and Performance*, vol. 27, pp. 3–21.

Savage, S.W., Potter, D.D. and Tatler, B.W. (2013) 'Does preoccupation impair hazard perception? A simultaneous EEG and eye tracking study', *Transportation Research Part F: Traffic Psychology and Behaviour*, vol. 17, pp. 52–62.

Shaffer, L.H. (1975) 'Multiple attention in continuous verbal tasks', in Rabbitt, P. and Dornic, S. (eds) *Attention and Performance: V*, New York, Academic Press.

Shallice, T. and Burgess, P.W. (1991) 'Deficits in strategy application following frontal lobe damage in man', *Brain*, vol. 114, pp. 727–41.

Shiffrin, R.M. and Schneider, W. (1977) 'Controlled and automatic human information processing: II. Perceptual learning, automatic attending, and a general theory', *Psychological Review*, vol. 84, issue 1, pp. 127–190.

Shinar, D., Meir, M. and Ben-Shoham, I. (1998) 'How automatic is manual gear shifting?', *Human Factors*, vol. 40, no. 4, pp. 647–54.

Shinar, D., Tractinsky, N. and Compton, R. (2005) 'Effects of practice, age, and task demands, on interference from a phone task while driving', *Accident Analysis and Prevention*, vol. 37, no. 2, pp. 315–26.

Spelke, E.S., Hirst, W. and Neisser, U. (1976) 'Skills of divided attention', *Cognition*, vol. 4, pp. 215–30.

Strayer, D.L., Watson, J.M. and Drews, F.A. (2011) 'Cognitive distraction while multitasking in the automobile', in Ross, B. (ed.) *The Psychology of Learning and Motivation*, vol. 54, Burlington, MA, Academic Press.

Stuss, D.T., Shallice, T., Alexander, M.P. and Picton, T.W. (1995) 'A multidisciplinary approach to anterior attentional functions', *Annals of the New York Academy of Sciences*, vol. 769, pp. 191–212.

Telford, C.W. (1931) 'The refractory phase of voluntary and associative responses', *Journal of Experimental Psychology: General*, vol. 14, pp. 1–36.

Treisman, A. (1960) 'Contextual cues in selective listening', *Quarterly Journal of Experimental Psychology*, vol. 12, pp. 242–8.

Treisman, A. (1969) 'Strategies and models of selective attention', *Psychological Review*, vol. 76, pp. 282–99.

Watson, J.M. and Strayer, D.L. (2010) 'Supertaskers: profiles in extraordinary multitasking ability', *Psychonomic Bulletin and Review*, vol. 17, issue 4, pp. 479–85.

Welford, A.T. (1952) 'The "psychological refractory period" and the timing of high- speed performance – a review and a theory', *British Journal of Psychology*, vol. 43, pp. 2–19.

Wertheim, A.H. (1991) 'Highway hypnosis: a theoretical analysis', in Gale, A. G., Brown, I.D., Moorhead, I., Haslegrave, C.M. and Taylor, S.P. (eds) *Vision in Vehicles III*, Amsterdam, Elsevier.

Wickens, C.D. (1984) 'Processing resources in attention', in Parasuraman, R. and Davies, D.R. (eds) *Varieties of Attention*, New York, Academic Press.

Wickens, C.D. (2002) 'Multiple resources and performance prediction', *Theoretical Issues in Ergonomics Science*, vol. 3, no. 2, pp. 159–77.

Wickens, C.D. (2008) 'Multiple resources and mental workload', *Human Factors*, vol. 50, pp. 449–55.

Wollesen, B. and Voelcker-Rehag, C. (2014) 'Training effects on motor–cognitive dual-task performance in older adults: a systematic review', *European Review of Aging and Physical Activity*, vol. 11, pp. 5–24.

Chapter 3

Is seeing believing? Visual perception and attention for dynamic scenes

Gemma Briggs and Simon J. Davies

Contents

1 Introduction

TMA ⌀2

Under normal everyday conditions the experience of our senses gives rise to a correct interpretation of the world. However, we've also seen some instances of how the information taken in by our senses is not translated into an accurate reflection of the world, for example when viewing visual illusions. This chapter will look at a variety of experiments, some of which show there are surprising differences between what we *think* we see and experience, and what we *actually* see and experience. It will further explore the critical role that attention plays in how we experience and understand the world. Given what you have learned about attention and perception so far, it is clear that we can be selective in the information we attend to, but can also process unattended information, albeit at a cognitive cost.

The two main areas to be explored to highlight the role of attention in accurately representing and perceiving the world are:

- the ability to notice when change occurs

- the impact that focusing attention on one object or event has on our ability to notice other changes to a scene.

On that basis, this chapter should not only give you a better appreciation of the apparent disconnect between the biology of vision and what we perceptually experience, but also draw your attention (pun intended!) to bigger questions regarding the **phenomenology** of visual experience and attention.

Phenomenology
The way things appear or are experienced subjectively.

Learning outcomes

On completing this chapter you should:

- have an understanding of the importance of the interplay between attention and perception in everyday tasks

- have an understanding of key psychological theories and research on change blindness, inattentional blindness and choice blindness

- have an awareness of the applications of research findings in these areas.

---

2   The visual world

2.1   Is the visual world an illusion?

To start this chapter have a go at Activity 3.1. This activity requires you do something that most of us rarely do: to reflect on the day-to-day routine of paying attention to things in the world and how they appear. The rest of this chapter is concerned with developing a clearer understanding of the mechanisms of visual awareness and, on occasion, how they differ to the subjective 'feeling' we experience.

Activity 3.1: A moment of reflection

What are you experiencing right now? Move your eyes around the room. Blink. Focus on one object, and then broaden your attention to a larger part of the visual world in front of you.

Take a minute to reflect on what your perceptual experience is like. What are its contents? What does it 'feel' like? What will you remember from what you are experiencing now, in one minute's time?

If, like us, you report you are aware of everything within the scope of your visual field that you sense a fully colourful panorama, that there is equal detail across the visual field, that you could recall all the details you witnessed, and that your experience is continuous, despite the saccade and fixations you make, then you are sharing in a universal illusion. This is what it *feels* like to visually perceive the world, but what we feel and what is actually going on are very different.

Over the past 30 years the revolution in understanding how we perform cognitive tasks, such as perceiving and attending to the world, has been overhauled through a series of counter-intuitive discoveries in the field of cognitive science and philosophy. These discoveries are so dramatic that the new view is that we all share in what is now called the '**grand illusion**' (Noë, 2002). It is grand because it is universal, and it is illusory because our experience does not seem to match reality when we measure performance objectively. Chapter 1 described some interesting examples that demonstrate a mismatch between anatomy and subjective perceptual experience. One example is the blind spot

Grand illusion
The suggestion that our lived perceptual experience is fundamentally different from what is actually being accomplished by our sensory systems.

and how we do not notice an absence of signal coming from two large holes in our vision. Another is the perceptual inferences we make that cause us to flip reality with the Necker cube and other multi-stable illusions.

So what are we actually experiencing? Well, first it is known that the proximal retinal image is upside down with reference to the distal visual world, yet we perceive things the right way up. The vast majority of photoreceptive cells on the retina have only **achromatic sensitivity**, yet as we look out on to the world we see a vista of colour. The distribution of cells on the retina means that sensitivity diminishes dramatically from the fovea towards the periphery, leading to less and less detail. Finally, most eye movements are rapid shifts of focus from one location to the next, rather than continuous scans of the environment. So how does this biological information map on to our subjective assessment of our experience?

Subjectively, everything *feels* colourful yet we now know that only a small fraction of the retina processes colour. We also *feel* that the world is equally detailed across the visual field, yet we know this isn't the case. If you look at Figure 3.1 you can see that for objects to be equally discernible they need to increase in size substantially as they move away from the centre of your vision. So although everything in the visual field *feels* equally detailed, it is not. Lastly, we experience a sense of the world that is continuous and smooth. It feels very much as though the world is ever present and when we move our eyes we sweep through it. In fact, as most eye movements are discrete jumps, and as the information available during an eye movement is suppressed (so-called '**saccadic suppression**'), in reality what we are left with is a series of snapshots that somehow feel as though they are connected in time and space. The subjective sense we have is therefore not what we seem to be objectively experiencing.

Achromatic sensitivity
The sensitivity of some photoreceptive cells to overall levels of illumination (i.e. dark/light) and contrast rather than colour.

Saccadic suppression
The reduction of input from the eyes to the brain during an eye movement. Suppression is thought to assist with our ability to focus on specific objects and also to prevent the experience of blurred vision due to eye movement.

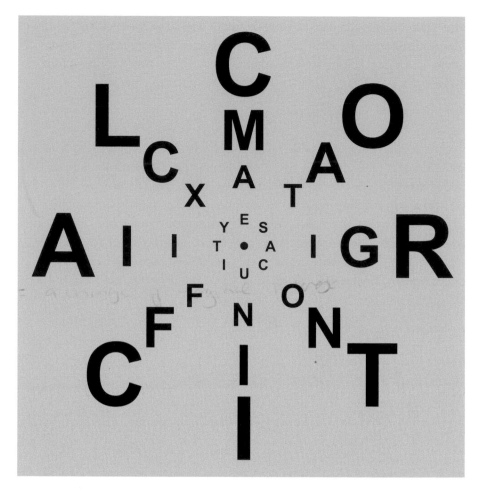

Figure 3.1 A chart that shows the size objects need to be across the visual field to be equally discriminable

The grand illusion hypothesis seeks to make sense of these disparities, and many more that you will meet throughout this chapter. Some of the disparities can be reconciled through new ways of understanding human visual perception and particularly the role of visual attention.

2.2 Do my eyes deceive me?

In Chapter 1 you learned how the visual system processes information. Nevertheless, there are certain aspects of our vision that offer additional insights. For example, our eyes make saccades as well as blinks and, when they do this, either they are entirely blind (blink) or else the visual input is drastically reduced to the level of functional blindness (saccade). These interruptions to our visual experience are not inconsequential; every second, on average, we make three or four rapid saccades (of about 30 milliseconds) and longer fixations (of about 300 milliseconds; Rayner, 1998), meaning that in a 16-hour day we make 172,800 eye movements adding up to 90 minutes of blindness (Irwin and Brockmole, 2004). But it is not the amount of overall blindness that is interesting, rather the frequency of interruptions we experience without really noticing. What we do notice is a continuous visual experience that is stable and without obvious gaps.

In an intriguing series of experiments, Irwin and colleagues (e.g. Irwin, 1996) sought to explore this experience by studying the fate of visual information when eye movements are made. They initially hypothesised that the coherence of our perceptual experience was achieved by a **visual buffer** that integrated information about the whole scene from different fixations. They failed to show this, but instead found that when eye movements are made we are good at detecting previously seen objects (i.e. within the last few seconds), but are not as sensitive to the background context. That is, we don't integrate snapshots to build up a detailed representation of the whole world; rather, we track specific objects. In one study, participants were asked to fixate on one point in a picture and then to make an eye movement to a specified object (Currie et al., 2000; see Figure 3.2). During the saccade some aspect of the display changed: the target object moved, the whole display including the object moved, or the whole display moved but the object remained in its original location. Their results indicated that participants were sensitive to the object moving on its own or with the rest of the scene, but were not sensitive to a situation where the object stayed in the same location but the background moved. (They didn't notice when the background changed!) This shows we perceive stability in the world across eye movements as long as the saccade target (object) maintains its position or expected position. While this ability has an evolutionary, adaptive benefit because it is more important to keep track of a potential predator than monitor the horizon, this effect can also cause potential danger, as you will discover later in the chapter.

Visual buffer
A short-lived mechanism for the storage of visual information for later processing.

Saccade target object (sign) →

Initial eye location in picture →

All shift down

Object shift down

Background shift up

Figure 3.2   Examples of Currie et al.'s stimuli

Short-term memory
A mechanism for the brief storage (in the order of a few seconds) of information to assist current thinking and awareness.

Executive control
The overall management of cognitive resources, including the ability to regulate and monitor how information is being processed.

Why might we be insensitive to some changes occurring in the world? Well, we normally aim to keep track of objects, and they tend to be fairly constant in terms of where they are from one moment to the next. We also have a **short-term memory** that is thought to be more concerned with objects than with separate features or spatial areas (Luck and Vogel, 1997; Walker and Davies, 2003). Currie et al. propose that eye movements are dedicated to tracking objects rather than re-mapping the entire visual scene for later recall (see also Hollingworth et al., 2008). Given the limitations of visual short-term memory, **executive control** and attention (Pylyshyn and Storm, 1988), it makes sense that we are not highly sensitive to changes in the environment because we do not have the capacity to represent them all. One theory for why we might not need detailed internal representations of the external world is that the world acts as its own memory and therefore does not need to be represented (O'Regan, 1992). We don't notice a shift in the world because the world is normally a reliable source of information.

2.3 Summary

The perceptual experience we have in many ways does not match what we objectively understand about our sensory systems, leading to the conclusion that we all share in a 'grand illusion'. A good example of the degree of sensory blindness most of us share is the spacing between our fixations on the environment. In terms of vision, it is known that information processing is suppressed during a saccade, so we only really see what we sample of the world through a fixation. There also appears to be an emphasis on certain aspects of the environment, such as objects, which most likely reflects the inherent limitations of our sensory and attentional systems. We can therefore begin to explain part of the grand illusion by the need to maximise the limited cognitive resources we have at our disposal, as well as the chief purpose of perception, which is to track and understand the objects in the world.

3   Why don't I always notice change?

3.1   What is change blindness?

Before you read on, have a go at Activity 3.2.

Activity 3.2: Spot the difference

Look at Figure 3.3 and see if you can tell what the difference is between the two pictures. Time yourself and compare your time with the answer later in the text.

= a change of marginal interest

Figure 3.3   Spot the difference

30 seconds!

The ability (or inability) to detect change has been used to develop increasingly complex accounts of visual memory, perception and attention. According to Gibson (see Chapter 1), perception is an act of exploration in a rich environment where objects are viewed in context, and with the perceiver's ability to act upon the environment for a protracted period of time. However, contemporary investigations in visual perceptual ability have explored the reasons for *failures* in detecting changes in a scene, rather than emphasising our *ability* to detect change. They are therefore interested in explaining why we can, on occasion, apparently be *change blind*.

One activity that requires us to attend to the material of interest is what you are doing right now: reading. Given what you have just learned about a functional blindness during an eye movement, what would you expect to happen if a change was made to the text you are reading at the same time as you made a saccade? Well, obviously you would not 'see' the change happening, but you might expect to notice the difference.

← probably not!

Pause for thought

Reflect on what you are experiencing now as you read these words. Do you notice the other words in the sentence? Do you think you would notice if some characteristics of the words changed, such as the case they are presented in?

In an early experiment on reading and eye movements, McConkie and Zola (1979) asked participants to read text where the letters alternated between upper and lower case, e.g. cHaNgE bLiNdNeSs. The twist in their experiment was that every time the participant made an eye movement the text case changed: so cHaNgE bLiNdNeSs would become ChAnGe BlInDnEsS. As the meaning of the words remained intact, one could still read the text. However, none of the participants reported ever noticing that anything had changed, despite the overall shape of each word they were about to fixate completely changing as they made an eye movement towards the words. Given the contention of Currie et al. (1995) that we are unperturbed by changes, other than the target our eye movement is aiming for, this result seems odd. However, it is known that the representations in visual short-term memory are somewhat abstract, and in this case the meaning of the word (i.e. the saccade target) was consistent in all cases. The target of the saccade was also there, as expected. Furthermore, objects in the real world can change their appearance when we move our eyes, but they remain what they are.

3.2   How is change blindness investigated?

One of the earliest papers on what is now called **change blindness** sought to explore change detection that was not contingent upon either eye movements or very brief displays. Rensink et al. (1997)

Change blindness
The inability to notice changes in a visual scene.

a typical feature

developed what is now the paradigmatic method within the field: the *flicker method*. Here, the participant is presented with a real-world scene for 240 milliseconds (ms), and then a brief intervening blank for 80 ms. After the blank, the original scene is reinstated, but with a change to the image of some sort (see Figures 3.4 and 3.5 for examples of changes made). The sequence then repeats with a brief blank 'flicker' between the changed and unchanged images until the participant notices the change. Changes could be to areas of central or marginal interest within the context of the scene. One might expect attention to be drawn to areas more meaningful to the scene.

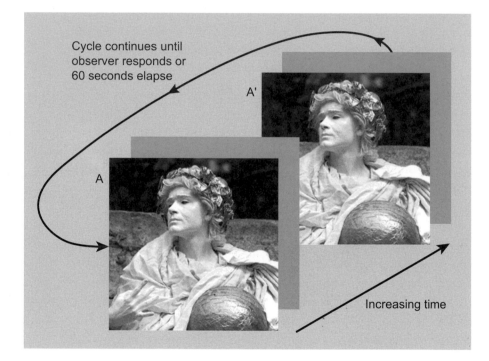

Figure 3.4   Flicker method
(Source: Rensink et al., 1997)

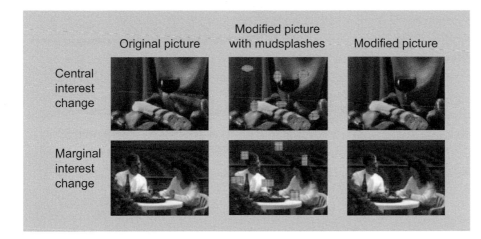

Figure 3.5   Example scenes from O'Regan et al. (1999)

Rensink et al. (1997) showed that it took participants many iterations of the flicker cycle to detect a change. In their original experiment they found it took on average 11 seconds to notice a marginal interest change, and 5 seconds to notice a central interest change. In a second experiment they increased the duration of the scene before each flicker to 560 ms, and still observed the same effects.

In Activity 3.2 you should have found it took you some time to detect that the change was the trees missing behind the Sphinx's head in the right-hand picture: a change of marginal interest.

The theoretical explanation for these prolonged failures to detect change involves both visual memory and visual attention. The argument is that without focused attention objects are not entered into visual short-term memory. In fact, without focused attention we can fail to see something in the centre of our gaze, so it is hardly surprising that it would not be remembered. The brief blank between images also serves to overwrite the contents of visual memory. If you had not recently attended to the object that was the subject of change, then you would not notice a subsequent change occur.

In a further study, O'Regan et al. (1999) removed the intervening blank between the changed and unchanged scenes. Without this break between the images one would imagine that change detection would be effortless. To make the task harder, when the scenes changed they added an 80 ms, non-relevant change to the scene by adding six salient patches. They refer to these as 'mudsplashes' (see Figure 3.5), and these never covered the change itself.

Their results again showed that it took a long time to see the change (up to 40 seconds), and also that central changes were easier to detect than marginal changes. A possible explanation for change blindness in this instance is that the sudden onset of the mudsplashes diverted attention from the less salient change to the scene. It is well-known that abrupt changes in the environment can capture attention, causing an individual to orientate their visual attention automatically to the new information (i.e. in a bottom-up fashion). This makes change detection all the more difficult (Posner, 1980).

To what extent might these findings extend to more real-world situations involving motion? We are all familiar with the idea of continuity errors in films: that some feature of the set or actors is inconsistent between camera cuts. These are difficult to spot, and are a real-world example of change blindness. Levin and Simons (1997) used film cuts to further develop an account of change blindness. In one experiment they used pairs of actors to act the same role and, across a film cut, the actor's identity would change (see Figure 3.6(a)). Viewers only noticed that the actor had changed 33 per cent of the time, despite giving accurate accounts of what they had seen in terms of the film's content.

Perhaps the ultimate example of change blindness in the truly ecologically valid sense was a study conducted by Simons and Levin (1998). Pushing their idea of real-world examples to the limit, they set up an interaction where an actor asked directions of a member of the public. During the conversation two people carrying a door walked between the pair. During this interval, the actor swapped places with one of the people carrying the door. The conversation then continued until the member of the public was asked whether they noticed anything different. Only 47 per cent noticed that they were now talking to a different person (see Figure 3.6(b))! In a follow-up experiment Simons and Levin explored whether social group membership played a role in change detection by having the actors dress as construction workers. The undergraduate student sample tested only noticed the person change 33 per cent of the time. Belonging to a different social group influenced the level of detail to which the students paid attention.

Figure 3.6   (a) An example of a film cut where the actor is swapped between cuts; (b) Actors swap places during a conversation with a member of the public

3.3   Theoretical explanations for change blindness

Much research has now explored the nature of what we see, how we see, and what we represent in visual short-term memory. Over the intervening years, theoretical models have been applied to try to explain some of the experimental findings. There does not appear to be any one model to explain all the phenomena discussed so far (and what will be discussed in the next sections). This is because there are a multitude of methodologies used and also a range of cognitive mechanisms that fully, or partly, determine any effect (e.g. attention, perception and visual short-term memory).

One candidate model for understanding our apparent lack of ability to detect changes to objects that we are not attending to (or have recently attended to, but have now disengaged from) is Anne Treisman's feature integration theory (FIT) (Treisman and Gelade, 1980). Her theory, which is too detailed to elaborate on fully here, considers attention as the 'glue' that establishes temporary representations in short-term memory. She considers that we have an ability to detect basic visual features in the environment with little effort, but to integrate features to form a lasting representation requires us to focus on the object. When we do this, we are said to establish a representation known as an 'object file'. This is considered to be a 'file' that contains information about the object's features as well as a way of tracking changes in its spatial and temporal characteristics. Importantly, without focused attention we can have an incorrect or false model of the world (Treisman and Schmidt, 1982), sometimes remembering an illusory combination of features from the environment.

A more recent model from within the change blindness community has a very similar structure to that of Treisman's FIT. Rensink's *coherence theory* (Rensink, 2000, 2002) argues for structures similar to object files that are established and maintained by attention. In the absence of attention, candidate objects are seen as volatile 'proto-objects' that are easily replaced by new features of a scene, and therefore are more likely to go unnoticed. The application of attention to these candidate objects establishes a more coherent form of representation that better supports our ability to detect change, but these too can become volatile and be easily replaced once attention is disengaged.

The involvement of attention seems critical for detecting change. Alongside this is the role of the representations that we can support within the capacity of visual short-term memory, presumably through the actions of attention. Failing to attend to an object, the withdrawal of attention from a critical part of a scene, or an impoverished representation in visual memory, can all account for the failures discussed. In the next section you will learn that attention is critical for being consciously aware of events, and also that in some cases we can be unaware of the very things we are physically looking at.

3.4 Summary

In this section you have learned that human observers are poor at detecting changes to scenes, a phenomenon referred to as change blindness. The flicker method is the most common technique employed to explore change blindness, though it can be criticised as lacking ecological validity. More ecological methods have been developed, such as film cuts and real-world interactions, with similarly striking results. The explanations for change blindness seem to involve several cognitive mechanisms and processes (depending upon the method), including short-term memory and attention. It is now widely accepted that attention is a critical mechanism for creating lasting representations of the world. In the absence of attention, or the disengagement of attention, representations are either not set up or can fade.

4   Why can't I see what I'm looking at?

Pause for thought

Have you ever had the experience of failing to find something you are actively searching for, only to then discover the object was right in front of you all the time? (This all too often seems to be the case with car keys!) Given what you know about attention and perception, why might this happen? What other factors might interfere with your ability to find what you are searching for?

4.1   How important is attention for accurate perception?

Inattentional blindness
The inability to notice events in a visual scene due to attention being applied elsewhere or due to current cognitive resources being exhausted.

Following on from investigations into change blindness comes the phenomenon of **inattentional blindness**. This is the inability to notice highly visible items, even when we look directly at them, due to our attention being applied elsewhere. Thus, the distinction between change blindness and inattentional blindness is that the former can be demonstrated when participants are simply asked to pay full attention to the task of detecting a change in a visual scene, whereas the latter demonstrates that when attention is applied to another task, events in a visual scene can seemingly go undetected. When frantically searching for your car keys, while trying to collect everything (or everyone) you need to take with you when you are running late, it may well be the case that inattention, rather than poor eyesight, is what prevents you from finding your keys. Many of us will have had experiences such as this where our attention has been applied elsewhere, meaning we miss important aspects of a scene.

Mack and Rock (1998) coined the term 'inattentional blindness' following on from their own investigations and earlier work carried out by Neisser (1967) and Neisser and Becklen (1975). They suggested that to fully appreciate the need for attention in order to drive perception, investigations need to remove the effect of expectation on perception. They claimed that because many previous investigations in this area adopted procedures where participants were *expecting* to search for a target among distractors, this expectation affected the participant's perception to the extent that it was not possible to investigate any perceptual processing of the unattended stimuli. For this reason, Mack and Rock distinguished between '**conscious perception**' – that which we subjectively experience, and '**implicit perception**' – processing that we are unaware of. They devised a procedure that could investigate both types of perception.

In their computer-based experiment, Mack and Rock flashed a black cross on a white screen for 200 ms. Participants were asked to judge which of the two arms of the cross was longer. On the third screen viewed by participants there was also an unexpected object (a small square) that appeared at the same time as the cross. This screen was known as the 'critical trial'. After viewing it, participants were asked if they had seen anything other than the cross on the screen. Once they had answered, participants were then asked to carry on with the remaining trials presented to them. At this point, regardless of the participant's answer to the question, they now had the suggestion in their mind that something unexpected might appear on the next screen. For this reason, the next screen (containing the cross and an unexpected object) was called the 'divided attention' trial, as participants would now be looking for unexpected objects as well as attempting to complete their primary task. Finally, participants were asked to complete a trial called the 'full attention' trial, where they were asked to ignore the cross, but to report whether or not an unexpected object appeared. Figure 3.7 shows the different trials in order.

Performance in the critical trial was then compared with that in the divided attention and full attention trials in order to identify the degree of inattentional blindness participants demonstrated. In this way, Mack and Rock were able to distinguish between perception *without* expectation for an unexpected object and perception when attention was divided between tasks.

Conscious perception
The subjective experience and awareness of perceiving something.

Implicit perception
Cognitive processing that the individual is largely unaware of. Although we are unaware of what we are processing, it can nevertheless have an influence on our behaviour.

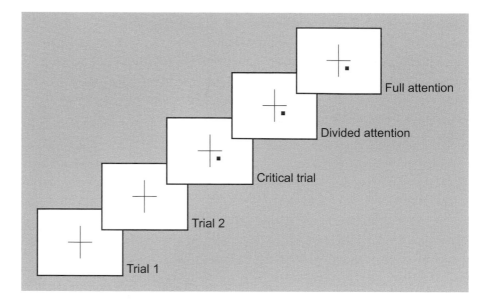

Figure 3.7   The five stages of Mack and Rock's experimental procedure

(Source: Mack and Rock, 1998)

Their results showed that around 25 per cent of participants failed to notice the unexpected object in the critical trial. Conversely, most participants detected the unexpected object in the divided and full attention trials, presumably because they were expecting to see it. Mack and Rock then varied the position of the cross and the unexpected object, either by moving the cross from the centre of the screen (the participant's fixation point) to one side (in a parafoval position), or the unexpected object from the side to the centre. In this case, they found that around 75 per cent of participants failed to detect the unexpected object if it was presented at the centre of the screen (at fixation) and the cross was presented parafovally (at one side). This striking finding led Mack and Rock to claim that rather than applying our attention to a specific visual object, we focus our visual attention on the area *around* the object. Therefore, when the cross was presented away from fixation, participants shifted their focus of attention to a different area, thus failing to detect the unexpected object presented at the centre of the screen.

Mack and Rock found similar effects when they varied the colour, orientation and duration on screen of the unexpected object. However, when the unexpected event was changed to the participant's name or a smiling face icon, participants in the critical trials tended to detect it, suggesting some processing of the unattended information, at a semantic level, had occurred. These simple, computer-based approaches allowed for a demonstration of the effect of expectation on perception, while also clearly revealing how focused attention can impair visual perception. However, in order to ascertain whether these effects were more pronounced according to the type of task presented, further researchers attempted to replicate these findings using a video-based approach.

4.2   Inattention: gorillas, umbrellas and attentional sets

Building on Mack and Rock's findings, Simons and Chabris (1999) questioned whether inattentional blindness could be sustained over a period of time longer than the 200 ms demonstrated previously, and whether a video study could offer more ecological validity. They recruited four groups of participants and asked them to watch a short film where two teams of three people played basketball: one team wore white shirts and the other wore black shirts. The players moved around randomly, but passed the ball to one another in a pre-arranged order. The players passed the ball to one another either by bouncing it on the ground or by an aerial throw. After 45 seconds, an unexpected event occurred: either a woman carrying an umbrella walked across the screen, or a person dressed as a gorilla walked across the screen. This unexpected event lasted for 5 seconds, giving participants plenty of time to see it. Two different types of video were used:

- in the 'transparent' condition, three films (one of each of the teams and one of the unexpected event) were made separately and were then made semi-transparent before being superimposed

- in the 'opaque' condition, one film (containing both teams and the unexpected event) was made, meaning there were points at which the players and the unexpected event occluded other parts of the scene (see Figure 3.8).

These different types of video were used because previous research had used the transparent approach (Neisser and Becklen, 1975), and Simons and Chabris were keen to identify if this was why the inattentional blindness effect appeared to be so strong.

Figure 3.8   (a) A woman walks through the game; (b) A person dressed as a gorilla walks through the game

(Source: Simons and Chabris, 1999)

Participants in each of the four groups watched just one version of the film. They were asked to track the passes made by either the white or the black team. Some participants were asked to count the number of bounce passes their team made (this was termed the 'hard' condition) and others were asked to count the number of aerial passes their team made (the 'easy' condition). After watching the film, participants were asked to write down the number of passes they had counted. They were then asked the following questions:

- Did you notice anything unusual in the film?

- Did you notice anything other than the six basketball players?

- Did you notice anyone else, other than the players?

- Did you see the gorilla or a woman carrying an umbrella?

Results showed that 46 per cent of participants demonstrated inattentional blindness and failed to detect the unexpected event. While more participants noticed the event in the opaque version (67 per cent) than in the transparent version (42 per cent), around a third of those in the opaque version still failed to notice the unexpected event. Moreover, those in the 'easy' condition (64 per cent) were far more likely to notice the unexpected event than those in the 'hard' condition (45 per cent), and this effect was more pronounced in the transparent version (27 per cent) than in the opaque version (62 per cent) suggesting that the harder task required more attentional resources than the easy task and even further resources were required when the stimuli were difficult to track. Finally, it was found that the woman carrying the umbrella was more likely to be noticed (65 per cent) than the gorilla (44 per cent), perhaps because she was more salient. However, those who were tracking the black team were more likely to detect the gorilla than those watching the white team. This effect was not found for the woman carrying the umbrella. Simons and Chabris suggest that this supports the view that individuals are more likely to notice an unexpected event that shares some basic visual features with the primary task – in this case, colour.

In a final version of the task, Simons and Chabris extended the amount of time that the gorilla was visible to the viewer from five seconds to nine seconds. In this version, the gorilla enters the scene, stops in the middle, beats its chest and then exits. Again, they found that when distracted by the same counting task, around 50 per cent of participants failed to detect the gorilla, even when presented at fixation. These findings are particularly interesting when we consider the movement of the players, the ball and the gorilla around the scene. As the players moved, they occluded each other as they passed one another. Similarly, there were moments when the ball itself was occluded by both the players and the gorilla. Given that the participants' task was to track the ball, and count the number of passes made, it is surprising that so many failed to notice this occlusion or the unexpected event that temporarily blocked their view of their primary task. Simons and Chabris conclude that the level of inattentional blindness demonstrated depends on the difficulty of the primary task: the more taxing the task, the more likely unexpected events will be missed. From an attentional resources standpoint this seems plausible: participants with a higher cognitive workload dispensed with processing other, irrelevant, information in order to reduce overall workload and maintain performance. However, further investigations have suggested that this may be only part of the explanation. The next section will consider the effect of expectations on visual perception.

4.3   'I wasn't expecting that!' Can expectation affect perception?

The above investigations have highlighted that when our cognitive workload is high, we are more likely to demonstrate inattentional blindness. From the research covered in Chapter 2, we know that as task demands increase, we tend to adopt strategies to reduce cognitive workload in order to maintain performance. If this is the case, it could be that we tend to rely upon our expectations for a given situation and therefore adopt a visual attention strategy based on these expectations. This allows us to ignore irrelevant information, and attend to pertinent information, but could also explain why seemingly obvious, but unexpected, events can go unnoticed.

Most et al. (2001) investigated this possibility with their target tracking experiment. They asked participants to fixate on a central point and count the number of times a target letter (either a 'T' or an 'L') bounced off the sides of the display. These letters were either black or white (there were four of each colour) and participants were asked to track just one colour of letter and to press a button if anything unexpected happened. In the critical trial, a cross (an unexpected event) which was either white, grey, dark grey or black, entered the display from the right-hand side and exited on the left-hand side, appearing on the screen for 5 seconds (see Figure 3.9). Note that in the figure, the white letters are shown in orange for clarity.

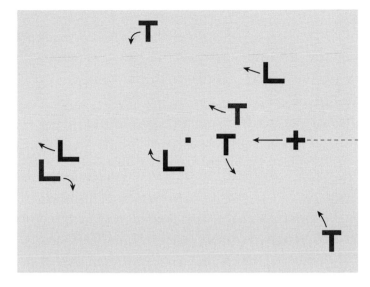

Figure 3.9   Letters move about a display screen. The arrows show their direction of travel
(Source: Most et al., 2001)

Results from a first experiment showed that when the cross was the same colour as the set of objects attended to (i.e. tracking white objects and the cross was white) 94 per cent of participants noticed it. However, in a second experiment, when the cross was a different colour from the attended set, only 3 per cent noticed it. Most et al. claim that these findings support the assumption that expectations affect perception, particularly as when the counting task was removed all participants noticed the unexpected events. They suggest that the 'mental set' adopted by participants led to a biased sampling of information, meaning not all of the available information was fully processed; rather, a selective attention strategy was employed.

If someone's attentional set affects what they perceive, does this mean they are looking at a scene differently? Richards et al. (2012) investigated how we allocate our visual attention by measuring the eye movements of participants completing inattentional blindness tasks. They presented participants with a slightly adapted version of Most et al.'s procedure. Participant instructions were the same as in the original investigation but the number of targets and distractors were varied to make two conditions: a 'simple' condition, where there were four targets and four distractors and the targets bounced 14 times; and a 'complex' condition, where there were six targets and six distractors and the targets bounced 24 times. After six seconds, in the critical trial, a red cross appeared on the screen, moving from right to left for 11.5 seconds. As with the earlier studies, participants were asked to report if they saw anything unexpected before they were asked to complete a 'full attention' trial, where they were not required to count the movement of targets.

Consistent with previous research, Richards et al. found that 47 per cent of their participants demonstrated inattentional blindness, with those in the complex condition being more likely to miss the unexpected event than those in the simple condition. However, the eye tracking data revealed further interesting results: not all participants who fixated on the red cross reported having seen it (only 65 per cent of those who fixated on it reported seeing the cross). Furthermore, some participants who did not fixate on the red cross *still* reported having seen it (40 per cent of those who did not fixate). These findings demonstrate two effects: first, fixating on an object does not guarantee that an individual has the experience of seeing it – it is possible to look without seeing; second, it is possible to process visual information without fixating on it, suggesting that perhaps our visual attention is more widespread than Mack and Rock proposed.

Richards et al. also found that those who demonstrated inattentional blindness were more likely to fixate on distractor letters more often and for longer than those who detected the unexpected event. This could suggest there are individual differences in how we apply our visual attention, with some being more able to focus their attention than others. This issue will be returned to later in the chapter.

4.4   Summary

When applying attention to one task, it is easy to miss aspects of a visual scene, leading to inattentional blindness. Furthermore, as task demands vary, and cognitive workload changes, individuals alter their visual attention strategy. What an individual expects to see in a given situation can affect their attentional set, leading them to miss important aspects of a scene. These findings demonstrate that fixating on an object does not equate to perceiving it, highlighting that there needs to be interplay between attention and perception for full awareness of a scene to be achieved.

5 Dual tasking while driving: is looking enough?

Given the apparent 'failures' in visual perception demonstrated by change and inattentional blindness investigations, how do we cope when faced with more cognitively challenging tasks? This section returns to the example of phone use while driving discussed in Chapter 2, and will move on to question how attention and visual perception interact in this instance.

Pause for thought

When driving, what other tasks do people routinely complete? Do these tasks vary in difficulty, and if so, how might they affect the driver's perception of the driving scene?

5.1 Does dual tasking affect visual perception?

Chapter 2 revealed that a driver talking on the phone can experience increased cognitive workload and decreased executive control, which can lead to deteriorated hazard perception as well as failures in the secondary task. However, in addition to this research, other investigations have focused on how dual tasking affects visual attention and perception.

Theoretical models of visual attention provide the backbone for investigations in this area. Posner's (1980) 'spotlight' model of attention suggests that individuals can move their focus of attention to different areas in a visual scene. Stimuli that are included within the current focus of attention are processed accordingly (a contiguous area of attention). If something else in the scene then captures attention, the spotlight will be shifted to focus on that area. It has been demonstrated that attentional acuity declines the further away a stimulus is presented from the central fixation point (LaBerge, 1983). This would suggest that most drivers will perceive and interpret the information presented ahead of them (that is in their 'spotlight') but they will be less attentive to stimuli presented in the periphery: a phenomenon known as *visual tunnelling*.

Eriksen and St James (1986) suggested that rather than a spotlight, visual attention is allocated in a fashion similar to a *zoom lens*: information from a wide range can be processed in a general way, but a smaller area can be selected for analysis in finer detail. This theory could be seen to support Richards et al.'s finding that participants who did not fixate on a cross were still able to report its presence because they had a broader area of processing (see Figure 3.10 for a comparison of the two models). In the context of driving, this would suggest that drivers should be capable of perceiving and interpreting all visual information, whether it is centrally located or in the peripheral fields. Moreover, they should be able to perceive two simultaneous events – even if one is at the point of fixation and the other is in the peripheral area.

However, although this may be the case for driving without distraction, research has revealed that introducing a secondary, attention-demanding, task interferes with visual perception and attention, meaning these abilities may be diminished.

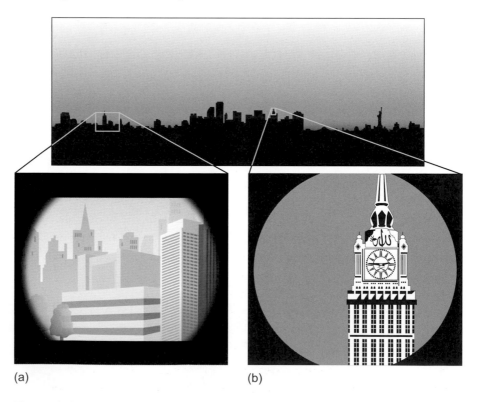

(a)   (b)

Figure 3.10   The (a) spotlight and (b) zoom lens models of visual attention

5.2   Is looking enough?

As we have discovered, we cannot assume that fixating on an object equates to perceiving it. Rensink et al. (1997, p. 369) claim: 'Although people must look in order to see, looking by itself is not enough.' So what does this mean for the dual-tasking driver? Strayer et al.'s (2003) simulator study directly assessed the impact of increased cognitive workload on eye movements and driving performance. They asked participants to 'drive' a simulated vehicle either without distraction or while completing a secondary, conversation task of varying difficulty. Those who were 'deep' in conversation on the phone were compared with control participants who didn't use the phone. It was found that those who were on the phone were twice as likely to miss traffic signals, displayed greater braking latencies when faced with unexpected events, and were less likely to recall billboards they had 'passed'. From a cognitive resources point of view, it could be suggested that participants on the phone diverted spare attention from the driving situation to the phone task, and therefore did not look at the signals. However, not only were the signals presented at their point of fixation, but also eye-tracking data indicated that both groups looked at the signals in equal proportions. For this reason, Strayer et al. contend that the telephone users viewed the signs but failed to perceive them because their attention was distracted by the phone conversation. In other words, they 'looked but failed to see', demonstrating both inattentional blindness and visual tunnelling.

If there is a mismatch between 'looking' and 'seeing', what can eye movement measures tell us about attention and perception? Recarte and Nunes (2000) addressed this question and found that when dual tasking, a driver's functional visual field is reduced both vertically and horizontally and the frequency of glances towards mirrors decreases significantly (see Figure 3.11). Similar effects were demonstrated by Briggs et al. (2011), who further highlighted that the type of secondary phone task engaged in can also selectively affect visual scanning behaviour. Participants engaged in an emotionally involving phone conversation or a conversation requiring mental imagery (Briggs et al., in preparation) noticed significantly fewer hazards than controls, showed increased cognitive workload and tended to focus their visual attention to a highly concentrated area of the driving scene, largely ignoring the peripheral fields.

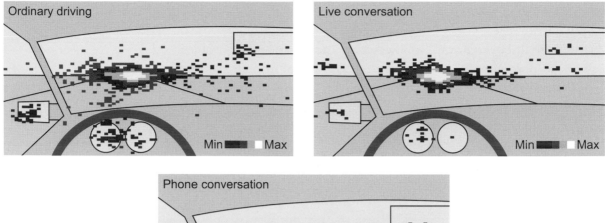

Figure 3.11   Eye glance behaviour when dual tasking and driving without distraction
(*Source: adapted from Nunes and Recarte, 2002*)

Harbluk and Noy (2002) also showed that as the difficulty of the secondary task increases, a driver makes fewer saccades. In their real-world experiment drivers who were dual tasking spent more time looking straight ahead and less time looking at instruments, and braked more often when the secondary task became more challenging. Moreover, the eye movement patterns of individual drivers differed according to task demands: when dual tasking, many drivers changed their inspection patterns in the central field compared with when they were driving without distraction, apparently focusing their visual attention on a smaller area of the driving scene.

Bringing all of these effects together, Tsai et al. (2007) asked participants to complete three tasks: 'driving' a simulator with no distraction, completing a paced mathematical addition task (presented auditorily), and then performing both the 'driving' and addition task together. In each case, measures were taken of blink frequency, fixation duration, number of mirror glances and lane position. It was found that when participants were dual tasking, there was an increase in blink frequency and a decrease in number of mirror glances, and visual tunnelling was observed. Furthermore, reduced fixation duration was a significant predictor of upcoming errors in the secondary task. Tsai et al. claim that these findings demonstrate how increased cognitive workload can selectively affect visual attentional ability, and how attention tends to be shifted between two concurrent tasks.

Taken together, these investigations reveal that dual-tasking drivers tend to focus their visual attention in a highly concentrated area of the driving scene – usually directly ahead of them. While this strategy makes sense in terms of the immediate danger of a head-on collision, it is also very worrying that seemingly little notice is being taken of the peripheral fields. While our peripheral vision is more specialised for motion detection, if our attention is focused elsewhere, in the time it takes to reallocate our 'beam' of visual attention we may fail to notice a child stepping into the road or another vehicle pulling out in front of us. These striking effects led one group of researchers to suggest that dual-tasking drivers not only shift their attention between tasks, but may also rely on their expectations for a given driving scene when their cognitive workload is high. They claim that drivers:

> ...develop a visual scanning strategy which concentrates on detection of more frequent and major dangers but ignores and may even mask visual information on less frequent dangers.
>
> (Summala et al., 1996, p. 147)

If we think back to Posner's spotlight model, this observed visual tunnelling seems to make sense. However, it is important to identify specifically what causes this tunnelling effect: is it simply due to a general increase in cognitive workload or are other aspects at play? Some suggest that a driver's expectations and attentional set can affect their **situational awareness**, which could explain inattentional blindness and increased crash risk. If this is the case, perhaps a better term would be *cognitive tunnelling*, as the alteration in workload directly affects visual attention strategies.

5.3   Expectations and situational awareness

As demonstrated by Most et al., what we expect to see can affect how we process information that can contribute to inattentional blindness. In the context of driving, we have seen that dual taskers can look but fail to see, and can fail to detect important aspects of a driving scene. However, there are further factors involved in the perception of a scene that may, in turn, be disrupted by the introduction of a

Situational awareness
An individual's understanding and perception of their environment, and their position in that environment both in the present and the near future.

secondary task. Endsley (1988) suggests that in order to drive safely we need to demonstrate good situational awareness. This is defined as an individual's perception and understanding of their environment at any given time, and their position in that environment both in the present and the near future.

When driving a vehicle, an individual must take in information from the environment and combine it with previous knowledge and experience in order to comprehend the scene ahead of them, as well as anticipating changes in the driving situation. Endsley (1995) formalises this approach by proposing three levels, based on multiple resource theory: *perception* of cues, *comprehension* (by integrating multiple pieces of information and appraising them in relation to individual goals), and *projection* (anticipating future events and changes). These levels are further affected by *temporal* (the time pressures imposed by a task) and *dynamic* (the changing nature of a scene) aspects of the situation. The former are crucial for an individual to predict accurately how much time they have before an event occurs (e.g. how long before the traffic lights will turn red). The latter are important for the understanding, by the driver, that as the situation is dynamic and constantly changing, their situational awareness must also constantly be updated (Endsley, 2000).

Given the difficulty of maintaining so much information at the same time as completing a potentially dangerous activity, it seems apparent that drivers use top-down, goal-directed behaviour to control the driving task. So a driver with the primary goal of travelling from A to B may only select information from the driving scene that is relevant to that goal. However, research has revealed that situational awareness can be affected by expectations and goals, suggesting that if information is inconsistent with past experiences, or with the goal in hand, it may not be processed. Instead, schema-driven processing will occur, leading to decreased situational awareness (Endsley, 2000).

In the case of driving, it could be argued that an individual with the mental set of reaching a destination in a given time may not notice subtle changes in the driving scene if they are irrelevant to this primary goal. Gugerty and Falzetta (2005) investigated this assumption with their simulator study in which participants were asked to detect changes in the driving scene. They were asked to complete a primary task of 'driving' the simulator, maintaining a constant speed of 40–50 mph, and to stop when a red traffic light appeared. At the same time, they were asked to react to unexpected events in the driving scene.

These could be another car either quickly decelerating (from 45 mph to 1 mph) or swerving out of its lane, and could occur ahead of the participant's vehicle in the same lane, behind the participant's vehicle, or ahead but in the oncoming lane.

Results revealed that participants detected more events that were presented ahead of them in the same lane, supporting Rensink et al.'s claim that relevant changes in a scene are more likely to be noticed. Furthermore, participants showed less awareness of events occurring behind them and ahead of them in the oncoming lane, suggesting that the mental set they had adopted for completing the primary task (of maintaining a constant speed and looking for red traffic lights) affected what they perceived. Gugerty and Falzetta suggest that such findings support the contention that situational awareness decreases in a dual-task situation, leading to shifts in attention and failure to detect important events in the driving scene.

Lee et al. (1997) further suggest that situational awareness decreases when attention is drawn towards an in-vehicle device. They found that participants took longer to react to critical events, or failed to notice them altogether, when a secondary task was introduced that involved either a mobile phone or satellite navigation system. Situational awareness detriments were not observed when no secondary task was present. Lee et al. also measured drivers' confidence in their performance in a hazard-detection task while they were dual tasking. They found that higher levels of confidence in performance did not correlate with accurate hazard detection, suggesting that drivers were largely unaware of the hazards they had missed and therefore the negative effects on performance of dual tasking when driving.

5.4 The interplay between attention and perception while dual tasking

---

Pause for thought

Based on the driving research covered both here and in Chapter 2, what are the main theoretical issues with dual tasking while driving? Can we separate attention and perception in this instance?

The introduction of a secondary task can interfere with a driver's goals, which in turn can affect visual attention and subsequent perception of a scene. This can result in inattentional blindness and decreased driving performance, both of which can have serious consequences. It seems apparent that the secondary task can disrupt attention both by introducing competition for attentional resources (see Chapter 2), and by interfering with the visual attention strategy employed by a driver, leading to failures in visual perception.

As the main goal of controlled attention is to orient to sensory stimuli, engage in processing and remain alert to changes in the situation (Posner and Peterson, 1990), it appears that dual tasking interferes at all of these levels. For example, drivers may decrease their range of fixations and therefore fail to orient attention to the pertinent areas of the visual scene; if the information is not attended to, it will not be wholly processed and as a result drivers may be less alert to changes in the environment. If drivers must perceive, comprehend and project information (Endsley, 1995), they must have the resources available to do so. The use of top-down processing, limited resource pools, increased load and decreased central executive control may mean that although information is seen, it is not perceived, preventing comprehension and projection of highly relevant information relating to the driving situation. Furthermore, increased demands on perceptual and attentional resources, although sometimes compensated for by alterations in behaviour (Hockey, 1997), can lead to increased processing of distracting information (Lavie, 2005), resulting in even higher load on central executive resources, and greater potential for deteriorated driving.

5.5   Summary

In this section you have been introduced to evidence showing that dual tasking while driving leads to increased cognitive workload and alterations in visual scanning patterns. These changes to scanning patterns can lead to both visual and cognitive tunnelling which can, in turn, affect perception of the driving scene. This means that a dual-tasking driver can easily miss important aspects of a driving scene. Given that a driver talking on the phone can also have altered situational awareness, their perception of the driving environment may not be entirely accurate.

6   Am I really so cognitively blind?

So far, this chapter has demonstrated the apparent disparity between our experience of the visual world and the reality of it. Experimental methods have enabled us to understand how and why we often fail to notice changes in a scene, either when paying full attention to a task or when our attention is divided between tasks. Theoretical models of attention and visual perception also shed light on the phenomena of change and inattentional blindness, demonstrating the need for interplay between attention and perception as well as memory. However, our subjective experience of the world is built not just on processing visual information but also by internalised goals for particular tasks (which may introduce competition for resources), and individual differences in ability to control attention, memory, task preference and processing capacity. Thus, although the brain is a highly efficient information processor it is not immune to these effects. The next section examines the extent to which we consciously make everyday decisions.

6.1   Do I know the reasons for the decisions I make? Choice blindness for facial attractiveness, tea and jam

In the world of decision making we assume there is a relationship between what we seek to achieve and what we actually achieve. That is, if you set out to buy a car and ended up with a bicycle, you wouldn't be happy with the outcome. We assume that some thought is given to the process of decision making, in that one has some form of detailed introspective process that establishes reasons for a desired outcome when confronted with a choice. However, a recent set of studies in what has become known as **choice blindness** has challenged these fundamental assumptions.

Choice blindness
The inability to notice when a less-preferred choice is presented as a replacement for the choice one has already made.

Johansson et al. (2005; also Johansson et al., 2008) used a form of change blindness to see what would happen if there was a mismatch between an individual's decision for a specific outcome and a different outcome occurring. To achieve this they showed participants 15 pairs of photographs of faces that were either similar or dissimilar. The participant was asked to choose which of each pair they found more attractive (see images (a) to (d) in Figure 3.12 for an example of the procedure). After making a decision, on some trials, the face they chose as more attractive was re-presented and they were asked to give the reasons for the decision they had made. Unbeknownst to the participants, on some of these trials the face that they had actually rejected (as the less attractive face) was re-presented as if it were the face they had chosen.

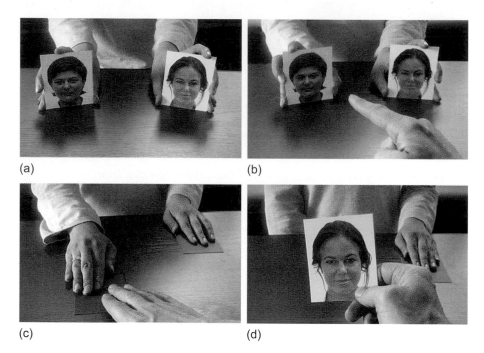

(a)   (b)

(c)   (d)

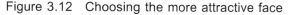

Figure 3.12   Choosing the more attractive face

In a situation where you are asked to evaluate the relative characteristics of something (in this case facial attractiveness) one would imagine you would be aware of the decision you made and the reasons for it. In fact, Johansson et al. found that on the trials where participants were duped, only 13 per cent of the deceptions were noticed. This level varied depending on the amount of inspection time the participant was given, with the level rising to 27 per cent of trials when there was an unlimited amount of time to inspect. Remarkably, there was no significant difference between picture pairs that had previously been categorised as similar or dissimilar in their facial appearance. When asked to give their reasons for the decision they made (i.e. for the rejected face that they now thought was their chosen face), participants managed to give clear and justified reasons.

In a follow-up study, Hall et al. (2010) explored the choice blindness phenomenon by looking at decisions for the taste of jam or the smell of tea. They asked participants in a supermarket to sample jams and teas. Again, people were given two alternatives and asked to make a preferred choice. They were then asked to re-smell or re-taste their preferred tea or jam and give reasons for their choice. At this point the experimenters secretly swapped the preferred tea or jam for the non-preferred tea or jam. Over a variety of conditions, only around 30 per cent detected the deceptive smell or flavour swap, even for smells and flavours that were quite distinct (e.g. cinnamon-apple tea versus grapefruit tea). It seems it is not only our sense of vision that can be change blind; our other senses are not immune.

Activity 3.3: Flavour pairs

For this activity try to taste test some common and less common pairs of flavours (e.g. jams, juices, teas). When you do this have someone to help you so that you do not know which you are tasting. Once you have a preference, re-sample the two choices (in a random order) and see whether you are always correct in identifying your preferred choice. Make sure not to look. As you learned in Chapter 1, incorporating more than a single sense can often enhance your perception.

It appears from this emerging literature that even when attending to a familiar experience or performing a familiar action we are easily misled when an unexpected change is introduced. Unlike the examples from performing more than one task at a time, or for changes occurring to marginal areas of a scene, here we have an example of people making a conscious decision between two options. This process, one presumes, relies upon us laying down some form of criteria upon which the decision is to be made by exploring the relative pros and cons for each choice. Why don't we then notice the dupe? Perhaps we behave as though these criteria are also part of the outside world, and therefore permanent, and can be sampled again at a moment's notice. It seems that we do rely on the external world as its own memory (O'Regan, 1992), and the experiences we have, and the decisions we make may not be as detailed or as informed as we subjectively believe, precisely because they don't always need to be (see Box 3.1).

Box 3.1   Crossing boundaries: if I am unaware of some things, am I more aware of others? Clinical applications

We have so far given examples that all have one thing in common: failure to detect some aspect of the environment changing. It seems reasonable to think we might also have evolved a capacity to have an enhanced sensitivity to relevant aspects of the environment. When we looked at change blindness we learned that if we make sudden salient changes to a scene (i.e. mudsplashes) at the same time as making another less salient change, the less salient change was rendered very difficult to detect. What is salient normally depends on the individual and their lived history. When things are salient we are more likely to notice them, and we are more likely to pay attention to them, or have our attention 'grabbed' by them. This attentional sensitivity is referred to as attentional bias.

Research into attentional bias has focused on two areas: bias for things we crave (either good or bad) and bias for things we wish to avoid (e.g. threats). For those with a bias driven by threats this can either be a normal response to factors of risk, or it can be a heightened response that is found with people who are classed as clinically anxious (Bar-Haim et al., 2007). Indeed, anxiety is sometimes viewed as a more extreme sensitivity to threat, whether learned or innate. People with a bias driven by addiction become more reactive to cues that are related to their substance of abuse. The most commonly accepted reason for addiction bias is a classically conditioned response that is evoked by an automatically learned relationship between a cue related to a substance and the response one normally has to the substance (Field and Cox, 2008).

Typical ways of studying attentional bias are either to compare an individual's response to neutral versus threatening or addictive stimuli, or to compare the response of anxious/addicted and non-anxious/non-addicted people to the same stimulus. Bias of attention can also cross from one modality to another. For example, Harrison and Davies (2013) showed that sounds heard in different spatial locations that were either unpleasant, neutral or pleasant differently affected the speed with which visual attention was deployed to regions of space from which the sound was emitted. Unpleasant sounds (i.e. threatening) were responded to very differently from either neutral or pleasant sounds.

One method commonly employed to research attentional bias is a modified Stroop task. Stroop (1935) asked participants to respond to the colour of ink a word was written in but ignore the word's meaning. When the word was a colour word (e.g. red) but written in another colour (e.g. blue ink), responses were slower (i.e. they showed Stroop interference) than when the colour word and ink colour were the same. In studies of addiction and anxiety, participants are asked to name the ink colour but ignore the word. If the word is related to the addiction or anxiety, then attention is biased towards the word, slowing response time. This has also been used with those suffering from depression where they are asked to read a word that is printed over a set of faces showing a range of emotions. For those suffering depression, it is more difficult to ignore sad expressions and read the word compared with non-depressed controls.

Another method, familiar to us now, is the use of the flicker paradigm from change blindness research. Jones et al. (2002) sought to explore the relationship between substance use and attentional bias in detecting change. The displays they used were either cannabis or alcohol themed (see Figure 3.13), and in each display they made two changes: one substance-related and one neutral. Participants were simply asked to respond once they had detected a change in the display. Jones et al. showed that whether they detected a cannabis or alcohol-related change was significantly determined by the amount of either substance they used. In other words, the use of such substances affected the detail in the displays they paid attention to, with heavier users showing a greater bias for the substance-related changes.

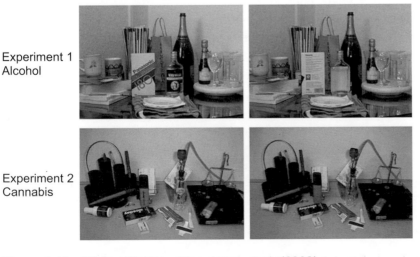

Figure 3.13   Flicker displays from Jones et al. (2002)

Research has also looked at more basic human needs, such as eating and whether one is more or less sensitive to food cues in the environment (e.g. the smell of a hamburger). Brignell et al. (2009) explored individual differences in terms of reactivity to food cues, with the assumption that those with a higher reactivity would find food items more pleasant, and would show an attentional bias to food-related items. Participants were assessed as being either high or low in terms of their sensitivity to external food cues. They were then asked to rate pictures of food and non-food items in terms of their perceived pleasantness. Finally, they undertook an experiment probing their degree of attentional bias. The experiment displayed a series of pictures, two at a time side-by-side, and these were followed by a cue located either on the left or right of the screen. The participant simply needed to respond to the cue location as fast as they could. When the cue appeared on the side of the food item, they expected participants more sensitive to food cues to respond most quickly.

The results showed that those classed as more sensitive to external food cues rated food items as more pleasant, but also showed a significant attentional bias for food, but not for non-food items. Thus, sensitivity to food cues preferentially directed attention towards the food items. The conclusions suggest that those with greater sensitivity to food will allocate their attention more readily to food-related cues. The authors suggest that those with such an attentional bias might be more vulnerable to obesity.

For a variety of reasons our visual attention seems to be more sensitive to some aspects of the environment than others. In situations where cues in the environment are salient to us, then our attention appears to be biased for those items, making them more likely to be detected. Whether this is a good or a bad thing really depends on the nature of the cue.

6.2   Summary

The final section of this chapter has focused on cases where we are either explicitly directed to pay attention to stimuli, or where our attentional systems appear to seek out, or be sensitive to, some things more than others. Choice blindness demonstrates an apparent *lack* of sensitivity to things people are asked to specifically pay attention to and make a decision about. Attentional bias demonstrates the *increased* ability of some aspects of the environment to capture our attention, particularly when they are linked to pleasure or aversion. Attention is therefore a complex system driven both by cues in the world, the complexity of a task, and individual differences.

7   Concluding thoughts

This chapter started by implying that we all partake in a grand illusion (Noë, 2000). It then explored a range of ways in which this illusion is revealed, frequently in situations that are only easily observable in the laboratory. We have learned that we cannot always take for granted that what we see is the whole picture; that we can easily fail to notice prominent features of the world; that we can look directly at something and still not consciously perceive it; that the sense of visual continuity is really a series of snapshots; that our decisions based on what we see can also be flawed; but also that attentional biases can help make some features of the environment more noticeable.

The grand illusion does exist, and there has been plenty of evidence for it provided here. However, for most situations the illusion is inconsequential and we can happily go about our business. It is mainly when we alter the world in ways that are unusual that we reveal the illusion. Although many criticise the lack of ecological validity created in some laboratory experiments, the experiments themselves are highly informative and revealing about the nature of our perceptual experience and the consequences for how we allocate our attention.

Further reading

- This collection of essays by a wide range of psychologists and philosophers tackles some of the key ideas you encountered in this chapter. If you are interested in inattentional blindness and change blindness and what these might tell us about perceptual consciousness, then this collection offers a range of opinions on the degree to which we are living in a Grand Illusion:

Noë, A. (2002) *Is the visual world a grand illusion?*, Thorverton, Imprint Academic.

- This book was originally a special issue of the *Journal of Visual Cognition* in 2000. It represents a point in time when interest in change blindness reached a critical mass. This collection of articles ranges from proposed theoretical models attempting to explain change blindness to original research exploring the phenomenon in more depth:

Simons, D.J. (2015) *Change Blindness and Visual Memory* , Hove, Psychology Press.

- This classic paper outlines some of the earlier research on change blindness and introduces the use of the flicker paradigm for research – the approach that is now most commonly used by psychologists:

Rensink, R.A., O'Regan, J.K. and Clark, J.J. (1997) 'To See or Not to See: The Need for Attention to Perceive Changes in Scenes', *Psychological Science*, vol. 8, pp. 368–73.

- This text provides further explanation and evidence on the phenomenon of inattentional blindness. It is highly accessible, funny and engaging:

Chabris, C. and Simons, D. (2011) *The Invisible Gorilla*, London, HarperCollins.

References

Bar-Haim, Y., Lamy, D., Pergamin, L., Bakermans-Kranenburg, M.J. and van IJzendoorn, M.H. (2007) 'Threat-related attentional bias in anxious and nonanxious individuals: a meta-analytic study', *Psychological Bulletin*, vol. 133, pp. 1–24.

Briggs, G.F., Hole, G.J. and Land, M.F. (2011) 'Emotionally involving telephone conversations lead to driver error and visual tunnelling', *Transportation Research Part F: Traffic Psychology and Behaviour*, vol. 14, pp. 313–23.

Briggs, G.F., Hole, G.J. and Land, M.F. (in preparation) 'Imagery-inducing distraction leads to cognitive tunnelling and deteriorated driving performance.'

Brignell, C., Griffiths, T., Bradley, B.P. and Mogg, K. (2009) 'Attentional and approach biases for pictorial food cues. Influence of external eating', *Appetite*, vol. 52, pp. 299–306.

Currie, C.B., McConkie, G.W., Carlson-Radvansky, L.A. and Irwin, D.E. (2000) 'The role of the saccade target object in the perception of a visually stable world', *Perception and Psychophysics*, vol. 62, pp. 673–83.

Endsley, M.R. (1988) 'Design and evaluation for situation awareness enhancement', *Proceedings of the Human Factors Society 32nd Annual Meeting*, Santa Monica, CA, pp. 97–101.

Endsley, M.R. (1995) 'Toward a theory of situation awareness in dynamic systems', *Human Factors*, vol. 37, no. 1, pp. 32–64.

Endsley, M.R. (2000) 'Theoretical underpinnings of situation awareness: a critical review', in Endsley, M.R. and Garland, D.J. (eds) *Situation Awareness Analysis and Measurement*, Mahwah, NJ, Lawrence Erlbaum Associates.

Eriksen, C. and St James, J. (1986) 'Visual attention within and around the field of focal attention: a zoom lens model', *Perception and Psychophysics*, vol. 40, no. 4, pp. 225–40.

Field, M. and Cox, W.M. (2008) 'Attentional biases in addictive behaviours: a review of its development, causes, and consequences', *Drug and Alcohol Dependence*, vol. 97, pp, 1–20.

Gugerty, L. and Falzetta, M. (2005) 'Using an event-detection measure to assess drivers' attention and situation awareness', *Proceedings of the 49th Annual Meeting of the Human Factors and Ergonomics Society*, Santa Monica, CA, Human Factors and Ergonomics Society.

Hall, L., Johansson, P., Tärning, B., Sikström, S. and Deutgen, T. (2008) 'Magic in the marketplace: choice blindness for the taste of jam and the smell of tea', *Cognition*, vol. 117, pp. 54–61.

Harbluk, J.L. and Noy, I.Y. (2002) 'The impact of cognitive distraction on driver visual behaviour and vehicle control', *Transport Canada Report*, Ergonomics division, Road Safety Directorate and Motor Vehicle Directorate.

Harrison, N.R. and Davies, S.J. (2013) 'Modulation of spatial attention to visual targets by emotional environmental sounds', *Psychology and Neuroscience*, vol. 6, pp. 247–51.

Hockey, G.R.J. (1997) 'Compensatory control in the regulation of human performance under stress and high workload: a cognitive-energetical framework', *Biological Psychology*, vol. 45, pp. 73–93.

Hollingworth, A., Richard, A.M. and Luck, S.J. (2008) 'Understanding the function of visual short-term memory: transsacadic memory, object correspondence, and gaze correction', *Journal of Experimental Psychology: General*, vol. 137, pp. 163–81.

Irwin, D.E. (1996) 'Integrating information across saccadic eye movements', *Current Directions in Psychological Science*, vol. 5, pp. 94–100.

Irwin, D.E. and Brockmole, J.R. (2004) 'Suppressing where but not what: the effect of saccades on dorsal- and ventral-stream visual processing', *Psychological Science*, vol. 15, pp. 467–73.

Jones, B.C., Jones, B.T., Blundell, L. and Bruce, G. (2002) 'Social users of alcohol and cannabis who detect substance-related changes in a change blindness paradigm report higher levels of use than those detecting substance neutral changes', *Psychopharmacology*, vol. 165, pp. 93–6.

Johansson, P., Hall, L. and Sikström, S. (2008) 'From change blindness to choice blindness', *Psychologia*, vol. 51, pp. 142–55.

Johansson, P., Hall, L., Sikström, S. and Olsson, A. (2005) 'Failure to detect mismatches between intention and outcome in a simple decision task', *Science*, vol. 310, pp. 116–9.

LaBerge, D. (1983) 'The spatial extent of attention to letters and words', *Journal of Experimental Psychology: Human Perception and Performance*, vol. 11, pp. 583–97.

Lavie, N. (2005) 'Distracted and confused?: Selective attention under load', *Trends in Cognitive Sciences*, vol. 9, no. 2, pp. 75–82.

Lee, J.D., Morgan, J., Wheeler, W.A., Hulse, M.C. and Dingus, T.A. (1997) *Development of human factors guidelines for advanced traveller information systems (ATIS) and commercial vehicle operations (CVO): description of ATIS/CVO functions* (FHWA-RD-95-201), Washington, DC, Federal Highway Administration.

Levin, D.T. and Simons, D.J. (1997) 'Failure to detect changes to attended objects in motion pictures', *Psychonomic Bulletin and Review*, vol. 4, pp. 501–6.

Luck, S.J. and Vogel, E.K. (1997) 'The capacity of visual working memory for features and conjunctions', *Nature*, vol. 390, pp. 279–81.

Mack, A. and Rock, I. (1998) *Inattentional Blindness*, Cambridge, MA, MIT Press.

McConkie, G.W. and Zola, D. (1979) 'Is visual information integrated across successive fixations in reading?', *Perception and Psychophysics*, vol. 25, pp. 221–4.

Most, S.B., Simons, D., Scholl, B.J., Jimenez, R., Clifford, E. and Chabris, C.F. (2001) 'How not to be seen: the contribution of similarity and selective ignoring to sustained inattentional blindness', *Psychological Science*, vol. 12, no. 1, pp. 9–17.

Neisser, U. (1967) *Cognitive Psychology*, New York, Appleton-Century-Crofts.

Neisser, U. and Becklen, R. (1975) 'Selective looking: attending to visually significant events', *Cognitive Psychology*, vol. 7, pp. 480–94.

Noë, A. (2002) 'Is the visual world a grand illusion?', *Journal of Consciousness Studies*, vol. 9, pp. 1–12.

Nunes, L.M. and Recarte, M.A. (2002) 'Cognitive demands of hands-free-phone conversation while driving', *Transportation Research Part F: Traffic Psychology and Behaviour*, vol. 5, no. 2, pp. 133–44.

O'Regan, K. (1992) 'Solving the "real" mysteries of visual perception: the world as an outside memory', *Canadian Journal of Psychology*, vol. 46, pp. 461–88.

O'Regan, K., Rensink, R.A. and Clark, J.J. (1999) 'Change-blindness as a result of "mudsplashes"', *Nature*, vol. 398, p. 34.

Posner, M.I. (1980) 'Orienting of attention', *Quarterly Journal of Experimental Psychology*, vol. 32, pp. 3–25.

Posner, M.I. and Peterson, S.E. (1990) 'The attention system of the human brain', *Annual Review of Neuroscience*, vol. 13, pp. 25–42.

Pylyshyn, Z.W. and Storm, R.W. (1988) 'Tracking multiple independent targets: evidence for a parallel tracking mechanism', *Spatial Vision*, vol. 3, pp. 179–97.

Rayner, K. (1998) 'Eye movements in reading and information processing: twenty years of research', *Psychological Bulletin*, vol. 124, pp. 372–422.

Recarte, M.A. and Nunes, L.M. (2000) 'Effects of verbal and spatial-imagery tasks on eye fixations while driving', *Journal of Experimental Psychology: Applied*, vol. 6, no. 1, pp. 31–43.

Rensink, R.A. (2000) 'The dynamic representation of scenes', *Visual Cognition*, vol. 7, pp. 17–42.

Rensink, R.A. (2002) 'Change detection', *Annual Review of Psychology*, vol. 53, pp. 245–77.

Rensink, R.A., O'Regan, K. and Clark, J.J. (1997) 'To see or not to see: the need for attention to perceive changes in scenes', *Psychological Science*, vol. 8, pp. 368–73.

Richards, A., Hannon, E.M. and Vitcovitch, M. (2012) 'Distracted by distractors: eye movements in a dynamic inattentional blindness task', *Consciousness and Cognition*, vol. 21, pp. 170–6.

Simons, D.J. and Chabris, C.F. (1999) 'Gorillas in our midst: sustained inattentional blindness for dynamic events', *Perception*, vol. 28, pp. 1059–74.

Simons, D.J. and Levin, D.T. (1998) 'Failure to detect changes to people during a real-world interaction', *Psychonomic Bulletin and Review*, vol. 5, pp. 644–9.

Strayer, D.L., Drews, F.A. and Johnston, W.A. (2003) 'Cell phone-induced failures of visual attention during simulated driving', *Journal of Experimental Psychology: Applied*, vol. 9, no. 1, pp. 23–32.

Stroop, J.R. (1935) 'Studies of interference in serial verbal reactions', *Journal of Experimental Psychology*, vol. 18, pp. 643–62.

Summala, H., Nieminen, T. and Punto, M. (1996) 'Maintaining lane position with peripheral vision during in-vehicle tasks', *Human Factors*, vol. 38, no. 3, pp. 442–51.

Treisman, A. and Gelade, G. (1980) 'A feature integration-theory of attention', *Cognitive Psychology*, vol. 12, pp. 97–136.

Treisman, A. and Schmidt, H. (1982) 'Illusory conjunctions in the perception of objects', *Cognitive Psychology*, vol. 14, pp. 107–41.

Tsai, Y-F., Viirre, E., Strychacz, C., Chase, B. and Jung, T-P. (2007) 'Task performance and eye activity: predicting behavior relating to cognitive workload', *Aviation, Space and Environmental Medicine*, vol. 78, no. 5, pp. 76–85.

Walker, P. and Davies, S.J. (2003) 'Perceptual completion and object-based representations in short-term visual memory', *Memory and Cognition*, vol. 31, pp. 746–60.

Chapter 4

Can you do what I do?
Learning: from conditioning to collaboration

Jane Barrett and Helen Kaye

Contents

1 Introduction

Imagine you have started a new job where you are part of a team developing ways of detecting abnormalities in human cells. You will need to learn a lot of different kinds of things. When you first look down the microscope at a mixture of normal and abnormal cells it is extremely difficult to tell them apart, but the more you look the more apparent the differences become. Soon the abnormal cells seem to jump out at you; your perception of them has changed. This is called **perceptual learning**. Also in your job you have to make sure the cell cultures are removed from the incubator at the right time. Just before the cells are ready there is a buzzing noise and after a few experiences of this happening, every time the buzzer sounds you stop what you are doing and attend to the culture. In fact, even when you are having a break and someone else is looking after the incubator the sound of the buzzer makes you stop what you are doing. You have learned to associate the buzzer with the cells being ready; this is *conditioning* or **associative learning**. You are not alone in your new job and you watch carefully how more experienced colleagues use the apparatus more efficiently than you do, and by copying their behaviour your performance improves. This is *imitative learning*, which is a type of **social learning**. Another kind of social learning also occurs when a piece of equipment arrives and you and your colleagues together work out how to use it. This is *collaborative learning*. We will explore each of these different kinds of **learning** – perceptual, associative and social – in this chapter. They are all included in our study of learning because they all fit the module's working definition: learning is a change, or potential change, in behaviour that occurs as a result of experience.

In this chapter, learning is looked at from several different perspectives: perceptual learning, associative learning, social learning and sociocultural theory. The discussions will be wide ranging because the topic of learning overlaps with many other areas of psychology. You will consider whether aspects of learning and teaching are uniquely human by looking at evidence from studies of an array of non-human animals. Learning occurs across the lifespan – there is always a new skill to learn or new knowledge to gain, so we will include evidence from infants, young children and adults in our discussions.

Perceptual learning
The enhancement of learning about a stimulus by exposure to that stimulus.

Conditioning

Associative learning
Learning about the relationship between or among stimuli.

Social learning
A theory of learning based on observing and imitating the behaviours of others.

Learning
A change, or potential change, in behaviour that occurs as a result of experience.

Learning spans different areas of psychology: biological, cognitive, social and developmental. There will be an opportunity to consider our own learning and to think about how best we learn: is learning rooted in the individual and what do we learn from one another? What happens to our learning? Does it stay within us or do we pass it on to others, even across generations? Does knowledge get changed along the way? This leads into links between learning and culture. Finally, consideration is given to the implications of the way learning is regarded in the study of psychology and wider society.

Learning outcomes

On completing this chapter you should:

- have an understanding of the different perspectives on and approaches to learning

- have an understanding of key psychological theories and research about the concept of learning, along with comparisons of human and non-human animal learning

- have an awareness that learning continues across the lifespan.

2 Perceptual learning

In the previous three chapters you studied the ways in which we perceive the world, i.e. how we make sense of the information gathered by our sensory organs of sight, hearing, etc. This chapter turns to how our perception changes simply as a result of experience: perceptual learning. Anecdotally we know that our sensations can change with experience. People who are new to drinking wine are often unable even to distinguish between red and white (with their eyes closed!) but wine experts can identify not only the grape used to make a wine, but also the year it was grown and in which country. Research has confirmed that people more used to drinking wine are better than less experienced drinkers at identifying which wine they are presented with in a laboratory setting (Hughson and Boakes, 2009). Another example of how our perception changes is the way that unfamiliar music 'all sounds the same', but the more we hear the music the more distinctive it becomes.

Perceptual learning was first studied in the laboratory by the American psychologist Eleanor Gibson (reported in Gibson and Gibson, 1955). Participants were briefly shown a scribble, such as the one labelled 'standard' in Figure 4.1(a).

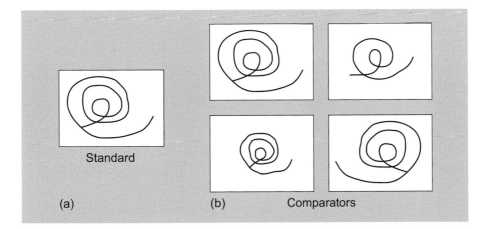

Figure 4.1   Scribbles: (a) the 'standard' scribble; (b) comparator scribbles *(Source: Gibson and Gibson, 1955)*

They were then asked to sort through several packs of cards, some of which bore an identical scribble, others with subtly different scribbles (the 'comparators' in Figure 4.1(b)). The participants had to pick out the cards bearing the target scribbles. After working through each pack of cards, the target was shown briefly again and the number of correct identifications of the target scribble and number of false identifications (picking out one of the cards with a different scribble) were counted. It was found that as people progressed through the experiment they made more correct and fewer incorrect identifications. So a scribble that was initially difficult to identify became easier simply with experience; the participants were never told which cards they had correctly identified. Many years later, Dwyer and Vladeanu carried out a similar experiment where participants were required to identify a particular face from a set of similar looking faces (Dwyer and Vladeanu, 2009). They reported that, if the participants had seen the face before, they performed much better than if they had not seen it previously. In other words, a familiar face was much easier to identify than an unfamiliar one. This finding fits well with the experience of meeting people who look identical to us at first (they might even be identical twins) but, as we interact with them and get to know them, we can reliably tell them apart.

There is a good deal of evidence, then, that our perception changes with experience: we see, hear and taste things differently. As psychologists we are interested in why these changes occur and what learning mechanisms are involved in perceptual learning. The examples so far could be explained by the participants actively trying to learn about the stimuli as they are being exposed to them; for example, it is beneficial to learn to distinguish your friend from her twin sister who you perhaps do not get on with so well. In experiments, people often try to second guess what the point of the study is: when the participants in Gibson's study were presented with the first scribble they may have anticipated they would be seeing that scribble again.

However, Gibson also demonstrated that perceptual learning occurs in rats (Gibson and Walk, 1956), where 'second guessing' seems unlikely to occur. She reared two groups of rats in standard animal cages, but for one group (the experimental group) she hung metal shapes (triangles and circles) on the walls. The other group (the control group) did not have shapes hung in their cages. Later, both groups of rats were given a choice (discrimination training) where approaching one of the shapes (for half of the animals in each group it was a triangle, for the other half a circle) resulted in food being presented. Approaching the other shape had no consequences. Animals in both groups learned to approach the shape that signalled food, but those who had the shapes in their cage learned much more quickly than the others. Activity 4.1 explores what happened for those rats that were fed only when they approached the triangle.

Activity 4.1: Discrimination training

Figure 4.2 illustrates the choice of shape on the first day of discrimination training when the rats were given food when they selected the triangle, but not when they selected the circle. As you can see, both groups chose the triangle and circle more or less equally; this is important because it indicates no initial preference for either shape and no difference between the groups. Subsequently, however, the experimental group (i.e. those exposed to the shapes) began to choose the triangle more often than the circle so that by day 10 around 90 per cent of the choices were for the triangle. For the control group a preference for the triangle also developed, but more slowly. By day 15 they were responding to that stimulus on only an average of around 60 per cent of trials. Eventually the control group learned the discrimination, but much more slowly than the experimental group. A similar pattern was seen when the circle was the rewarded shape: the experimental group learned to approach that shape more quickly than the control group.

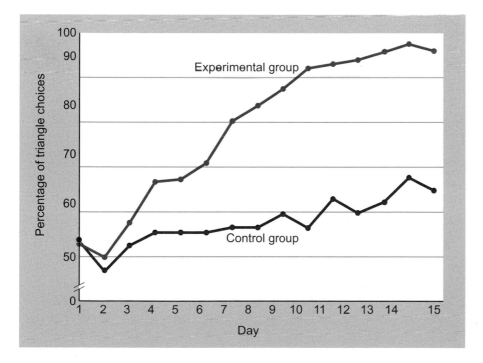

Figure 4.2   Learning curves, in percentage of correct responses per day, for the experimental and control groups

The graph illustrates two important features of learning. First, conditioning usually requires multiple trials; and, second, discrimination is rarely complete: rats continue to make the occasional response to the 'wrong' shape.

Why might it usually be advantageous to:

(a) learn over multiple trials?

(b) make the wrong response occasionally?

Adaptive?

learning over time & adapting on environment. on adaptive environment?

Both features are ways of adapting to variability in the environment. The first time a response is reinforced it could be a chance occurrence or it could be some particular aspect of the response (for example, how hard the lever was pressed or which part was pressed) that resulted in the reward; gradual learning allows the exact form to be selected. Always choosing the reinforced shape would be a good strategy in a constant environment, but rats naturally live in an inconsistent environment, so the occasional 'wrong' response acts a check that the consequences have not changed.

Animals can also demonstrate perceptual learning about flavours. Mackintosh and colleagues added a few drops of lemon juice to rats' drinking water together with a little saccharine on some days and a pinch of salt on other days (Mackintosh et al., 1991). After experiencing these flavours for several weeks, the rats were made nauseous after drinking 5 ml of the salty lemon. They subsequently avoided the salty lemon taste but continued to drink the sweet lemon. The control group was initially given only plain drinking water before the 5 ml of salty lemon that made the rats nauseous. Subsequently these rats drank similar amounts of the sweet lemon and the salty lemon. The authors concluded that prior experience with both flavours helped the rats to distinguish between them.

So, exposing rats to complex stimuli affects their behaviour too: they demonstrate perceptual learning and distinguish between familiar stimuli more quickly than novel ones. It seems unlikely that the rats anticipated the need to discriminate between the patterns on the walls of their cage or the mild flavours of their drinking water. In fact, as the shapes and differences were literally part of the background, it is more likely the rats would ignore them. So why did they learn more quickly?

A number of explanations have been proposed and the matter is far from resolved. Gibson argued that exposure to a set of similar stimuli draws attention to their differences; others have argued that attention to the common features of stimuli declines. Other explanations (such as those of Mackintosh and colleagues) propose that exposure permits learning about which stimuli occur together and which never occur together.

2.1 Summary

Our perception, and that of other animals, is not fixed but changes as a function of experience. We can measure this change by comparing how quickly learning about familiar and unfamiliar stimuli occurs.

Classical conditioning

Conditioning in which a stimulus acquires the capacity to trigger a response by virtue of its pairing with an unconditional stimulus.

Instrumental conditioning

A form of conditioning in which the outcome depends upon the action of the animal, as exemplified by obtaining food on turning a latch or negotiating a maze.

Unconditional stimulus (US)

A stimulus that evokes a response without any conditioning taking place; for example, the smell of food will evoke a salivation response in hungry dogs.

Unconditional response (UR)

The unlearned reflexive behaviour evoked by a stimulus, for example salivation in response to the presence of food in the mouth.

Conditional stimulus (CS)

A stimulus that evokes a response after being

3   Associative learning

As the term suggests, associative learning is learning that two or more events are associated with each other. There are two basic types of associative learning: **classical conditioning** and **instrumental conditioning**.

3.1   Classical conditioning

Classical conditioning was reported by Pavlov in 1927 and involves associating two stimuli or events with each other. A neutral stimulus, such as a tone, light or perhaps a flavour, is followed by a biologically important stimulus, such as food, water or something painful. The biologically important stimulus is termed the **unconditional stimulus** (usually abbreviated to US) and the response it causes, such as salivation or nausea, is termed the **unconditional response** (usually abbreviated to UR). The neutral stimulus becomes a **conditional stimulus** (usually abbreviated to CS) and it elicits a **conditional response** (usually abbreviated to CR) that is usually similar to the UR. For example, a puff of air (an unconditional stimulus) on your eye automatically makes you blink (an unconditional response). If the machine that produces the puff of air makes a clicking sound just prior to delivering the puff of air then the click will become a conditional stimulus and elicit the conditional response of blinking – the blinking will occur before the puff of air.

Pavlov's original study paired a bell with the presentation of meat powder to dogs. The meat powder was the unconditional stimulus that elicited the unconditional response of salivation. The sound of the bell became a conditional stimulus as it preceded the meat, and with training the dogs salivated (the conditional response) during the ringing of the bell, i.e. before the meat was presented (Figure 4.3).

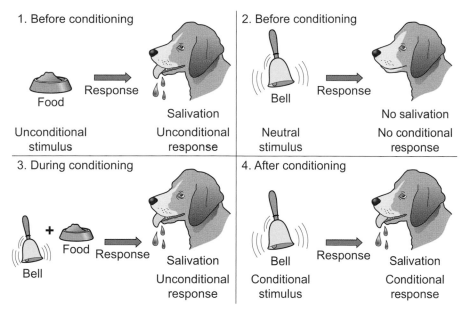

Figure 4.3 Classical conditioning

paired with an unconditional stimulus via conditioning. For example, the sound of a bell will evoke a salivation response in hungry dogs after being paired with the presentation of food.

Conditional response (CR)
The behaviour evoked by a conditional stimulus as a result of that stimulus predicting an unconditioned stimulus.

Activity 4.2: Humans salivate too, of course!

Look at Figure 4.4.

[handwritten annotations]
US = lemon = food = mouth waters?
UR =
CS = Sight becomes stimulus
CR = elicits salivation.

Figure 4.4 A cut lemon

Can you explain in terms of classical conditioning why looking at the cut lemon makes your mouth water? Use the terms US, UR, CS and CR in your explanation.

Tasting lemon juice causes us to salivate. The lemon juice is a US that elicits a UR of salivation. You would not have salivated the first time you saw a lemon; it was a neutral stimulus at that point. However, tasting lemon juice frequently follows seeing a lemon; the sight of the lemon is paired with the taste of the lemon. So the sight of the lemon becomes a CS that elicits the CR of salivation.

3.2   Instrumental conditioning

The other type of associative learning is instrumental conditioning that involves an individual associating an action they do with a stimulus or event. An animal or human performs a particular behaviour and its consequences make it more or less likely that the behaviour will be repeated. One of the most common ways of investigating instrumental conditioning is using a 'Skinner box' (see Figure 4.5). These are chambers typically equipped with a lever for a rat to press, or a coloured disc or key for a pigeon to peck. There is also a mechanism for presenting food. Typically the rat is first accustomed to being in the Skinner box, and as rats are naturally inquisitive it will discover the food hopper and may touch the lever while exploring the chamber. If that lever contact is followed by food then the likelihood of the rat contacting the lever again is increased. This is an example of **positive reinforcement**; lever pressing is termed an operant response and the food is the reinforcer. (Instrumental conditioning that occurs in a Skinner box is often referred to as 'operant' conditioning because the animal 'operates' upon the environment.) Conversely, the rat's behaviour might be followed by an unpleasant consequence, a loud noise for example, and then the likelihood of that behaviour reoccurring will be less. This is an example of **punishment**. Another term you may encounter in instrumental conditioning is '**negative reinforcement**'. This is where responding increases when it results in the removal of an unpleasant stimulus, e.g. taking paracetamol to cure a headache. Here the reduction in pain reinforces taking the drug so it is more likely that next time you have a headache you will take paracetamol to ease it.

Positive reinforcement
The process of giving something as a consequence of a particular behaviour, which increases the frequency of showing that behaviour.

Punishment
An event that follows a response and that leads to a decrease in the frequency of that response.

Negative reinforcement
The process of removing something as a consequence of a particular behaviour, which increases the frequency of showing that behaviour.

Figure 4.5   Skinner boxes designed for: (a) rats; (b) pigeons

Instrumental conditioning is easy to demonstrate in humans, and using
the techniques can tell us about important aspects of human behaviour.
For example, young babies have quite limited behaviours that can be
measured and the practicalities of studying infants are notoriously
difficult. However, they can turn their heads and are attracted to
brightly coloured moving toys. A technique known as conditioned head
turning uses instrumental conditioning to assess what babies can hear
(see Figure 4.6). The baby is fitted with earphones through which
speech sounds can be played. At first, each time the baby turns her
head towards the toy it beats the drum for a five-second period – the
head-turning response is reinforced by the toy's activity. The baby
learns this quickly, then the experimenter changes the conditions
slightly; now head turning only switches on the toy when the baby
hears a particular sound. The experimenters can therefore know which
sounds the baby can hear and, importantly, which sounds she can
distinguish between. Tsao and colleagues played six-month-old babies a
background soundtrack of a particular vowel sound and every so often
changed it to a short burst of a different vowel sound (Tsao
et al., 2004). When the change occurred, head turning was reinforced
by the toy becoming active. Head turning at other times had no effect.
This is quite a difficult discrimination for a baby, and Tsao and
colleagues found a correlation between how successfully individuals
managed to distinguish between the sounds and their language abilities
two years later. So a simple instrumental conditioning procedure can

provide an early diagnosis of possible language delay and allow a timely intervention.

Figure 4.6   When the baby hears a change in the vowel sound played through the headphones, turning her head will cause the toy to start drumming

To recap, the distinction between classical and instrumental conditioning is that, in the former, one stimulus or event (CS) is followed by another stimulus or event (US) regardless of the behaviour of the animal or human participant. In instrumental conditioning the behaviour of the animal or human (the CR) determines whether or not the second stimulus or event is presented; the response is reinforced or punished.

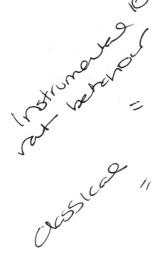

Activity 4.3: Classical or instrumental?

In Gibson and Walk's procedure, after rats had been exposed to the triangles and circles they were placed in an experimental chamber and given food when they approached one of the shapes.

In Mackintosh et al.'s procedure, after the rats had been exposed to salty lemon and sweet lemon they were given a taste of salty lemon followed by a dose of a drug (lithium chloride), which produces mild nausea.

Which of these procedures is an example of classical conditioning and which is instrumental conditioning?

Mackintosh et al.'s procedure is classical conditioning. The salty or sweet lemon taste (the CS) was followed by lithium chloride (the US)

regardless of the rats' behaviour. Gibson and Walk's procedure is instrumental conditioning. The rats' behaviour determines what happens to them. If they choose the correct shape they get food; if they select the wrong shape they don't get food.

3.3 Associative learning phenomena

3.3.1 Superstition

We have characterised instrumental conditioning as a situation in which the investigator rewards or reinforces the action that an animal or a human makes. However, it is sometimes the case that the behaviour that is strengthened is not the one the investigator intended. In a classic paper, the American psychologist B.F. Skinner reports a study where he placed pigeons in a box and gave them a few grains of food every few seconds. The grain wasn't signalled (as it would be in a classical conditioning procedure) and the pigeons did not have to do anything to obtain the grain (as they would in an operant procedure) (Skinner, 1948). However, most of the birds began to emit particular behaviours between presentations of the food, which included head bobbing, turning in circles, and brushing the floor with their beaks. The more often grain was presented the more the birds performed these responses and the more stereotyped they became. Skinner argued that these responses had undergone **adventitious reinforcement**, perhaps the first time the grain was presented the pigeon had just turned around in the box. The grain would strengthen (reinforce) that behaviour so it would recur and might again be followed by grain. Skinner drew parallels with superstition in humans; we dress in a particular way and our football team happens to win, so next time we decide to dress the same way, and our team wins again. These then become our 'lucky clothes'. Similarly some people adopt rituals in exam situations, using a special pen, parking in a particular spot, etc. The fact that every occurrence of the response isn't reinforced actually increases the amount and persistence of responding (the **partial reinforcement** effect, see Toates, 2014). Perhaps one difference between the pigeon and human superstitions is that the pigeons adopt idiosyncratic patterns of behaviour, i.e. each pigeon displayed its own particular ritual, whereas humans will sometimes share superstitions, e.g. not walking under a ladder, touching wood for luck, etc. Instances of widely held beliefs that are in fact superstitious are frequent in history. The miasma theory of disease is one such. Miasma theory holds that diseases are caused by foul smells, and may well have

Adventitious reinforcement
Unintentional strengthening of a response by its coincidence with a positive event.

Partial reinforcement
Responses that are reinforced only occasionally.

originated in the many pairings of bad smells and disease: poor sanitation was associated with dysentery, stagnant water with malaria (which literally means 'bad air'), etc. Furthermore, actions that reduced the bad smells, such as improvements in sewers that reduced reflux into homes, also reduced the incidence of sickness. Associative learning principles can clearly explain why miasma theory was widely accepted, and it was not until the late nineteenth century that a 'germ theory' of illness gained popularity.

3.3.2   Generalisation and discrimination

One powerful aspect of learning is that its effects are not confined to the exact training situation. For example, if you learned to play a piece of music on one piano you would be able to play it on a different piano; similarly, learning to drive one car transfers quite well to another car. In animal conditioning the CR generalises to other stimuli that are similar to the CS, and a pigeon that learns to peck a particular coloured key to get grain will peck a key of a slightly different shade almost as quickly. **Generalisation** is rarely perfect; for example, driving a different car involves adapting to changes such as the sensitivity of the brake pedal. However, as a rule the more similar the new situation is, the more generalisation is observed.

Generalisation
Responding in the presence of a stimulus that is similar to the trained stimulus.

Sometimes generalisation is not beneficial. Mushrooms (which are usually harmless) and toadstools (which are often poisonous) may look similar, but generalising that a toadstool omelette would be just as good to eat as a mushroom omelette would be a bad idea! In some circumstances **discrimination** is more appropriate than generalisation. Discrimination is quite straightforward to demonstrate with animals and the literature contains many slightly bizarre examples with pigeons. For example, pigeons can learn that pecking a key when music by Bach is playing results in grain, but pecking when Stravinsky music is presented has no consequences (Porter and Neuringer, 1984). Similarly, they can learn that pecking when they are shown a picture of a Picasso painting results in food, but pecking while a Monet painting is shown has no effect (Watanabe et al., 1995). Interestingly, the birds generalise within each category, i.e. the pigeons peck the key when a new piece of Bach is played or a novel Picasso is shown. However, new examples of the non-reinforced music (Stravinsky) or paintings (Monet) don't elicit pecking. These are both instrumental conditioning examples, but similar discriminations have been shown with classical conditioning procedures.

Discrimination
Learning to respond in the presence of one event (e.g. a green light) but not in the presence of another (e.g. a red light).

There have been a number of explanations of generalisation and discrimination and one of the most influential regards stimuli as compounds of unique elements and elements that are shared with other stimuli. Generalisation is mediated by shared elements, and discrimination by the unique elements. For example, imagine you give someone who is familiar with strawberries a raspberry for the first time. They may generalise between the fruits on the basis of their shared properties – red, soft, small, fruity – or discriminate between them on the basis of their differences: flavour, shape, location of seeds, etc.

3.3.3   Predicting the future

Learning that two events tend to occur together is important, but that is not enough. The natural environment contains lots of events that occur together and associative learning allows animals to pick out the really important events, such as good predictors of food, predators, potential mates, etc.

To illustrate this, think about the following situation.

You eat a new variety of fruit (A), a superfruit, and find that you feel happy and full of energy for about an hour afterwards. You eat that fruit again the next day and get the same effect. This happens a few times. Then you eat that fruit together with another new food (B) and feel exactly the same: happy and energetic for an hour. What do you think made you feel happy and energetic after eating that meal with A and B in it?

You'd be unlikely to believe that food B was the cause because you've already learned that fruit A is a good predictor of just that effect. This is called '**blocking**' and it was described by Kamin (1969). Kamin initially pre-trained rats with a light as a conditional stimulus that signalled a particular unconditional stimulus. He then presented the light together with the tone, following this with the same US. Finally he presented the tone alone and found it elicited no conditional response. The tone would normally make a perfectly good CS, and indeed did so in a control group. However the pre-trained light, which was a good predictor of the US, blocked conditioning to the tone.

Blocking
A situation in which prior learning about one stimulus reduces learning about another stimulus.

Pause for thought

Suppose the size of the US was also increased when the tone was added to the light. What do you predict would happen to the tone?

(Hint: thinking back to the example of a superfruit, suppose you felt even better after eating the superfruit with food B. What would you conclude about food B?)

You might expect that animals would learn that the tone and light together predict a bigger US, so the tone will become a CS and elicit a CR when it is presented alone. This is what experiments on 'unblocking' typically find.

Humans and other animals are not passive viewers of their environment. They do not sit back and calculate what might happen next; rather, they are active and seek to control what happens. It is important, therefore, to be able to predict the effects of one's actions, and research into instrumental conditioning suggests this happens. This might seem fairly obvious when we think about our own behaviour: we put on a sweater (or the central heating) when it is cold because it will warm us up; we buy a cold drink in summer to cool us down; we study to get good grades. However, there is evidence too that animals anticipate the results of their actions. In a very early study of animal behaviour (Tinklepaugh, 1928), macaque monkeys observed their trainers hide either a piece of banana or a lettuce leaf under one of two cups. Monkeys prefer bananas but will eat lettuce too. The monkeys were then taken out of the experimental room for a few minutes, then returned and allowed to select a cup. They quickly learned to choose the cup concealing the banana or lettuce and readily ate the food they had seen hidden there. Occasionally, however, the trainers swapped the banana for lettuce when the monkey was out of the room. Tinklepaugh describes what happens when the monkey returns:

> She jumps down from the chair, rushes to the proper container and picks it up. She extends her hand to seize the food. But her hand drops to the floor without touching it. She looks at the lettuce, but (unless very hungry) does not touch it. She looks around the cup and behind the board. She stands up and looks

under and around her. She picks the cup up and examines it thoroughly inside and out. She has on occasions turned toward observers present in the room and shrieked at them in apparent anger.

(Tinklepaugh, 1928, p. 224)

The description makes it difficult not to conclude that the macaque expected banana and was frustrated when she got lettuce. More recently, experimenters have systematically examined the effects on operant conditioning of changing the value of the reinforcer (e.g. Colwill and Rescorla, 1985; Kosaki and Dickinson, 2010). In a typical experiment using rats in a Skinner box, pressing the left-hand lever was reinforced with food pellets and pressing the right-hand lever was reinforced with a sucrose solution. After pressing was established to both levers one of the reinforcers was devalued; rats were fed the pellets or the sucrose in their home cage then were given a low dose of lithium chloride, which produces mild nausea. In most of the experiments when they were returned to the Skinner boxes the rats did not press the lever that had been associated with the devalued reinforcer but did continue to press the other lever. This is evidence that the rats had a good representation of the reinforcer. It wasn't simply the case that responses were associated with positive consequences: they associated one response specifically with sucrose and a different response specifically with food pellets. This would be a good clear conclusion to this section. However, not all of the studies have found that devaluation of the reinforcer affects lever pressing. Sometimes pressing continues even when the presented food was not always collected (Dickinson et al., 1983). Exactly why and when this happens is still under investigation.

Dickinson and colleagues have demonstrated similar effects in young children using a touch screen computer (Klossek et al., 2008). Two groups of children (one aged around two years, the other three to four years old) were shown one type of cartoon film when they touched a green butterfly icon and a different cartoon when they touched a red butterfly. The cartoon films reinforced touching the butterfly icon. Initially the children touched both butterflies equally, suggesting they had no particular preference for either colour or film. Then one of the cartoon types was devalued, by being repeatedly played in the absence of the butterfly icon. Although there was evidence that the devalued cartoon was less attractive to all of the children – they were bored by its repeated playing – only the older children subsequently avoided the butterfly that had produced that cartoon. The younger ones continued to touch both butterflies. Based on a series of such experiments the researchers concluded that children develop the ability to form a detailed representation of the consequences of their actions at around three years old.

3.4 Summary

Classical and instrumental conditioning can be demonstrated in humans and animals. Behaviour can change depending on its consequences and detailed representations of those consequences, the unconditional stimulus and reinforcer are created in both types of conditioning.

4   Can we learn from others?

4.1   Learning from others by conditioning

Up until now we have concentrated on how the behaviour of individual animals and people changes as a result of their learning. However, there is a growing body of evidence that an individual's behaviour is also affected by what happens to another individual.

An experiment demonstrated that people watching videos of others being conditioned made conditional responses to an observed conditional stimulus (Olsson et al., 2007). The experimenter showed participants films of people (who were actually accomplices) receiving presentations of a blue shape that appeared to be followed by a painful electric shock. After a few such viewings the participants made conditioned fear responses (galvanic skin response) when they saw the blue shape even though they had never personally experienced pairings of that stimulus with a shock. This phenomenon has been linked to the development of phobias; for example, a child may observe a parent's fear of a spider and develop a similar fear themselves. Gerull and Rapee showed toddlers toy snakes and spiders while their mothers expressed fear of one type of toy but not the other type (Gerull and Rapee, 2002). Later the toddlers were frightened when they saw the toy their mother had apparently been afraid of. Animals too learn from each other. Galef and colleagues have investigated food preference in rats (Galef et al., 1985). They fed 'demonstrator' rats on chow flavoured with either cinnamon or cocoa, then allowed them to interact with 'observer' rats that had no experience with either flavour. The observer rats subsequently preferred the flavour their demonstrator had consumed.

Pause for thought

Why might it be adaptive for rats to prefer to consume food that other rats eat?

Rats have evolved to eat a wide range of foodstuffs, and they will try almost anything. However, not all foods are good to eat. Some foods may be poisonous, and to survive rats must learn to eat only non-poisonous food. Smelling or tasting a particular food on another, healthy, rat is a good clue that the food is not poisonous.

> Note: this doesn't mean the rats have to make a conscious decision to preferentially eat food their companions eat; it may simply be that rats that do so live longer and breed more than those that don't!

The next section continues to consider how animals learn from others, but steps away from conditioning to explore social learning and how behaviour becomes embedded in tradition and culture.

4.2   Social learning and imitation

Imitation
Learning by copying a behaviour.

The ability to imitate is present from birth in humans and some primates (such as chimpanzees), since neonates can imitate human facial expressions, such as tongue protrusions (Meltzoff and Moore, 1977; Myowa-Yamakoshi et al., 2004). Neonatal **imitation** may be a survival mechanism and, in humans, may be a precursor for understanding others and developing social interactions skills (Meltzoff and Moore, 1977; Myowa-Yamakoshi et al., 2004). The previous section set the scene by discussing vicarious reinforcement in animals, but here social learning theory gives imitation in humans centre stage as a mechanism for learning.

4.2.1   Can we learn just by watching?

Imitation can be defined very simply as 'learning to do an act from seeing it done' (Thorndike, 1898, cited in Whiten et al., 2009, p. 2422). However, Thorndike's definition does not tell the entire story. For Bandura (1971), imitation is not just a stimulus response; instead, observers process the information from watching others to gain a symbolic representation of the observed activity which they can access in the absence of the person modelling the behaviour.

Let's illustrate Bandura's social learning theory by considering an example. Pilates is an exercise regimen where correct placement is essential for developing core muscle strength. It is a useful example of learning by observing and imitating because it requires a novice to learn the moves from an expert and then practise. Jane goes to a Pilates class each week because she wants to know how to do it properly. She finds an exercise called the Hundreds particularly challenging (Figure 4.7(a)). This exercise involves using the core muscles to stabilise and protect the back while simultaneously elevating the upper torso and legs and patting the air with one's arms – its purpose is to improve breathing.

(a)   (b)

Figure 4.7   Learning the moves: (a) by observing; (b) in a class

Her teacher demonstrates the exercise and Jane tries to copy the moves, but finds it really difficult and doubts whether she is doing it correctly. Her teacher gives her some individual tuition and explains in detail how to do the exercise, how to position her body and which muscles are being used. Jane tries again under supervision and with, encouragement from her teacher, then practises the exercise at home. During class the following week she finds it easier and is pleased with her progress. Her teacher and the rest of the class comment on her improvement (Figure 4.7(b)). How can this learning process be explained in terms of social learning theory?

Developing a representation of the exercise involves several different cognitive processes, which Bandura called attentional and retention processes, and motoric reproduction. Jane must pay attention to her teacher in order to understand how to do the exercise (attentional processes). She then needs to memorise how the teacher did the exercise, storing it so that she can do it again after the class (retention processes). She needs to use symbolic coding such as imagery to remember the name of the exercise and associate the name with how to do the exercise. She also has to remember what her teacher has told her about placement of her body on the mat and muscle movements (verbal encoding). Practising the exercise helps Jane to remember it and to reproduce it after the class. The movements themselves (i.e. lying on a mat, lifting the legs, positioning the arms, and the location of the abdominal muscles which will provide stability during the exercise) need to be remembered (motoric reproduction). Jane knows there are limitations to her performance of the exercise because she finds lifting her head and her legs is quite a strain. Also, she realises she did not observe one part of the modelled exercise, but is able to fill that gap because of her general knowledge of Pilates exercises. Finally, her teacher's praise and encouragement provides a reward for her hard work in learning and practising the exercise (as in instrumental conditioning), as is her pleasure in her improvement (self-reinforcement).

Social learning does not stop at modelling a particular behaviour, because what is learned could be modified in various ways. For instance, Jane learns from her teacher how to do the exercise and then, by watching others in subsequent class sessions, realises that she doesn't need to lift her back so high above the ground. In this way, the exercise she practises has become an amalgam of the different models she has observed. Of course, there is a limit to the modifications that can be made. For instance, when learning to drive, there are certain rules about what you can and cannot do – so although you may observe someone driving on the wrong side of the road, it is unwise to imitate it!

Pause for thought

Can you think of some downsides to social learning where you learn by imitating others?

How did you get on? Unfortunately, there is evidence that antisocial or risky behaviour, such as aggression, can be imitated, although it is unclear how long-lasting the effect is. Bandura (1971) highlighted the powerful effect of visual media, such as television. For example, his studies of aggression demonstrated that children who have observed someone behaving aggressively are more likely to model that aggressive behaviour than children who have not seen the behaviour modelled (Bandura et al., 1963).

4.3   Is social learning singularly human?

Social learning occurs in other species and Alex Thornton's meerkat research (Kalahari Meerkat Project) is interesting on a number of different conceptual and methodological levels. According to Thornton (2008), meerkats are interesting creatures because they quickly habituate to the presence of humans, they can be easily spotted in their home terrain, and they live in cooperative groups. So their social behaviour can be studied 'in the field' with seemingly little disruption to their behaviour, rather than in laboratories.

Meerkat pups learn by observing others, and in particular learn in a progressive way from adults about how to hunt and eat scorpions, gaining experience with handling live prey while being protected from harm. One study (Thornton, 2008) explored how pups learn that scorpions are a good food to eat and discovered that the pups who observe others eating scorpions start doing so themselves more quickly than pups who are presented with dead scorpions.

Activity 4.4: Learning by observation

The bar chart in Figure 4.8 shows the average number of times meerkat pups were presented with scorpions before they ate one.

1   Which group was quickest to eat the scorpions?
2   Why was one of the groups given saliva-coated scorpions?

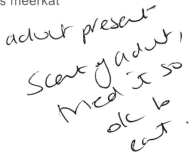

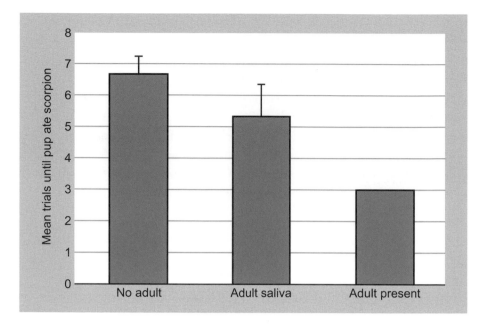

Figure 4.8   Three groups of meerkat pups were presented with dead scorpions in a number of separate trials. In one group (adult present) this occurred in the presence of older meerkats who were eating scorpions, in a second group (adult saliva) there were no adults present but the scorpions were covered in meerkat saliva, and in the final group (no adult) unadulterated dead scorpions were presented

Discussion

1   The group where there was an adult present was the quickest to eat.

2   The saliva-coated scorpion was presented to check how much the effect of the adult being present was due to the saliva they left on the scorpion. The middle bar suggests that meerkat saliva made the scorpion more attractive to the pups, but there was also an added effect of the adult being physically present.

Social learning is apparent in other species: chimpanzees and human children can learn by imitating the actions of others or emulating use of tools (Flynn and Whiten, 2013; Whiten et al., 2009). Research in this area highlights some intriguing differences and similarities between humans and non-humans.

Whiten and colleagues suggested that social learning comes in different forms and levels of cognitive sophistication (see Figure 4.9) (Whiten et al., 2009). In particular, they distinguished between imitation and emulation, which are about copying from another individual, as distinct from learning about the properties of an object (affordance learning). They suggested that learning by imitation involves copying the demonstrator's bodily actions and learning a behaviour that does not already exist in the individual's repertoire of behaviours. On the other hand, **emulation** involves a focus on the goal – for example, a chimpanzee might observe another chimpanzee using a hammer to crack a nut, but might then focus on cracking the nut rather than using the hammer. So, are there inter-species differences? Are chimpanzees emulators whereas human children are imitators?

Emulation
Learning by copying the product or outcome of a behaviour.

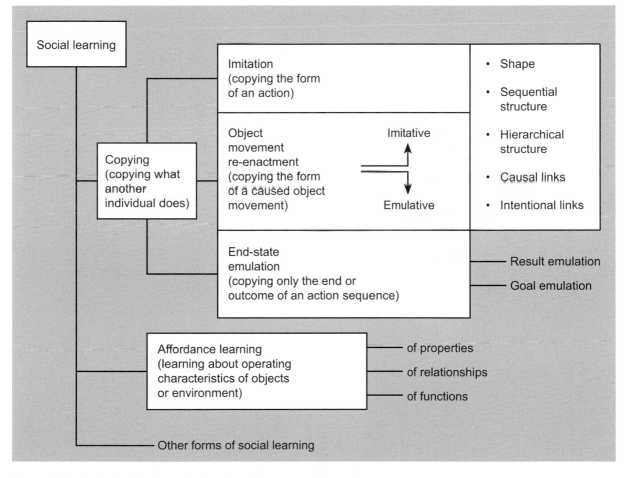

Figure 4.9   Imitative and emulative learning processes
Source: (Whiten et al., 2009)

Lyons and colleagues found that four-year old children don't always get it right when imitating a demonstrator because they faithfully copy the actions whether or not the movement is relevant to the solution (Lyons et al., 2007). For example, in an experimental situation to obtain a toy from a puzzle box, the demonstrator adult performed irrelevant actions like touching the box with a feather before unscrewing a lid to retrieve the toy. The irrelevant actions were copied by the children, and they were surprisingly resistant to change. The researchers performed a series of experiments where the child was given explicit training about these actions prior to the experiment, and where they were told not to copy irrelevant (silly) actions; in all cases, the children continued to copy all of the adults' actions. The researchers termed this 'over-imitation', and say it is due to the child including the actions in a causal, functional representation of the puzzle: in other words 'If I copy all the adult's actions, I'll get the toy'. There are parallels here with the adventitious reinforcement that led to superstitious behaviour in Skinner's pigeons. The children's 'over-imitation' was reinforced by the toy and this seems to have overridden the instruction. Perhaps this is a case of 'do what I do' rather than 'do what I say'?

Why does this happen? Whiten and colleagues suggested that, because human childhood is longer than that of apes, children have plenty of time to learn and adapt learned behaviours in response to real-world situations. Chimpanzees can copy sophisticated movements from a demonstrator, but once they have found a solution to a problem, they are less flexible about learning new solutions than human children (Whiten et al., 2009).

4.4   Cultural transmission and the cultural ratchet

Imagine you were the sole survivor of a shipwreck, who landed on a desert island. What would you do? Perhaps you would try to make a boat – but even if you built it, you would soon realise you would be unlikely to survive long enough to reach land in an open boat with no power, no sails, no fresh water and no food. So, if you cannot escape, what do you need to survive on the desert island? As a minimum, you require food, fresh water and shelter. How would you go about getting that food – maybe make a harpoon and spear fish? In walking around the island, you find a well-hidden community of indigenous people who are friendly and helpful. They invite you into their community, give you food and shelter and introduce you to their culture and traditions. One day, you decide to go fishing as an attempt to repay them for their kindness. You bring the fish back to the community as a gift. You are confused when your friends throw away some of the fish – you don't understand their behaviour because all the fish look the same to you. Now, what you don't know is that there are some lethally poisonous fish in the waters around the island and, furthermore, these fish seem to be indistinguishable from the edible variety. Over many generations of surviving on the island, the indigenous people have ways of identifying the poisonous fish and they communicate this cultural knowledge to you. You could not have learned this on your own, because sooner or later you would have eaten the poisonous fish and died.

There appear to be two processes at work and it seems that humans are good at both of them. The poisonous fish example gives an example of cultural transmission, and making a harpoon is an example of innovation and creativity. For instance, if you wish to make the best use of your harpoon when fishing, you may need to adapt it or change the design; this is when **cultural transmission** kicks in – you learn what works best by growing up as part of a group that has that knowledge within its culture, although you can learn some of those elements from others (social learning). Interestingly, you may not always understand why you use cultural traditions; for example, eating chilli peppers with meat protects against pathogens, and this practice continues in the New World although the original reason for using it is lost. The original (medical) reason for consuming chillies is lost and eating chillies causes a burning sensation, yet people learn to tolerate them because it is part of the culture (Boyd et al., 2011).

Cultural transmission
A learned behaviour or tradition that is passed on through the generations.

Although the fish story is fictional, there are many instances of adaptation and cultural transmission within human societies (Boyd et al., 2011). As a counter-example, in 1845, Sir John Franklin set out to find the Northwest Passage with an extremely well-provisioned expedition. But they got stuck in the Arctic winter ice on King William Island and, once the provisions had run out, they tried but failed to escape, dying of scurvy and starvation (Boyd et al., 2011). However, Inuits survive the winter on the island, which suggests that the sailors perished because they did not have the necessary cultural artefacts and local knowledge for survival, such as making clothing and shelter to protect them from the Arctic winter, as well as seal hunting and dog sledding skills (Boyd et al., 2011).

So, how does cultural transmission work and how are cultural traditions modified?

4.5   Cultural rachet

Tomasello and colleagues suggest that culture, our ability to collaborate with one another and to share intentions, ideas, beliefs, memories and other cognitions, defines the differences between species (Tomasello and Herrmann, 2010; Tomasello et al., 1993). Likewise, Hill argues that all human societies have culture and all humans belong to cultural groups, adopting their behavioural norms, whereas non-human animals develop behavioural traditions that are the building blocks of culture rather than culture itself (Hill, 2010).

As discussed above, chimpanzees and children do not learn in the same way. Social learning involves copying someone else, and comparative studies have demonstrated that where participants copy a demonstrator, chimpanzees focus on the outcome of the action (e.g. getting a banana from a puzzle box), whereas human children focus on what the demonstrator is doing (i.e. the process of getting the treat) (Tennie et al., 2009). Learning becomes a tradition that can be transmitted through the generations. The major difference between the two species is that humans (unlike chimpanzees) introduce modifications beyond their individual capabilities, called the '**cultural ratchet**'.

Cultural ratchet
The accumulation of modifications to learned actions that emerge because of uniquely human processes (such as teaching, social learning and normativity) that underlie the establishment and maintenance of social groups.

For instance, Boyd et al. (2011) recounted how West Greenland Inuit adapted their kayak keels to allow them to use guns rather than the lighter harpoons when hunting marine mammals. A much-esteemed Inuit hunter tried various methods, including a crude rudder. Although his attempts to adapt the keel were unsuccessful, other hunters imitated him because he was so prestigious. They were ashamed of their efforts and hid the rudders under the water, finding, to their surprise, that this adaptation allowed them to use their guns. Over the next 50 years and several generations later, the keel was improved further until the modern version was produced (see images (a) to (e) in Figure 4.10 for a demonstration of progression of the keel over generations).

Tennie and colleagues attribute this cultural ratchet effect in humans to our 'uniquely human forms of cooperation [which] make human social organisation in many ways different as well, as things such as teaching and norms of conformity contribute to the cultural ratchet' (Tennie et al., 2009, p. 2413). Our ability to use language as a means of information transmission in printed material and geographically distributed networks as well as proximal social interactions allows individuals to tap into knowledge from past as well as contemporary members of our species. For example, in a single lifetime Ache hunter-gatherers in Paraguay have adapted to new technology by using computers, smartphones and GPS rather than bone chisels and stone axes – essentially ratcheting up the cultural ratchet (Hill, 2010). In other words, as Tennie et al. argue, modifications to learned actions emerge because of uniquely human processes that underlie the establishment and maintenance of social groups: teaching, social imitation and normativity (i.e. behaviour considered to be right or wrong).

(a)

(b)

(c)

(d)

(e)

Figure 4.10   The West Greenland kayak: a cultural ratchet

Pause for thought

Think about how you are learning about learning by reading this chapter. Written language (or text) comes in many forms and media – books, newspapers, internet sources to name a few; it is a **cultural tool**. Through reading texts in a variety of media, you'll have access to centuries of knowledge – far more than you could amass in your own lifetime. Text conserves ideas and knowledge, and allows us to benefit from the wisdom and experience of previous generations. But such knowledge is never static: if you write an essay about learning, you'll use the information in the chapter, but you'll also adapt and modify it to answer a particular question, perhaps by reading other sources or discussing it with others.

Cultural tool
A means of achieving something that is passed on by cultural transmission (for example, a hammer is a physical cultural tool). Language is a psychological cultural tool: what we say and how we say it depends on how we interpret the words, which, in turn, reflect our culture.

4.6 Summary

We learn a lot by observation: for example, conditioned emotional responses, such as fear and phobia, can be learned from observing others. Social learning has been observed in several non-human species, as well as with human children. Although imitation is observed in humans, there is evidence that other species focus on the goal (emulation) rather than the process (imitation). Cultural transmission of learned behaviours is apparent in many species, but the cultural ratchet effect, whereby cultural tools become modified, appears to be singularly human.

5   Do others help me to learn?

5.1   Do I need a teacher?

Teaching is ubiquitous in human societies: we teach children to use a spoon, tie their shoe laces, read a book, etc. Can we find evidence that adult animals actively teach their young?

Research by Thornton and colleagues demonstrates social learning, but do the adult meerkats teach their young as opposed to the young imitating or emulating their elders' behaviour?

Caro and Hauser devised a working definition of teaching from their empirical work with animals (Caro and Hauser, 1992; Leadbeater et al., 2006):

- the naïve young should learn a new skill or knowledge more quickly than it would on its own

- the teacher (usually a close relative) demonstrates the behaviour only in the presence of the learner

- teaching is an altruistic act because there is a potential cost to the teacher.

Meerkat pups learn by observing others. They learn in a progressive way from adults about how to hunt and eat scorpions by gaining experience with handling live prey while being protected from harm: the adults bring dead scorpions to very young pups, then, as they mature, live scorpions without tails, and finally intact scorpions. The pups are learning a new skill – to catch prey without getting stung. However, bringing back dead or injured prey is not the usual behaviour of adult meerkats when hunting; and there is a cost – the adults expend energy on hunting without getting the food. On these criteria, Thornton's adult meerkats appear to be teaching the young pups. Using these criteria, it seems that even ants teach other ants how to find food by accompanying them to food sources, even adapting their pace to that of the learner ant so they don't get lost (Franks and Richardson, 2006, cited in Leadbeater et al., 2006). But is this the same kind of teaching that humans do? Anecdotally, when we teach our children we deliberately adapt our behaviour to what we know about their abilities, levels of understanding, etc. Does the adult meerkat understand what the young pups need or is there a simpler explanation that avoids theorising about empathy? In one experiment where adults were played a soundtrack of a young pup's begging cry, they brought dead prey to older pups. Similarly, they presented young pups with live scorpions after hearing the cries of older pups. So rather than an empathic understanding of pups' needs which invokes complex cognitive abilities, adult meerkats simply respond to the cries of the pups, which can result in inappropriate behaviour (Thornton and McAuliffe, 2006; Figure 4.11).

Figure 4.11   Meerkat pup begging for food

Intriguingly, given the ease with which rats learn to do new things, they do not always pass on their new-found knowledge. Galef and colleagues extended their earlier work on social learning in rats by examining whether active teaching also occurs. They conditioned rat mothers to avoid certain foods, then provided them with the opportunity for teaching their young. Interestingly, they found no evidence of the mothers passing on this learning to their young; they thus failed to protect them from potentially life-threatening toxic food (Galef et al., 2005).

So, some sort of teaching appears to be present in some animal species. But teaching seems to take a different form for humans and non-human species, with human teachers more actively anticipating the needs of their young. There are other differences too – for example, ants communicate about food (information transfer), whereas human teachers don't always tell you the answer, but help you to learn the skills to find it out for yourself (Leadbeater et al., 2006).

5.2   Can I learn from others?

The previous subsection looked in detail at how human and non-human individuals might learn from one another, and how social learning and cultural transmission are linked. As Hill (2010) indicated, the use of language is a key identifying feature of the human species and a tool for the development of human culture. The link between learning and culture is developed further in this section by considering how people (children and adults) develop and learn together. The focus is on tool use – in this case, how language is used in groups, how learning and thinking develop through talk, and how creative thought can sometimes emerge from working in groups, but is often inhibited. First, we will consider the origins of **sociocultural theory** by examining Vygotskyan developmental theory. We will then look at some examples from work by Littleton and Mercer, who bring together culture, social interaction, language and cognition under the umbrella of sociocultural theory to discuss how learning emerges from group interactions and shared understanding and knowledge within groups (Littleton and Mercer, 2013; Littleton and Wood, 2006).

Lev Vygotsky (1896–1934), a Russian psychologist with an interest in medicine, developed his theory in the post-revolutionary period (Cole and Scribner, 1978). The theory was heavily influenced by Marxist dialectical materialism, and a belief that development of mental functioning (or cognitive processes) is contextualised and rooted in society and culture. His theory has applications in learning and teaching, possibly as a result of the work he did as a psychologist in the People's Commissariat for Public Education, working with children who had special educational needs. As Cole and Scribner note, his writings and theory are not just of historical interest, but still contribute to debates about learning and development in contemporary psychology.

Vygotsky believed that the child is born into a social world and learns by interacting with adults and peers. He said: 'Learning and development are interrelated from the child's very first day of life,' (Vygotsky, 1978, p. 84). He distinguished between what the child knows now (the 'fruits' of development) and what they are capable of learning in interactions with others (the 'buds' or 'flowers' of

Sociocultural theory
A theory that stresses that learning involves the use of tools and artefacts and is embedded within the context of interpersonal relationships, which in turn are embedded in social and cultural systems.

development) in what he calls the **zone of proximal development (ZPD)**. The ZPD is the difference between what the child can do with and without the aid of others; this aid comprises encouragement, demonstrations, suggestions and general nudging rather than overt instruction, and is often referred to as 'scaffolding' (Littleton and Wood, 2006). The developing child becomes a sort of apprentice to other, more experienced individuals. These others are 'teachers' in a very broad sense of the word, comprising adults or older children who have more knowledge or expertise than the learner (Perret-Clermont et al., 2004).

Vygotsky said: 'Every function in the child's cultural development appears twice: first on the social level, and later, on the individual level; first, between people … and then inside the child' (Vygotsky, 1978, p. 57). Language, as a cultural tool, mediates between the child and the social world; such **mediation** means that interactions become internalised and the child reflects on discussions and conflicts with others, using these as the basis for reasoning and regulating their own behaviour. 'Consequently, meanings constructed through social interaction become embedded in individual thought processes' (Littleton and Wood, 2006, p. 211).

What happens when children work in groups on a problem? How do they reach decisions? In the extract below (Figure 4.12), four children are trying to decide how to categorise fish into carnivores or herbivores. Look at how the talk evolves. At first, they just pool their ideas; but in the last few interactions, they begin to work together. What's going on?

Zone of proximal development (ZPD)
The difference between what the child can do with and without the aid of others; this aid comprises encouragement, demonstrations, suggestions and general nudging rather than overt instruction and is often referred to as 'scaffolding'.

Mediation
In the sociocultural perspective, tools and technologies affect how we interact in the physical and social environments; and learning emerges from interactions with others and the tools they use.

Emmeline:	Now we've got a fish – uh – the ...
Oliver:	What sort, the piranha?
Emmeline:	No, the little, not the scaly one.
Maddy:	Lun, lungf ... (hesitating)
Oliver:	Lungfish.
Maddy:	It probably feeds on things in the river, because it's not going to go out and catch a monkey or something, is it? (all laugh)
Emmeline:	Yeah. Could bri ...
Oliver:	(interrupting) There is of course river plants, some of them do feed on river plants, and leaves that fall in the river.
Maddy:	Yeah, it's probably a herbivore.
Ben:	We haven't got anything to tell.
Emmeline:	What do you think it should be?
Oliver:	No, actually I think we should put it in 'carnivore', most fish are.
Emmeline:	No, because, ma ...
Oliver:	(interrupting) It's our best, and most fish are, isn't it?
Emmeline:	(interrupting) Yeah, but we've got this one here, and this one here (she indicates some fish cards in both 'carnivore' and 'herbivore' piles on the table).

Figure 4.12   Cumulative and exploratory talk in group work

Littleton and Mercer (2013) suggested that as well as mediating this transition from social to individual thought, language also mediates collective thinking. They demonstrated that certain types of talk engender creative thinking and innovation in people (children and adults). This creative context is more than the sum of its parts: by thinking together (or '**interthinking**') ideas emerge that wouldn't emerge by individual effort. Interthinking is facilitated by a particular type of talk that they call 'exploratory talk'. Exploratory talk is a collaborative activity where ideas are evaluated, interactants ask one another questions and attempt to reach agreement at different stages of a task, and joint reasoning and decision making are observable. This type of talk is distinguished from disputational talk or cumulative talk. Disputational talk involves frequent disagreements, no pooling of ideas or constructive criticism, and a competitive atmosphere. In cumulative talk, interactants share ideas, but are generally consensual and non-evaluative.

In Figure 4.12, you saw an example of children working together in a small group on a classification problem (you will meet this concept

Interthinking
When people think together, ideas emerge that wouldn't emerge by individual effort. Littleton and Mercer suggest that exploratory talk facilitates interthinking.

again in Book 3). In the first part of the extract, Emmeline, Oliver, Maddy and Ben are just pooling their ideas (cumulative talk). But when Ben says they haven't done the task ('We haven't got anything to tell'), there is some exploratory talk. Emmeline and Oliver interrupt one another, pose questions and give reasons for the decisions the group has made (Littleton and Wood, 2006, p. 218).

Littleton and Mercer (2013) analysed talk in different contexts and with different groups of people, and it became clear that exploratory talk is much rarer than the two other forms; but when it does appear, it leads to a qualitative change in the outcomes of the group activity. The researchers found that asking groups to formulate ground rules (see Figure 4.13) about working together had a transformative effect, so that language and talk became 'a tool for joint, reflective, critical consideration of how members work together': indeed, thinking about thinking enabled them to try to improve group dynamics (Littleton and Mercer, 2013, p. 105).

Class 7's ground rules

- When we work in a group:
    - everyone offers relevant information
    - everyone's ideas are treated as worthwhile – but are critically evaluated
    - we ask each other questions
    - we ask for reasons and give them
    - we try to reach agreement
    - people trust each other and act as a team.

Figure 4.13   Ground rules for exploratory talk

Activity 4.5: Working in a group

A, B, C and D are a team working on a project to organise a one-day seminar on team-working skills. A is always late for meetings, causing them to overrun, but he always does what he agrees to do. B works part time and has young children to collect from school. She is an experienced colleague who has worked on a number of successful teams and work groups. C always turns up on time, but is very quiet and doesn't contribute any ideas. C doesn't feel that he gets an opportunity to contribute anything. D is an experienced manager and knows the target audience for the seminar very well.

Think about sociocultural theory here and what you know about small groups (for example, see Book 1, Chapter 3). How can you make sure that the people in the group can contribute optimally? What expertise do they bring to the group and what are the perceived difficulties that need to be overcome? What ground rules would you suggest if you were a member of the team?

5.3   Summary

In this section, we have considered the contribution of others (animals and human) to learning. Although meerkats teach, it is unlikely that they adapt their behaviour to the needs of the learner; instead, they respond to external cues, such as pups' begging calls. In humans, working collaboratively is an important skill that is mediated by cultural tools (such as language). The adoption of ground rules may improve group dynamics.

6   Crossing boundaries and species

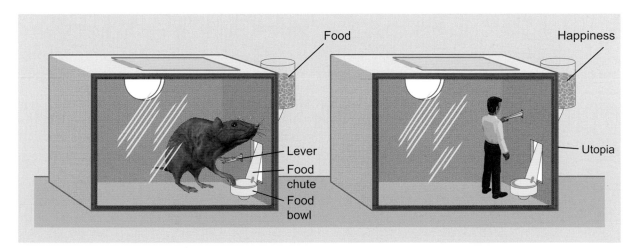

Figure 4.14   Utopia?

6.1   Social and political implications

Learning principles are used in many sectors of society such as health and education as well as in advertising and marketing. While conditioning might be effective in changing behaviour, the use of such techniques raises ethical issues and crosses boundaries into politics.

Skinner published a novel, *Walden Two*, that described a Utopian ideal for society where behaviourist principles could be used to tackle practical problems such as poverty, the destruction of the environment, crime, anti-social behaviour and consumerism (Skinner, 1976). The prime assumption of this approach is that human behaviour can be shaped, like that of pigeons and rats. In his introduction, he wrote:

> To induce people to adapt to new ways of living which are less consuming and hence less polluting, we do not need to speak of frugality or austerity as if we meant sacrifice. There are contingencies of reinforcement in which people continue to pursue (and even overtake) happiness while consuming far less than they now consume. The experimental analysis of behaviour has clearly shown that it is not the quantity of goods that counts (as the law of supply and demand suggests) but the contingent relation between goods and behaviour ... in an experimental community contingencies of reinforcement which encourage unnecessary spending can be corrected.

(Skinner, 1976, p. x)

Pause for thought

The idea of a Utopian society where people live in harmony and social problems are eliminated may sound very attractive. But think a little deeper about the underlying assumptions. How do you feel about the sort of social engineering that Skinner suggests? What does it imply in terms of free will?

6.2　Is social learning singularly human?

In Section 4.3 we asked: 'Is social learning singularly human?' and now we will try to unpack this a little more to highlight what are, in fact, some very contentious ideas about the assumptions of comparative psychology: although non-human animals are intrinsically interesting, one of the questions that arises is whether we can learn about human learning from studying animals. And, of course, this brings some assumptions to the fore: can we generalise from studies of pigeons, rats, meerkats and chimpanzees to humans?

As we have seen, it is quite difficult to pinpoint exactly how human behaviour is different from the behaviour of non-human animals. Once, it was thought that communication differentiated us from other animals, but studies of chimpanzees have demonstrated their ability to communicate in quite sophisticated ways using sign language. Instrumental conditioning appears to provide explanations for behaviours of both humans and non-human animals: pigeons can distinguish between Bach and Stravinsky because they are conditioned to respond to music by Bach and can generalise this learning to new music by Bach. In terms of social learning, meerkats can learn by copying others in their groups and can, on some level, teach, just as humans can differentiate and imitate. Some form of culture is evident in all the species considered so far. So, what is different?

Thornton's meerkats teach their pups how to hunt and eat scorpions safely, but rather than inferring the needs of the pups, they respond to external cues, such as begging calls. The distinction between imitation and emulation is also important here. In solving puzzles to get a reward, chimpanzees focus on getting the reward, but human children learn how to do the puzzle (the process). But perhaps the biggest difference lies in consideration of culture and the cultural ratchet: the transmission of local traditions by apes is not the same as the innovative process involved in the cultural ratchet that goes beyond individual capabilities. This is particularly so for language, our cultural tool, which, according to Vygotskyan theory and the sociocultural approach, mediates between us and the social world and allows us to construct meaning through interaction with others that goes beyond what is observable. Rather, our system of signs and symbols enables joint thinking, innovation and creativity.

Pause for thought

Studying animals is very helpful precisely because we can infer how they learn from watching their behaviour. As far as we know, although they can communicate, they have no human-like spoken language. But can we then generalise from animal studies to learn about our own learning?

7   Concluding thoughts

Our working definition of learning was 'a change, or potential change, in behaviour that occurs as a result of experience'. This seems to work well for animal learning. Human learning includes this simple definition, but needs expanding to include our capacity for self-reflection, self-regulation, innovation and creativity. As humans, we can think about our own thinking, and we can pass on what we learn to future generations, meaning that we have access to knowledge that transcends our individual capabilities. But it doesn't stop at passive transferal; indeed, what we learn as individuals can be passed on and, for humans, this cultural transmission can be modified (cultural ratchet) for future generations.

We have also considered what is uniquely human. The basic principles of associative learning seem to hold throughout the animal kingdom, including humans. Non-human animals have a capacity to learn from one another (and teach), but evidence suggests they may learn (and teach) differently from humans. Meerkats are not mind-readers, but respond to external stimuli; and chimpanzees focus on the goal, not the process, when learning a new skill. However, our ability to learn by making meaning with others appears to differentiate what we can do from what animals do.

In asking the question: 'Can you do what I do?', we have examined learning from several areas of psychology (perceptual, associative, social and sociocultural), which have different conceptual roots (behaviourism, social cognition and Vygotskyan theory) and, accordingly, different assumptions. (Figure 4.15 provides an amusing illustration of this.) For example, are we products of (determined by) external influences or do we construct our own environment through the mediation of language? Such fundamental differences suggest that these areas of psychology diverge and exist in parallel, rather than building on one another.

Figure 4.15 A range of approaches

Each area of psychology has particular underlying assumptions, as exemplified by the very brief discussion of social engineering and determinism that is a natural corollary to the behaviourist approach. So, we invite you to think about what all this means in terms of what psychology contributes to wider social and political agenda; and, perhaps as importantly, what does this mean in terms of our own responsibility as psychologists to contribute to these agenda?

Further reading

- This book by John Pearce is a fascinating and very readable account of animal learning. As well as expanding on associative learning he considers controversial topics such as animal language and intelligence:

Pearce, J.M. (2008) *Animal Learning and Cognition: an Introduction*, Hove, Psychology Press.

- These three papers are recommended if you'd like to read more about cultural transmission and the cultural ratchet:

Boyd, R., Richerson, P.J. and Henrich, J. (2011) 'The cultural niche: why social learning is essential for human adaptation', *Proceedings of the National Academy of Sciences*, vol. 108, Supplement 2, pp. 10918–25.

Tennie, C., Call, J. and Tomasello, M. (2009) 'Ratcheting up the ratchet: on the evolution of cumulative culture', *Philosophical Transactions of the Royal Society B: Biological Sciences*, vol. 364, no. 1528, pp. 2405–15.

Tomasello, M. and Herrmann, E. (2010) 'Ape and human cognition: what's the difference?', *Current Directions in Psychological Science*, vol. 19, no. 1, pp. 3–8.

- If you'd like to learn about methodology in this area then Flynn's papers about diffusion experiments are fascinating:

Flynn, E. and Whiten, A. (2010) 'Studying children's social learning experimentally "in the wild"', *Learn Behaviour*, vol. 38, no. 3, pp. 284–96.

Flynn, E. and Whiten, A. (2013) 'Dissecting children's observational learning of complex actions through selective video displays', *Journal of Experimental Child Psychology*, vol. 116, no. 2, pp. 247–63.

- We've provided a very brief overview of sociocultural theory and its roots; it makes fascinating reading, so if you'd like to learn more, the following are recommended:

Cole, M. and Scribner, S. (1978) 'Introduction and biographical note on L.S. Vygotsky', in Vygotsky, L.S. (ed.) (1978) *Mind in Society*, Cambridge, MA, Harvard University Press, pp. 1–16.

John-Steiner, V. and Souberman, E. (1978) 'Afterword', in Vygotsky, L.S. (ed.) (1978) *Mind in Society*, Cambridge, MA, Harvard University Press, pp. 121–33.

- Vygotsky's essays, published after his death, provide detailed explication of his theory, but they are rather dense. However, the Introduction, Biographical Note and Afterword written by the editors provide a useful overview, putting his work in context and explaining the historical–cultural approach and its links with educational theory:

Vygotsky, L.S. (1978) *Mind in Society*, Cambridge, MA, Harvard University Press.

- Littleton and Mercer's book provides some excellent illustrations from the perspective of sociocultural theory, which focuses on the role of language in learning and creative thinking:

Littleton, K. and Mercer, N. (2013) *Interthinking: Putting Talk to Work*, Oxford, Routledge.

References

Bandura, A. (1971) *Social Learning Theory*, New York, General Learning Press.

Bandura, A., Ross, D. and Ross, S.A. (1963) 'Imitation of film-mediated aggressive models', *Journal of Abnormal and Social Psychology*, vol. 66, no. 1, pp. 3–11.

Boyd, R., Richerson, P.J. and Henrich, J. (2011) 'The cultural niche: why social learning is essential for human adaptation', *Proceedings of the National Academy of Sciences*, vol. 108, Supplement 2, pp. 10918–25.

BPS (British Psychological Society), 2014 [online]. Available at www.bps.org.uk (Accessed 30 July 2014).

Caro, T.M. and Hauser, M.D. (1992) 'Is there teaching in nonhuman animals?', *Quarterly Review of Biology*, vol. 67, no. 2, pp. 151–74.

Cole, M. and Scribner, S. (1978) 'Introduction and biographical note on L.S. Vygotsky', in Vygotsky, L.S. (ed.) *Mind in Society*, Cambridge, MA, Harvard University Press, pp. 1–16.

Colwill, R.M. and Rescorla, R.A. (1985) 'Instrumental responding remains sensitive to reinforcer devaluation after extensive training', *Journal of Experimental Psychology: Animal Behaviour Processes*, vol. 11, no. 4, pp. 520–36.

Dickinson, A., Nicholas, D.J. and Adams, C.D. (1983) 'The effect of the instrumental training contingency on susceptibility to reinforcer devaluation', *Quarterly Journal of Experimental Psychology Section B*, vol. 35, no. 1, pp. 35–51.

Dwyer, D.M. and Vladeanu, M. (2009) 'Perceptual learning in face processing: comparison facilitates face recognition', *Quarterly Journal of Experimental Psychology*, vol. 62, no. 10, pp. 2055–67.

Flynn, E. and Whiten, A. (2013) 'Dissecting children's observational learning of complex actions through selective video displays', *Journal of Experimental Child Psychology*, vol. 116, no. 2, pp. 247–63.

Galef, B.G., Kennett, D.J. and Stein, M. (1985) 'Demonstrator influence on observer diet preference: effects of simple exposure and the presence of a demonstrator', *Animal Learning and Behaviour*, vol. 13, no. 1, pp. 25–30.

Galef, B.G. Jr, Whiskin, E.E. and Dewar, G. (2005) 'A new way to study teaching in animals: despite demonstrable benefits, rat dams do not teach their young what to eat', *Animal Behaviour*, vol. 70, no. 1, pp. 91–6.

Gerull, F.C. and Rapee, R.M. (2002) 'Mother knows best: effects of maternal modelling on the acquisition of fear and avoidance behaviour in toddlers', *Behaviour Research and Therapy*, vol. 40, no. 3, pp. 279–87.

Gibson, E.J. and Walk, R.D. (1956) 'The effect of prolonged exposure to visually presented patterns on learning to discriminate them', *Journal of Comparative and Physiological Psychology*, vol. 49, no. 3, pp. 239–42.

Gibson, J.J. and Gibson, E.J. (1955) 'Perceptual learning: differentiation or enrichment?', *Psychological Review*, vol. 62, no. 1, pp. 32–41.

Hill, K. (2010) 'Experimental studies of animal social learning in the wild: trying to untangle the mystery of human culture', *Learning and Behaviour*, vol. 38, no. 3, pp. 319–28.

Hughson, A.L. and Boakes, R.A. (2009) 'Passive perceptual learning in relation to wine: short-term recognition and verbal description', *Quarterly Journal of Experimental Psychology*, vol. 62, no. 1, pp. 1–8.

Kamin, L.J. (1969) 'Predictability, surprise, attention, and conditioning', in Campbell, B.A. and Church, R.M. (eds) *Punishment and Aversive Behaviour*, New York, Appleton-Century-Crofts, pp. 279–96.

Klossek, U.M.H., Russell, J. and Dickinson, A. (2008) 'The control of instrumental action following outcome devaluation in young children aged between 1 and 4 years', *Journal of Experimental Psychology: General*, vol. 137, no. 1, pp. 39–51.

Kosaki, Y. and Dickinson, A. (2010) 'Choice and contingency in the development of behavioural autonomy during instrumental conditioning', *Journal of Experimental Psychology: Animal Behaviour Processes*, vol. 36, no. 3, pp. 334–42.

Leadbeater, E., Raine, N.E. and Chittka, L. (2006) 'Social learning: ants and the meaning of teaching', *Current Biology*, vol. 16, no. 9, pp. R323–5.

Littleton, K. and Mercer, N. (2013) *Interthinking: Putting Talk to Work*, Oxford, Routledge.

Littleton, K. and Wood, C. (2006) 'Psychology and education: understanding teaching and learning', in Wood, C., Littleton, K. and Sheehy, K. (eds) *Developmental Psychology in Action*, Oxford and Milton Keynes, Blackwell Publishing Ltd in association with The Open University, pp. 193–229.

Lyons, D.E., Young, A.G. and Keil, F.C. (2007) 'The hidden structure of overimitation', *Proceedings of the National Academy of Sciences*, vol. 104, no. 50, pp. 19751–6.

Mackintosh, N.J., Kaye, H. and Bennett, C.H. (1991) 'Perceptual learning in flavour aversion conditioning', *Quarterly Journal of Experimental Psychology Section B*, vol. 43, no. 3, pp. 297–322.

Meltzoff, A.N. and Moore, M.K. (1977) 'Imitation of facial and manual gestures by human neonates', *Science*, vol. 198, no. 4312, pp. 75–78.

Myowa-Yamakoshi, M., Tomonaga, M., Tanaka, M. and Matsuzawa, T. (2004) 'Imitation in neonatal chimpanzees (Pan troglodytes)', *Developmental Science*, vol. 7, no. 4, pp. 437–42.

Olsson, A., Nearing, K.I. and Phelps, E.A. (2007) 'Learning fears by observing others: the neural systems of social fear transmission', *Social Cognitive and Affective Neuroscience*, vol. 2, no. 1, pp. 3–11.

Perret-Clermont, A.-N., Carugati, F. and Oates, J. (2004) 'A socio-cognitive perspective on learning and cognitive development', in Oates, J. and Grayson, A. (eds) *Cognitive and Language Development in Children*, Oxford and Milton Keynes, Blackwell Publishing Ltd in association with The Open University, pp. 303–32.

Porter, D. and Neuringer, A. (1984) 'Music discriminations by pigeons', *Journal of Experimental Psychology: Animal Behaviour Processes*, vol. 10, no. 2, pp. 138–48.

Skinner, B.F. (1948) '"Superstition" in the pigeon', *Journal of Experimental Psychology*, vol. 38, no. 2, pp. 168–72.

Skinner, B.F. (1976) 'Walden Two revisited', in Skinner, B.F. (ed) *Walden Two* (reissued), New York, MacMillan Publishing Company, pp. v–xvi.

Tennie, C., Call, J. and Tomasello, M. (2009) 'Ratcheting up the ratchet: on the evolution of cumulative culture', *Philosophical Transactions of the Royal Society B: Biological Sciences*, vol. 364, no. 1528, pp. 2405–15.

Thornton, A. (2008) 'Social learning about novel foods in young meerkats', *Animal Behaviour*, vol. 76, no. 4, pp. 1411–21.

Thornton, A. and McAuliffe, K. (2006) 'Teaching in wild meerkats', *Science*, vol. 313, no. 5784, p. 227.

Tinklepaugh, O.L. (1928) 'An experimental study of representative factors in monkeys', *Journal of Comparative Psychology*, vol) 8, no. 3, pp. 197–236.

Toates, F. (2014) 'Changing behaviour', in Brace, N. and Byford, J. (eds) *Investigating Psychology*, Oxford, Oxford University Press/Milton Keynes, The Open University.

Tomasello, M. and Herrmann, E. (2010) 'Ape and human cognition: what's the difference?', *Current Directions in Psychological Science*, vol. 19, no. 1, pp. 3–8.

Tomasello, M., Kruger, A.C. and Ratner, H.H. (1993) 'Cultural learning', *Behavioural and Brain Sciences*, vol. 16, no. 3, pp. 495–511.

Tsao, F.-M., Liu, H.-M. and Kuhl, P.K. (2004) 'Speech perception in infancy predicts language development in the second year of life: a longitudinal study', *Child Development*, vol. 75, no. 4, pp. 1067–84.

Vygotsky, L.S. (1978) *Mind in Society*, Cambridge, MA, Harvard University Press.

Watanabe, S., Sakamoto, J. and Wakita, M. (1995) 'Pigeons' discrimination of paintings by Monet and Picasso', *Journal of the Experimental Analysis of Behaviour*, vol. 63, no. 2, pp. 165–74.

Whiten, A., McGuigan, N., Marshall-Pescini, S. and Hopper, L.M. (2009) 'Emulation, imitation, over-imitation and the scope of culture for child and chimpanzee', *Philosophical Transactions of the Royal Society B: Biological Sciences*, vol. 364, no. 1528, pp. 2417–28.

Chapter 5

Why do I feel this way? Brain, behaviour and mood

Frederick Toates

Contents

1 Introduction

Within psychology, the term 'mood' refers to a state of the brain and mind, which makes some actions and thoughts more likely than others. Moods generally can fluctuate over hours, days or weeks. In such terms, different moods are associated with different patterns of activity by the brain. Psychologists assume that activity of the brain lies at the basis of thoughts, moods and behaviour. Alas, *how* a pattern of activity by one region of the brain is linked to the conscious sensation of joy and a different region is linked to sadness remains a mystery and an enigma.

Activity 5.1: Moods

Think about the various moods you have felt over the past few weeks. How would you classify your moods? When do mood changes occur? Consider also moods you observe in others and how they describe them. Think of the causes of these moods and changes in them. Knowing a person's mood, what does this suggest about their likely behaviour and thought processes?

You have probably described moods on a dimension of good versus bad. A bad mood might divide further into a sad mood or an irritable/angry mood, though these can coexist. You might also have classified moods in terms of a dichotomy between stressed/agitated and relaxed.

The possible causes of moods might be divided into external and internal. An external cause of a protracted bad mood might be repeated failure and frustration on having job applications ignored or being rejected by potential romantic partners. By contrast, a good mood might be associated with finding a suitable job or receiving praise. An internal cause of a mood change could be infection with a virus, such as influenza, causing a low mood, or, in the case of some women, differences in the phase of the menstrual cycle. So, understanding mood involves taking both external and internal events into account.

Regarding the behaviour that is related to different moods, you might have arrived at something like the following. A good mood is associated with laughing or smiling, and expressions of warmth towards others, for example, a wish to cooperate or give to charity, accompanied by positive thoughts. A bad mood might be associated with, say, irritability in dealing with others and obsessing over negative things. If it is characterised as sadness, it could be reflected in crying, withdrawal from engagement with the world and pessimism.

Biopsychosocial model
A model that recognises the importance of biology, psychology and social factors in the determination of mental states and behaviour. It incorporates interactions between these component factors.

Consideration of the determination of moods by internal and external factors leads to a **biopsychosocial model** (Figure 5.1), in which biological, psychological and social factors are involved. Those psychological factors that are external and contribute to our moods, such as relationship harmony, involve complex processing by the brain and then affect those parts of the brain underlying moods. Similarly, when an internal factor, such as an infection, influences mood, it is assumed to do so by its effects on the brain. Indeed, the importance of the role of both biology and psychology in mood can also be seen in terms of the interventions that are used to treat mood disorders, such as depression. While some interventions specifically target the mind (as in counselling or cognitive interventions), others target the brain (through the use of drugs). However, if either such technique works, it is assumed that both brain and mind are changed in parallel.

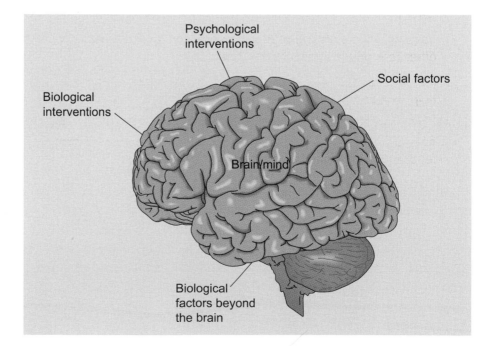

Figure 5.1   A biopsychosocial model

With improvements in technology, such as the development and improvement of **fMRI** techniques, psychologists are now able to identify parts of the brain associated with different moods. So it seems that to fully understand our moods and how they arise, we need to consider how our biology plays a role in what we experience. As such, this chapter primarily focuses upon the biological component of the biopsychosocial model.

Functional magnetic resonance imaging (fMRI)
A neuroimaging technique that measures brain activity by detecting changes in blood oxygen levels.

1.1   Summary

Mental events are assumed to correspond to brain events and the moods we experience are influenced by both external (e.g. social) and internal (biological) factors. A biopsychosocial model captures the interdependence between biological, psychological and social factors in the determination of moods.

Learning outcomes

On completing this chapter you should:

- have an understanding of the components and function of the central nervous system and the autonomic nervous system

- have an understanding of how neurons communicate with each other to produce effects on the brain

- have an appreciation of the biopsychosocial model's ability to help explain how positive and negative affect is produced and experienced

- have an understanding that mood can be affected by exercise, food and drugs, all of which act on the brain

---

2   What is the link between my brain and my moods?

While remaining aware of psychology and social context, it is now time to turn to biology to understand something of the biological bases of moods. The focus here is on the brain.

2.1   Some details of the nervous system

To understand the association between the brain and mood, you first need to consider how the brain works in conjunction with the rest of the body. Figure 5.2 shows the nervous system, consisting of the brain and other structures: the **spinal cord** and nerves that extend throughout the regions of the body.

Spinal cord
A column within the backbone consisting of neurons, as well as glial cells.

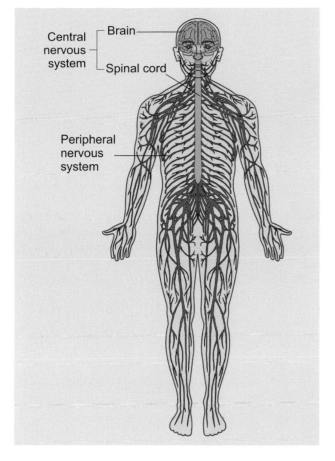

Figure 5.2   The nervous system

The nervous system is divided into the **central nervous system** (CNS), consisting of the brain and spinal cord, and the peripheral nervous system. The peripheral nervous system comprises all the nerves that extend from the CNS throughout the different regions of the body.

Let's now consider the structure of the brain. Figure 5.3 shows that much of the brain is divided into two halves, termed 'hemispheres'. These are the left hemisphere and the right hemisphere, defined from the perspective of the individual concerned.

Central nervous system (CNS)
The brain and spinal cord.

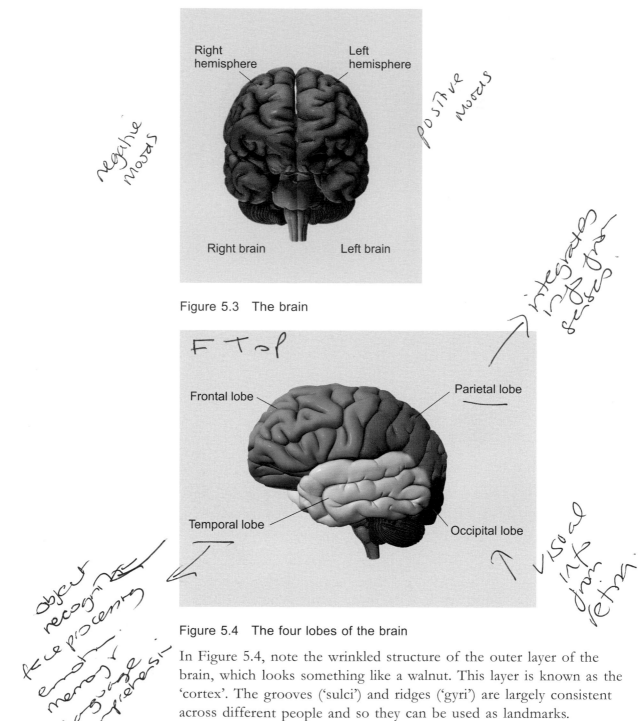

[handwritten annotations: "negative moods", "positive moods", "F Top", "integrated info from senses", "visual info from retina", "object recognit / face processing / emotion / memory / language comprehensi"]

Figure 5.3   The brain

Figure 5.4   The four lobes of the brain

In Figure 5.4, note the wrinkled structure of the outer layer of the brain, which looks something like a walnut. This layer is known as the 'cortex'. The grooves ('sulci') and ridges ('gyri') are largely consistent across different people and so they can be used as landmarks. Figure 5.4 also shows a mapping of the outer layer of the brain in terms of its four lobes: the frontal lobe, the temporal lobe, the parietal lobe and the occipital lobe. Particular sulci define the boundaries between the lobes.

Figure 5.5 shows a segment of the brain cut away to reveal the depth of the cortex. Note the difference in colour of this outer layer of the brain, grey (strictly grey(ish) or pink(ish)), and the regions just below this, white(ish). You might have heard an expression of the kind 'use your grey matter'. This implies that the cortex is used in higher intellectual tasks. Other structures are known as 'sub-cortical', since they are located at a level below the cortex.

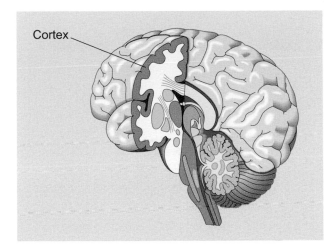

Figure 5.5   Cut-away view of the brain

By means of the technique known as neuroimaging, it is possible to look inside the brain and see its deep structures. Figure 5.6 shows two brains observed by a form of neuroimaging, known as **magnetic resonance imaging**. The different structures of the brains appear as different shades of grey, with black corresponding to fluid, known as 'cerebrospinal fluid'. This technique can reveal abnormalities in the brain's structure, e.g. changes as a consequence of disease. Figure 5.6 compares the brain of someone suffering from Alzheimer's disease and a healthy brain. In the brain of the person affected by Alzheimer's disease note the shrinkage of certain regions and corresponding filling of these spaces with fluid, most obviously the butterfly-shaped region. Research has shown that loss of tissue in some areas, e.g. the hippocampus, can be linked to loss of memory and to mood changes.

Magnetic resonance imaging (MRI)
A form of neuroimaging that examines either the structure of the brain or both the structure and activity of the different brain regions.

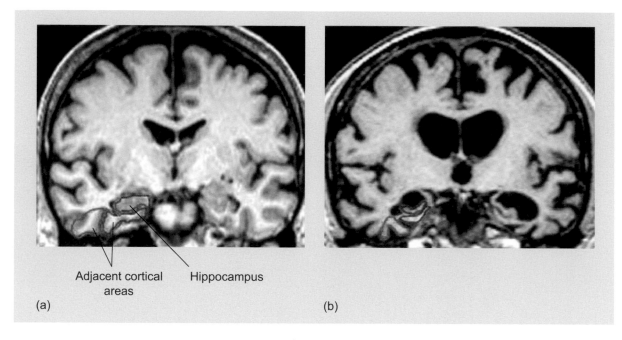

Figure 5.6   (a) A healthy brain (b) the brain of a sufferer of Alzheimer's disease

2.2   The cells of the nervous system

Cells
The basic building block of the body. The body is composed of billions of different cells, serving various functions. The primary interest here is in a type of cell known as neurons.

Looking at a microscopic level, the body is comprised of billions of tiny building blocks known as **cells**. These come in various shapes and sizes and serve correspondingly different roles. Figure 5.7 shows some cells and can be used to illustrate general features. Each cell requires a supply of nutrients and oxygen, and these are brought to it in the bloodstream. The blood carries away from the cell any waste products of the cell's activity, a kind of refuse disposal.

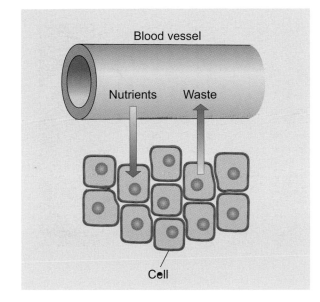

Figure 5.7   Cells of the body

Two types of cell that are of most interest to us are neurons and glial cells. Just as with the cells shown in Figure 5.7, these require a supply of blood to bring nutrients and oxygen to them. Figure 5.8 shows a representative neuron and some glial cells. Our principal focus will be on neurons as they are primarily responsible for the transmission of information within the nervous system, but we will not lose sight of glial cells. The nervous system consists of billions of neurons and glial cells, as well as the blood vessels that course through it and some spaces filled with cerebrospinal fluid. Figure 5.9 shows two types of neuron.

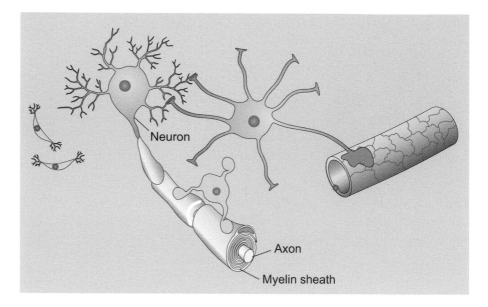

Figure 5.8   Neuron and some glial cells

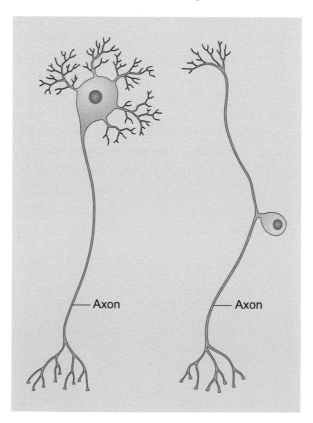

Figure 5.9   Two types of neuron

Neurons serve two related functions: to transmit and to process information. These can be illustrated by means of some familiar analogies. Consider a telephone wire. Information is communicated along it in the form of electrical activity. If it is transmitting Morse code, this takes the form of a series of long and short pulses. This is called the 'signal' and it is transmitted from one location to another. Neurons perform a similar function of communication; they transmit information over various distances, along their axons (Figure 5.9).

Now consider using a mobile telephone as a calculator. Information is fed in, e.g. 'what is 444 plus 654?' and the calculator processes this information and gives the answer as the output on the screen. By crude analogy, the brain takes in vast amounts of information and does computations on it. The billions of neurons of the brain constitute the physical basis of the computation. The output can be thought of as our experience or behaviour.

Neurons communicate information over distances by means of a series of electrical pulses, called **action potentials**, see Figure 5.10. These are identical and travel rapidly along the length of the neuron's axon. So, when, for example, you tread on a sharp object, this instigates electrical activity at the tips of neurons in the foot. The signal is transmitted along the axons and arrives at the brain. Further neurons then very rapidly *process* this information and *signal* damage at the foot, corresponding to the conscious sensation of pain with a feeling that this refers to events at the foot. This information is processed and instructions about how to respond are generated in the form of another electrical signal. This signal is sent back to the peripheral nervous system and along the relevant motor neurons. These are neurons that specifically stimulate muscles to contract or relax, in this case most likely resulting in the rapid movement of the foot from the sharp object!

Action potential
A spike of electrical change that forms the means of communication in neurons. Neurons transmit information by the frequency of action potentials that occur.

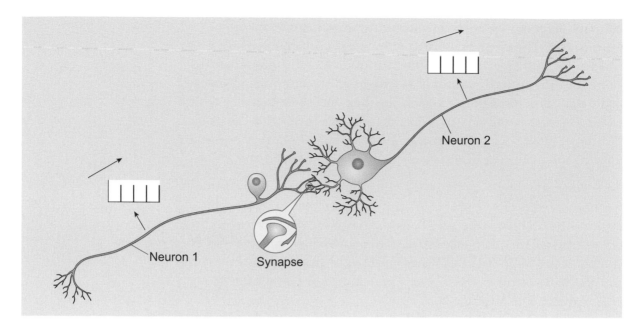

Figure 5.10   Action potentials in two neurons

Synapse
The junction between a neuron and another cell, either another neuron or a muscle cell.

Neurotransmitter
A chemical stored at the terminal of a neuron and which is released by the arrival of an action potential. It occupies receptors on a neighbouring cell.

Receptor
The structure on a cell that may be occupied by a chemical, either neurotransmitter or hormone.

You will see that the neuron of Figure 5.8 has associated with it a series of other cells. These are examples of glial cells and some of them wrap themselves around the length of the neuron. They speed up the action potential.

Figure 5.10 shows the action of neurons in transmitting information, where a series of action potentials is conveyed to the brain. Note the junction between neurons 1 and 2, which involves a small gap between these two neurons. This gap and the part of each neuron to each side of it are known as a **synapse**. Synapses located in the brain are crucial to understanding mood.

2.3   How do neurons communicate with each other?

In Figure 5.10, when an action potential reaches the end of neuron 1 (the terminal), it ceases to exist. However, it causes the release of a quantity of a particular chemical that is stored at the terminal (Figure 5.11). This chemical is known as a **neurotransmitter** (a general term for any chemical found in the brain is 'neurochemical'). Neurotransmitters very rapidly move across the minute gap ('synaptic gap') between the two neurons and occupy what are called **receptors** on the surface of neuron 2. The two parts of each neuron and the gap between them constitutes the synapse. By occupying the receptors on neuron 2, the chemical alters the activity of neuron 2. To take the simplest possible case as shown in Figure 5.10, it excites activity in neuron 2, such that a new electrical pulse (or action potential) arises in neuron 2.

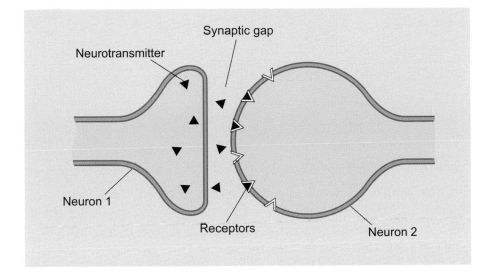

Figure 5.11   A synapse

Figure 5.12 shows the more general situation. There are multiple inputs to a neuron, each at a synapse. Simultaneous activity in a number of neurons might be needed in order to trigger activity in the neuron shown.

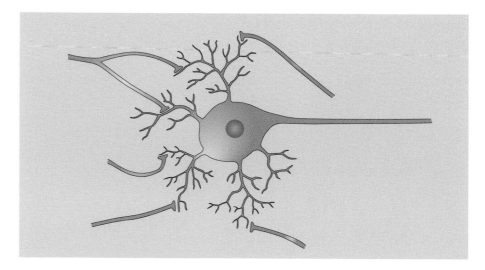

Figure 5.12   Multiple inputs

Synapses can be excitatory, as just described, but they can also be inhibitory, as shown in Figure 5.13. At an inhibitory synapse, activity in one neuron reduces the activity in another. A neuron that exerts such an effect is known as an 'inhibitory neuron'.

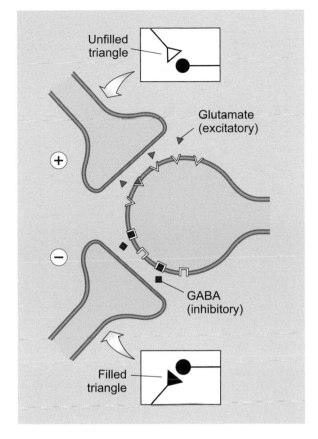

Figure 5.13   Excitatory and inhibitory synapses

2.4   What are neurotransmitters?

So far, we have mentioned neurotransmitters and distinguished between excitatory and inhibitory types. Figure 5.13 showed just two such neurotransmitters, their difference represented by their different shapes. Figure 5.14 shows two synapses with two different neurotransmitters.

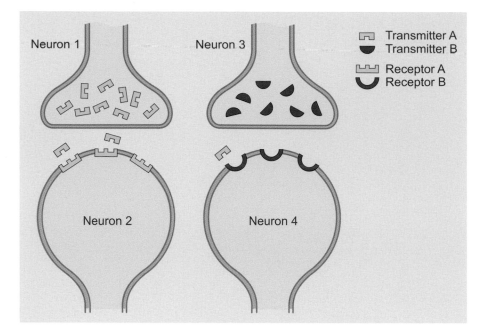

Figure 5.14   Two synapses with two different neurotransmitters

Note the correspondence between the shape of a neurotransmitter and that of its receptors. This is termed the 'lock and key principle': a particular neurotransmitter fits only a particular type of receptor, just as a particular key fits only one lock. If, as shown, a 'foreign' neurotransmitter finds itself in a synapse (in this case, between neurons 3 and 4), it does not fit the receptor and therefore has no influence. This could happen when some of the neurotransmitter released from neuron 1 escapes in the direction of neighbouring neurons such as 3 and 4.

The nervous system contains an array of different neurotransmitters, some excitatory and some inhibitory. A few of the better known neurotransmitters, which you are likely to meet in a study of psychology, include noradrenaline, dopamine, serotonin and glutamate. Some neurotransmitters act in an excitatory role throughout the nervous system, for example glutamate (Figure 5.13). Others act in an inhibitory role, for example GABA (Figure 5.13). The suffix 'ergic' is added to the name of a transmitter to form an adjective. For example, a dopaminergic neuron is one that releases dopamine.

After a neurotransmitter has been released, it is rapidly taken out of action in the synapse. This can occur in one of two ways. It can either be broken down (Figure 5.15(a)) or can be taken back into the neuron that released it (Figure 5.15(b)). The process shown in Figure 5.15(b) is known as **reuptake**. Either way, for neuron 1 to continue to exert an influence on neuron 2 it must continue to release neurotransmitters to replace that which is taken out of the synaptic gap.

Reuptake
The process by which a neurotransmitter released from a neuron is taken back into that neuron.

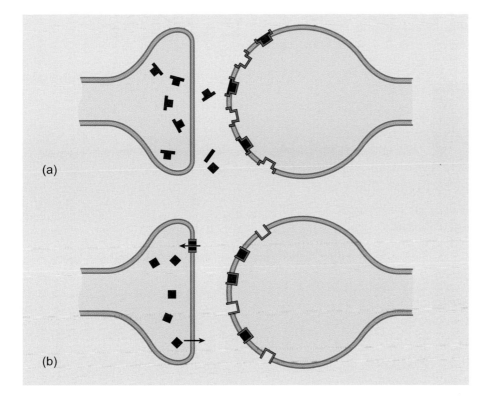

Figure 5.15   Removal of neurotransmitter: (a) broken down; (b) reuptake

2.5   Neurons, brain regions and whole brains

The characteristics of neurons can be investigated to gain an understanding of how brains work under different conditions. Changes in the brain as a result of disease or injury can sometimes be identified by changes in the activity of particular classes of neuron (e.g. dopaminergic) located in the affected regions. Investigators can sometimes link such changes in the activity of a brain region to psychological changes.

One technique, known as 'electroencephalography', exploits the fact that communication within neurons is by electrical means. Each neuron is like a miniature battery. The combined activity of millions of neurons can be detected by electrodes placed on the scalp and this record examined. Insights into the relationship between mood and sleep-cycle abnormalities have been obtained by examining changes in the electroencephalogram or EEG (Figure 5.16). People's brain activity can be monitored while they are sleeping and any unusual brain activity recorded by the EEG can serve as a warning of potential underlying abnormal function which may relate to specific psychological phenomena (e.g. anxiety or depression).

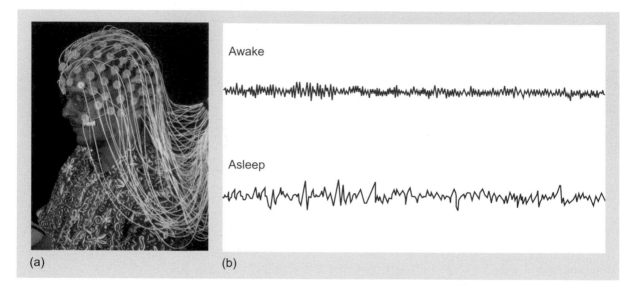

(a)   (b)

Figure 5.16   An EEG recorded during sleep

As noted in Section 2.2, all cells require a source of energy and oxygen in order to function. This is brought to the cells in the bloodstream. When a neuron is active it requires more energy than when it is inactive. A neuron is active when it is transmitting action potentials.

Positron emission tomography (PET)
A neuroimaging technique for examining the activity of different parts of the brain.

The higher the frequency of action potentials, the greater the energy needs of the cell and the higher the rate at which nutrients enter the cell. The movement of nutrients can be measured by a neuroimaging technique such as **positron emission tomography (PET)**. The technique can reveal the differences in energy consumption by neurons in different regions of the brain. Thereby it can suggest which regions are undergoing the most information processing under different conditions. So, for example, when a visual scene is being viewed, a relatively high activity will be shown by neurons in a region of the occipital cortex, known as the visual cortex (see Chapter 1, Section 2.3). If a person is exposed to sounds, relatively high activity will be measured in a brain region termed the 'auditory cortex', which is dedicated to processing sounds. Figure 5.17 shows a PET scan of a human brain obtained while a person with schizophrenia is experiencing auditory hallucinations. Those same brain areas that in controls are involved in sound processing are shown to be active, pointing to a biological basis of the 'hallucinatory' phenomenon.

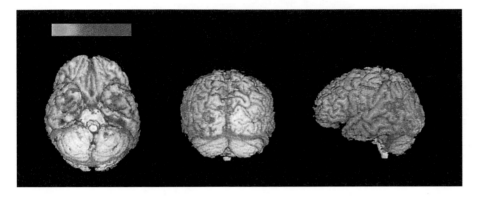

Figure 5.17   Active brain regions of a person suffering from schizophrenia. High activity indicated by red and yellow colour, highest being yellow

A PET scan can reveal which neurotransmitters are located where. In some cases, neurons that employ a particular neurotransmitter can be identified in particular parts of the brain. For example, the main dopaminergic neurons are shown in Figure 5.18. Some of them project to a region of the frontal cortex termed the 'prefrontal cortex'. Schizophrenia is associated with abnormality in these pathways.

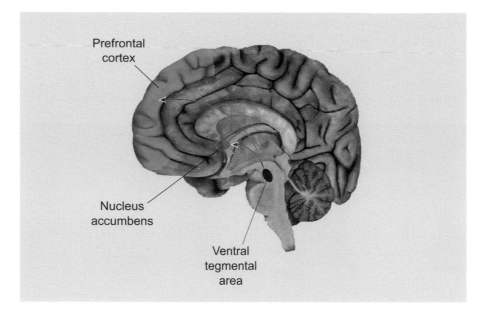

Figure 5.18   Two dopaminergic pathways of the human brain

2.6   The inputs to and outputs from the brain

The information on individual neurons, brain regions and neurotransmitters that you have gained so far will now enable you to understand some of the details of what the nervous system does.

Sensory neuron
The class of neuron that serves the role of detecting sensory information, e.g. light or pressure on the skin.

Look at Figure 5.19, which shows a neuron 1 with its tip at a finger. This neuron is one of a class termed **sensory neurons**, those specialised to detect sensory information. It is a 'cold neuron', meaning that it is specialised to detect cold. As the temperature of the water decreases, so the neuron increases its frequency of producing action potentials. Neuron 1 links to neuron 2 via a synapse within the spinal cord. Neuron 2 then conveys the message to the brain. Action potentials arrive at regions of the brain specialised to assess this information and translate it into the sensation of cold. The frequency of the action potentials translates into the intensity of the cold sensation.

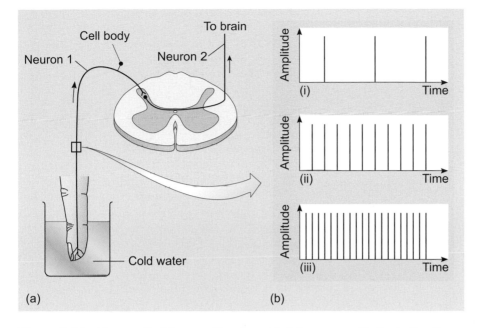

Figure 5.19   Neuron that is sensitive to cold: (a) neuron with tip in the finger (b) trace of activity as cold intensity increases (i) – (iii)

Figure 5.20 shows the pathways by which information leaves the brain in the form of action potentials in particular neurons. This information activates muscles, in this case both in the legs and at the heart. The brain controls the internal environment of the body (its 'housekeeping'), e.g. the frequency of beating of the heart (more on such control in a moment), and the external environment, e.g. via the muscles of the leg.

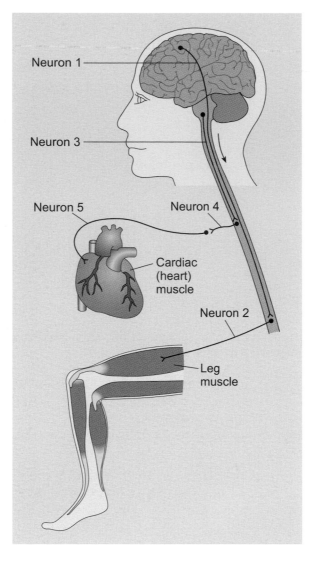

Figure 5.20   The control of the muscles. Neurons 1 and 2 control a muscle in the leg, while neurons 3, 4 and 5 adjust the frequency of the heartbeat

Imagine now that you put your hand on a very sharp object and jerk it away immediately. This is because of a reflex of neurons in sequence that convey an electrical signal to the muscles in your arm (Figure 5.21). You also emit an 'ouch' response. Information has been transmitted from your hand to your brain in the form of signals in groups of particular neurons. A bundle of axons of neurons in the peripheral nervous system is known as a 'nerve'.

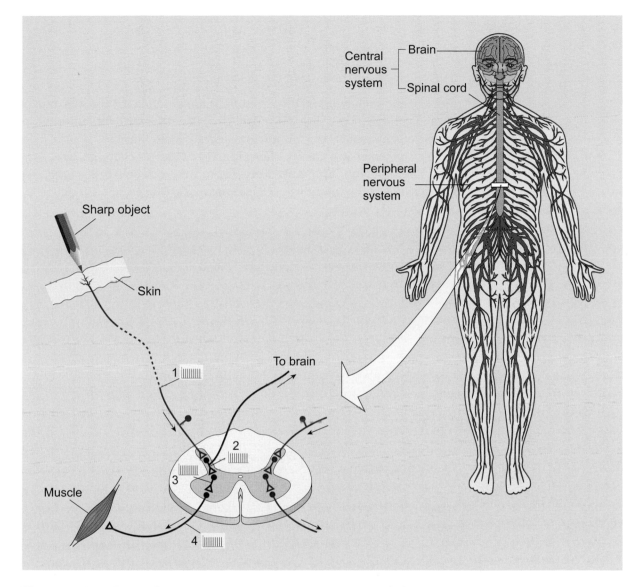

Figure 5.21   Effects of tissue damage at the skin. A sequence of neurons 1,
2, 3 and 4 within the spinal cord links the sensory input to the muscle
controlling movement. Neuron 2 also projects up to the brain

Pause for thought

Have you ever experienced the following?

Suppose that inadvertently you put your hand under a hot water tap and instantly jerk it away. A fraction of a second later, you feel a conscious sensation of pain and say 'ouch'. Note that the conscious sensation comes after the start of the reaction, so pain was not the trigger to the reaction. Try to work out how this might be explained. Can you think of circumstances when such a reaction is inhibited?

Try asking others whether it is familiar to them.

Look again at Figure 5.21. You will see the relatively short distance the signal travels from the skin to the muscle controlling the arm. By contrast, the signal has further to travel when going up the spinal cord to the brain. There could be circumstances when it is beneficial to survival to be able to inhibit such automatic actions. For example, you might be clinging for your life on to a thorn-covered edge of a mountain. It appears that the brain has some ability to inhibit activity in the pathway 1, 2, 3, and 4.

2.7   Hormones

Hormone

A chemical that is released into a blood vessel. It is then transported in the blood to a site where it occupies receptors and thereby effects action.

Synapses are not the only means of chemical transmission in the body. A **hormone** is a chemical that is released into a blood vessel at one location, travels in a blood vessel or the whole bloodstream to another location and then occupies receptors at that location. On occupying receptors, it changes the activity of the site. Figure 5.22 shows the sites of release of some of the principal hormones.

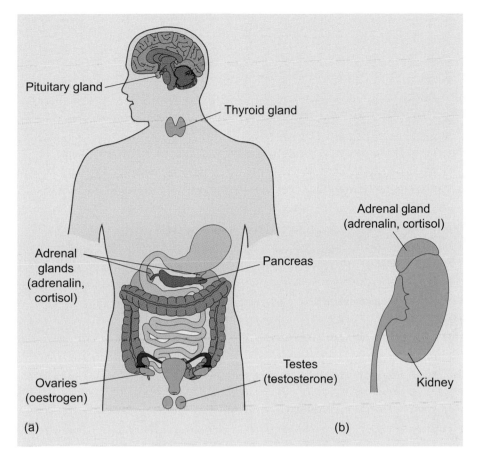

Figure 5.22   Site of release of some of hormones

Some hormones are released into the bloodstream and travel around the body in it, thereby reaching most, if not all, parts of the body. This is the type of hormone that will be discussed here. Insulin is a hormone of this kind. It is used by most cells. The adrenal gland is a source of several hormones that are of interest to psychologists: cortisol, adrenalin and noradrenalin (the latter two are termed 'epinephrine' and 'norepinephrine', respectively, in the American literature).

Another group of hormones is the 'sex hormones', so called because of their involvement in reproduction and, by their action on the brain, sexual desire. There are two broad classes of sex hormones: oestrogens and androgens. Oestrogens are secreted from the ovaries in women and their cyclical release corresponds to the menstrual cycle.

Activity 5.2: Neurotransmitters and hormones

Stop and think about neurotransmitters and hormones with the help of Figures 5.11, 5.12 and 5.23. From carefully examining these figures, try to describe some similarities and differences between communication by neurotransmitters and hormones.

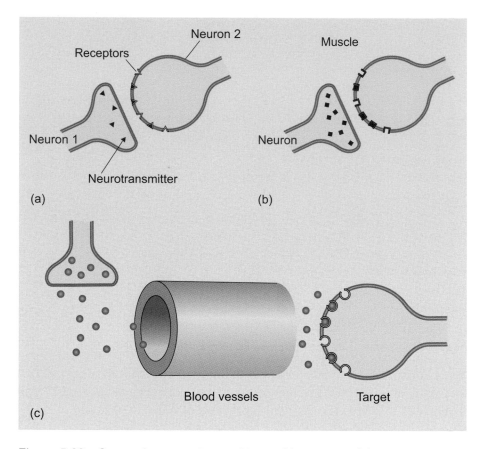

Figure 5.23   Comparing neurotransmitter and hormones: (a) a neurotransmitter; (b) another neurotransmitter; (c) a hormone

---

A similarity is that both serve a communication function by being released at one location and influencing events at another location. A difference is the distance between the site of release and the site of action. In the case of a neurotransmitter, the communication is one-to-one, cell-to-cell, the cells being separated by the minute distance of the synaptic gap. As just noted, a hormone is typically released into the bloodstream at one site, circulates in the bloodstream and affects many distant targets, after having travelled a relatively large distance.

2.8 The autonomic nervous system

That part of the peripheral nervous system that controls the internal housekeeping of the body, e.g. the heart, lungs, intestine and salivary glands, is known as the **autonomic nervous system (ANS)**. In Figure 5.20, neurons controlling the heartbeat, e.g. neuron 5, are part of the ANS.

Figure 5.24 shows that the ANS takes the form of two divisions (or 'branches'): the 'sympathetic division' and the 'parasympathetic division'. These divisions exert opposite effects on the organs of the body, as a kind of tug-of-war. Increased activity by the sympathetic division prepares the body for immediate action, as in running from a bear. Heart rate is accelerated and blood is pumped to the muscles of the legs at a high rate. Digestion of food by the gut is temporarily suspended, since the blood is needed elsewhere. Note the link from the sympathetic division to the adrenal gland. It is through this route that times of emergency are associated with triggering the secretion of adrenalin from this gland. Conversely, increased activity by the parasympathetic branch triggers, among other things, digestion by the gut and an inhibition of heart rate to a calmer level. It is the reaction that is appropriate to a psychological state of relaxation.

Autonomic nervous system (ANS)
The part of the nervous system responsible for controlling the internal activity of the body, e.g. heart rate and digestion.

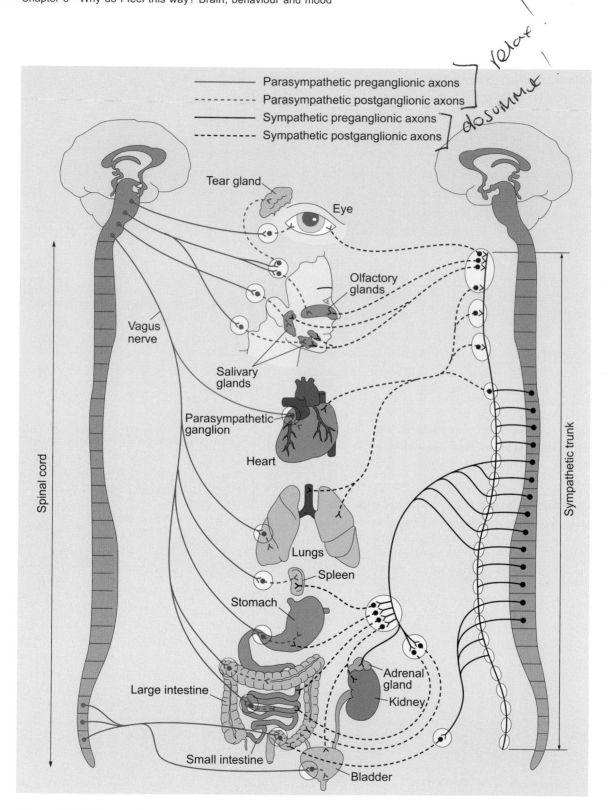

Figure 5.24 The autonomic nervous system

It is sometimes suggested that we live in a society dominated by the sympathetic branch, meaning that we are too often stressed and reacting to emergencies. Deadlines must be met and people spend hours stuck in traffic jams or on trains that have broken down. The circulation is put into top gear as if running from a bear but you are moving nowhere. This can take a toll on the stomach, circulation and heart.

2.9   Summary

In this section you have learned that the central nervous system (CNS) consists of the brain and spinal cord and nerves extend from the CNS throughout the body. A type of cell found in the nervous system and used for information transmission and processing is termed 'neuron'. Communication within neurons is by means of electrical pulses termed 'action potentials'. Neurons communicate with other cells at synapses. At a synapse, a neuron releases neurotransmitter, which occupies receptor sites on an immediately adjacent cell. Neurotransmitters can excite or inhibit. A hormone, on the other hand, is released at one site in the body and is transported to another site, in a blood vessel, where it occupies receptors and effects action.

Now you have considered the biological aspects of the brain and its place within the body, the next sections bring the focus back to psychological experience. Specifically, they investigate the interplay between biology and psychology, exploring the relationship between the brain and our mood.

3   Can I alter my moods by altering my brain?

3.1   Basic principles

Humans can change their own moods in various ways. Alcohol, nicotine and other substances can be taken into the body, with obvious effects on mood. When we are seriously distressed, we might seek medicines in the hope of improving our mood. All such effects are mediated by changing the activity of particular parts of the brain. How does this occur?

Drugs, whether taken recreationally, such as alcohol, nicotine or cocaine, or by prescription, such as anti-depressants, have their effects by altering the activity of synapses. Thereby, they alter the activity of the associated neurons and the collections of interacting neurons. Drugs have effects on one or more particular classes of synapse. Let us consider how certain drugs work.

3.2   The action of Prozac

One type of drug is known as 'selective serotonin reuptake inhibitors' (SSRIs), the best known being fluoxetine, also called Prozac. It is taken as a prescription for depression and obsessive compulsive disorder. Its action is to block the reuptake of serotonin and it selectively targets just this neurotransmitter. Figure 5.25 shows its action. Note that, after its release, serotonin is normally taken back into the neuron that released it (part a → b). Figure 5.25(c) shows the effect of Prozac in blocking the reuptake of serotonin. Note the increased density of serotonin in the synaptic gap and the correspondingly increased occupation of serotonin receptors on neuron 2. This increases the effect of activity of neuron 1 on neuron 2 by artificially amplifying the impact of the serotonin that was initially released. This, in turn, is thought to improve mood. There are a large number of such serotonergic synapses in the brain and Prozac has a wide influence.

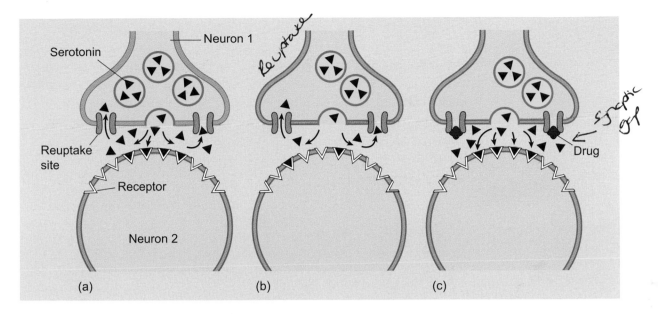

Figure 5.25   The action of Prozac

3.3   Some drugs not on prescription

It is not only prescription drugs that can influence mood. There are various recreational drugs (both legal and illegal) that have mood-altering effects. Depending on the drug, they act on different types of synapse in the brain, with some correspondingly different effects on mood.

Cocaine blocks the reuptake of dopamine and thereby boosts the activity of this neurotransmitter in the brain. This is felt as a short-lived 'high' and an energising of behaviour. It has a particular effect on synapses that are within the pathways shown in Figure 5.18. Under normal conditions, this pathway underlies our wanting and seeking of things in life, such as sex, food and exciting novel events. When it is strongly activated we are drawn to them. Cocaine tends to have the effect of making people want more cocaine. It does this by, among other things, forming conditioned associations (Chapter 4, Section 3.1) between cues that were around at the time of taking the cocaine and the wanting sensation (Robinson and Berridge, 1993). So, for example, the sight of the cocaine can set up an intense craving for it. This is a major problem for people who are trying to resist drugs.

Figure 5.26 shows a synapse that employs a substance known as an opioid. This neurochemical derives its name from the equivalent substances known as opiates, which include morphine and heroin. Figure 5.26 represents this near equivalence by a similarity in shape of the substance and the corresponding receptors. When these substances occupy receptors there is a shift of mood in a positive direction, with such effects as to lift pain or depression and to produce a euphoric mood. However, the effect is not long lasting because, in time, the chemical leaves the receptors and is lost from the body. Correspondingly, the 'high' lifts and a psychological rebound or 'low' can be experienced.

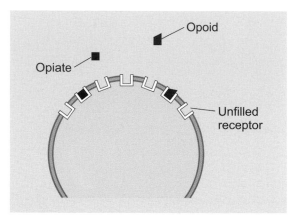

Figure 5.26   Opioidergic synapse

Heroin also affects the control of respiration, among other things. There is a risk that with an overdose a suppression of respiration will occur. A medical intervention for this is to inject a substance having a similar property to heroin, which will compete for occupation of opioid receptors but which is chemically inert.

Both heroin and cocaine trigger a desire for more of the drug, and the need to buy more and more is a major factor behind criminal acts. Such drugs not only instigate a transient change in mood but also alter the structure of the brain, a property known as plasticity (a topic discussed in detail in Chapter 6). This change means that the wanting increases over time, even though the pleasure does not necessarily increase in parallel. Figure 5.27 shows the apparent change in dopaminergic synapses by increase in receptors, brought about by extensive drug use. The plasticity takes the form of sensitisation.

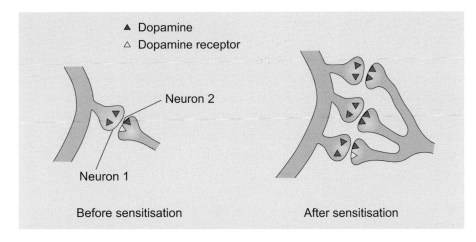

Figure 5.27   Sensitisation

There are other illegal drugs that also alter mood, but target different types of synapse. An example is ecstasy, which affects serotonergic synapses. The effect is to put the user in a mood of increased sociability but it does not lead to intense craving and is not addictive.

3.4   My pounding heart

Figure 5.24 described a flow of information from the brain to the organs of the body. However, in the reverse direction, signals also arise in the organs of the body and are transmitted via neurons to the brain. These carry information on the state of the organ, e.g. heart rate and degree of contraction of the gut. There is some evidence that such signals have an effect on our moods. For example, beta-blockers are drugs that attach themselves to receptors on the heart, slowing its activity. They are of some help to those suffering from various anxiety and panic disorders, including stage fright (Battes et al., 2012).

Now you have learned something about nervous systems, neurons and synapses and their relevance to moods, the relevance of this to understanding a range of mood-related phenomena can be explored. The next three sections are devoted to this.

3.5   Summary

In this section you have seen that psychoactive drugs exert their effects by altering the activity of particular types of synapse, thereby altering the activity of neurons. Prozac, for example, blocks the reuptake of serotonin while cocaine blocks the reuptake of dopamine. Such addictive drugs have long-term effects on the brain, with addicts' brains showing plasticity with increased use.

4   When does a change in mood represent an illness?

4.1   Introduction

Depression is much more than just a kind of transient mood state of sadness that we might all experience at times. Rather, it is a serious illness.

Pause for thought

Think of the characteristics of depression you might have observed. Are there common behaviours demonstrated by individuals suffering from depression?

You might well arrive at a chronic depressed or sad mood as the most obvious defining feature, sometimes associated with an inability or reduced ability to experience pleasure. We all experience sadness at stages in our life, for example when relationships end. However, clinical depression is different in that it tends to be unremitting and its intensity is sometimes out of proportion to any negative events in the person's life. Other features can involve feelings of helplessness, worthlessness, guilt, pessimism and lethargy.

In depression, activity by brain regions underlying mood shifts from its normal setting. Particular brain regions are either relatively underactive or overactive.

A biopsychosocial model highlights the fact that depression can arise from either intrinsic biological changes or from events in the person's life. Correspondingly, treatments can target the biology of the brain or the social context. Another common treatment for depression is termed 'cognitive therapy'. This directly targets the individual's thought processes by challenging modes of thinking that appear to be sustaining the depressed mood. If it is successful, an implicit assumption is that there are corresponding changes in the brain.

The following sections consider the relevance of features of the brain and the hormones to understanding depression.

4.2   Hormones

People suffering from depression often have elevated levels of cortisol in the body. This hormone is secreted from the adrenal glands in response to signals initiated in the brain and circulates throughout the bloodstream (Figure 5.28). Some of this arrives at the brain, where there are receptors at various sites. Stress is commonly a precursor to depression and stress elevates levels of cortisol in the body. Does the elevated cortisol cause the depressed mood? This could be so but, conversely, the depressed mood might have caused the excessive secretion of cortisol (see Figure 5.28). It is perhaps most likely that both factors are involved as a vicious circle, i.e. excessive cortisol levels promote depression, which in turn triggers still higher cortisol secretion.

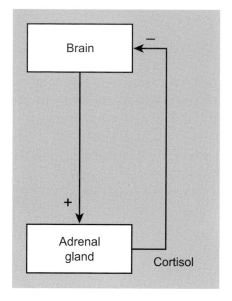

Figure 5.28   The brain and cortisol. The brain triggers the release of cortisol and cortisol normally inhibits its own release. In depression inhibitory feedback on the brain appears to be disrupted

Very high levels of cortisol damage neurons in parts of the brain, e.g. the prefrontal cortex and hippocampus (Figures 5.6 and 5.18). It is also known that these areas can be damaged in depression (Paul and Skolnick, 2003).

It would obviously be unethical to inject people with high levels of cortisol over an extended period to observe the result. However, nature has in effect done the experiment for us. A condition known as

Cushing's disease enables researchers to establish that a rise in cortisol levels is a factor in the causation of depression (Feelders et al., 2012). This disease consists of a tumour that triggers an elevated secretion of cortisol and an early indicator of the presence of the tumour is a depressed mood.

4.3   Neurotransmitters

A common assumption in the study and treatment of depression is that, at its biological basis, there is abnormality in one or more neurotransmitter. An observation of neurotransmitter abnormality might point to the initial cause of the depression. However, the initial cause might be a social event that subsequently exerts an influence on the brain so as to produce the profile characteristic of depression. Another possibility is that (a) social events and cognitive interpretations, and (b) biological events get locked into a vicious circle, with each reinforcing the other.

Anti-depressant medication is designed to correct the abnormalities in neurotransmitter level and hence, in principle at least, to ameliorate the depression. Abnormal activity by particular neurotransmitters implies abnormal activity in particular regions of the brain where the corresponding synapses are located.

There are various candidate neurotransmitters for investigation and therapeutic intervention. There might well turn out not to be one magic bullet to treat depression. Rather, abnormalities in more than one neurotransmitter could be implicated. Also, neurons using different neurotransmitters interact with each other. Therefore targeting neurotransmitter A, changing its activity and finding an effect could be because neurons that employ neurotransmitter A make synapses on neurons that employ neurotransmitter B. The change in activity of B could be necessary for therapeutic help and a drug to target B directly might be of greater efficacy.

One of the best-known classes of anti-depressant is the selective serotonin reuptake inhibitors (Section 3.2). These have been used extensively. Figure 5.25 showed the action of Prozac (fluoxetine) in blocking the reuptake of serotonin. This action is rapid, but any beneficial effects of fluoxetine in treating depression are only felt some three weeks later. So what could be happening during this three-week period? There might be changes in the structure of the brain that are triggered by the elevated serotonin levels and these could lie at the basis of the therapeutic effect: see Figure 5.29.

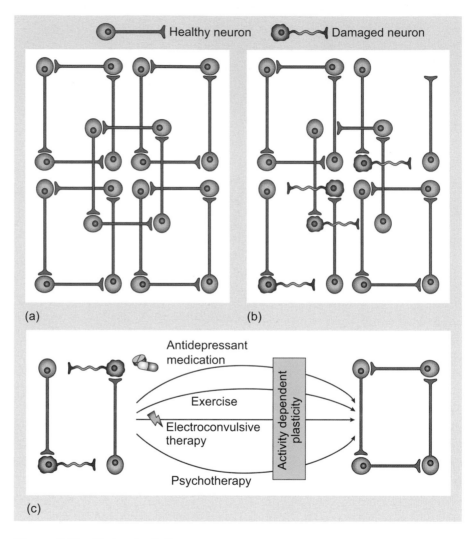

Figure 5.29   Brain plasticity

Unfortunately, Prozac is not invariably successful in treating depression. Estimates vary with an average of around 65 per cent of depressed patients benefiting (Paul and Skolnick, 2003) but with the lowest estimate suggesting that Prozac is no better than a placebo. A placebo is a chemically inert substance that is taken by a patient in the understanding and expectation that it is real medicine with an established efficacy.

More recently, attention has moved to another neurotransmitter: glutamate (Paul and Skolnick, 2003). Evidence suggests that the activity of glutamate might be abnormal in depression and that correcting this could bring relief. Some drugs that have an anti-depressant effect block a class of glutamate receptors, known as NMDA receptors, thereby reducing activity at the corresponding glutamatergic synapses; see Figure 5.30. Inert substances that block neurotransmitters in this way are termed **antagonists**. Ketamine is an example of such a drug that has potential to treat depression but, alas, has undesirable side-effects.

Antagonists
A type of chemical that occupies the receptors for a particular neurotransmitter but that is chemically inert and therefore blocks the action of the natural substance.

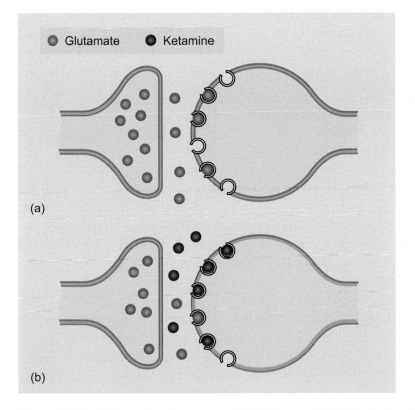

Figure 5.30   Glutamatergic synapse (a) before and (b) after ketamine use

4.4   Brain hemispheres

Neurotransmission is not the only aspect of brain function that has been implicated in mood changes; the broader brain structure may also have a part to play. There appears to be an asymmetry in the responsibility of the two hemispheres of the brain (Figure 5.3) for the control of moods (Cozolino, 2002). The frontal lobe of the left hemisphere has a greater control over positive moods and that of the right hemisphere has a greater control over negative moods.

Evidence for this comes from the effects of damage to the brain. When the damage is to the left, the result tends to be an increase in negative mood, whereas when it is to the right, there is an increase in positive mood. Increased negative mood follows if the left hemisphere is temporarily anaesthetised.

A method of providing stimulation to a hemisphere is to apply a powerful magnetic field alongside the head, specifically targeting either the right or the left hemisphere. If the left hemisphere is artificially stimulated there tends to be an increase in positive mood. Conversely, when the right hemisphere is artificially stimulated there tends to be an increase in negative mood, e.g. a shift towards a more depressed mood.

4.5   Vagal stimulation

The vagus nerve, part of the parasympathetic division of the ANS, was shown in Figure 5.24. The effect of activity by the parasympathetic branch is to calm the body. The vagus nerve contains neurons that transmit action potentials from the brain to the organs and others that transmit in the opposite direction, i.e. from the organs to the brain. For cases of chronic and unremitting depression, patients have had electrical stimulators surgically implanted to stimulate the vagus nerve, with some success (Marangell et al., 2002). Exactly what the stimulation is doing is unclear. While it may seem strange that patients should be given a treatment without actually understanding how it works, this is often the norm when treating mood disorders. As the underlying cause of depression is still not definitively recognised and understood, it is not possible to design a specific treatment that targets the known causes. Instead, possible treatments are developed in the hope that they will work, and their success (or failure) sheds more light on the possible mechanisms underlying the condition.

4.6   Electroconvulsive therapy

Perhaps the most controversial treatment for depression is that of Electroconvulsive Therapy (ECT). ECT consists of passing an electric current through the brains of severely depressed patients. This technique like few others evokes public unease. However, there is evidence that it is effective and worth the risks in some very severe cases (Nordanskog et al., 2014).

How does it work? It is assumed that ECT alters the brain state associated with depression, bringing it nearer to that of healthy controls. There is still some mystery surrounding exactly how it does this and the assumption has been that it is effective because it alters the release of certain key neurotransmitters. Could it also change the structure of the brain? Neuroimaging enables the brain to be examined before and after ECT. A region of the brain, known as the hippocampus, has been found to be enlarged following ECT, possibly involving the growth of new neurons and glial cells (Nordanskog et al., 2014). Among other things, the hippocampus is known to exert control over the secretion of cortisol from the adrenal glands and thus may account for its efficacy.

4.7   Post-natal depression

While studying successful treatments of depression can give us some insight into the biological mechanisms underlying it, so too can the investigation of specific instances of the illness. For example, insight into depression can be gained by considering a particular form: **post-natal depression** (also termed post-partum depression) (O'Hara and McCabe, 2013). Some term this 'post-natal illness', while others see it in terms of post-traumatic shock rather than depression. Post-natal depression is a serious condition that occurs in the period following birth, a time when heavy demands are placed on the mother. It is distinguished from so-called 'baby blues', a relatively mild and transient change in mood that occurs in a large percentage of women in the days immediately following birth.

Post-natal depression Depression experienced by a percentage of women following birth. It is also known as post-natal illness or post-partum depression.

Accompanying birth is a dramatic fall in the level of a number of hormones, e.g. oestradiol (one of the class of oestrogens) (O'Hara and McCabe, 2013). This suggests a causal link between hormones and depression but it is not enough to prove it. (Another contributory factor could be sleep deprivation.) All women experience these drops in hormone level but only a minority experience post-natal depression. So it seems that a sudden change in hormone level is a *necessary* but not *sufficient* condition to trigger depression. A minority of women appear to have a particular vulnerability to such a hormonal change. This suggests the use of supplementary hormone administration as a treatment, which has some success (McCoy, 2011).

Oestradiol interacts with a number of neurotransmitters, such as serotonin and dopamine (O'Hara and McCabe; 2013, see Figure 5.31).

By its loss from, say, serotoninergic neurons, a bias towards depression might be created. Women suffering from post-natal depression have relatively low levels of serotonin in their blood. Corresponding to these observations, drugs that target serotonin (e.g. fluoxetine) are used to treat post-natal depression. There is also a possible indication of increased glutamate activity in regions of the prefrontal cortex of women suffering from this illness (McEwen et al., 2012). If confirmed, this would fit the bigger picture that points to the involvement of this substance in depression and suggests multiple neurotransmitters may be involved simultaneously.

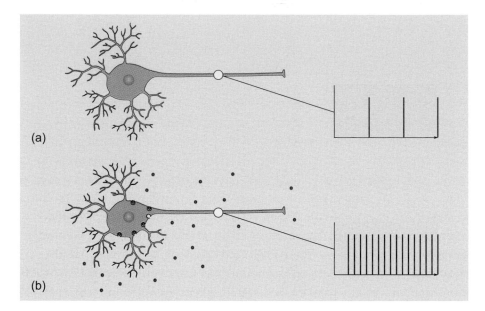

Figure 5.31   Interaction of hormone with a neuron: (a) without oestradiol; (b) with oestradiol

Box 5.1   Crossing boundaries: post-natal depression: the need to take more than one perspective

Social and cognitive factors appear to play a fundamental role in whether women develop post-natal depression (O'Hara and McCabe, 2013). Risk factors that increase the chances include depression experienced during the course of the pregnancy, stress, poverty, low self-esteem, a poor quality of relationship with the child's father and having little social support. Such considerations map on to the use of cognitive behavioural techniques and counselling as treatments.

Physical exercise has been found to have beneficial effects for sufferers from post-natal depression (McCoy, 2011). It could work through a combination of (a) triggering the body to produce substances called endorphins (discussed shortly), and (b) cognitions of the kind of gaining self-esteem and control over the situation.

It is clear that post-natal depression arises from a combination of cognitive, social and biological factors, with corresponding therapeutic interventions suggested at each level. In other words, a biopsychosocial model is applicable. This phenomenon illustrates how an approach that crosses boundaries is essential.

Could there be an animal model of post-natal depression? When levels of oestrogen are suddenly reduced in female rats they exhibit a depression-like reaction, indexed by greater passivity (Perani and Slattery, 2014). The death of neurons in a region of the brain, the hippocampus, was also observed.

4.8 Summary

In this section you have learned that depression can arise from internal (e.g. hormonal changes) or external (e.g. social disruption) events, or a combination of the two. The drugs used to treat depression target particular neurotransmitters and thereby alter activity at synapses. Post-natal depression arises from post-partum hormonal imbalances that occur and an adverse social context, leading a new mother to experience clinical depression. The finding that depression (post-natal or otherwise) can come about as the result of both biological and social factors (and the interplay between them) supports a biopsychosocial model of the condition. In the next section you will explore this model further in a different psychological context.

5   Can a biopsychosocial model explain self-harm?

5.1   Introduction

The phenomenon of deliberate non-lethal self-harm refers to the disturbing behaviour of people who inflict damage to themselves, typically knife cuts to the skin of the arms, legs or stomach. Reports of this behaviour go back thousands of years, though it appears to have increased in frequency in recent years (Nock, 2009). It is distinguished from self-harm with the intention of committing suicide.

This behaviour is a puzzle since it appears to defy rationality. Normally people try hard to avoid injury; humans and non-humans alike are equipped with brain mechanisms and reflexes that serve this function (Section 2.6). Evolution has favoured such processes because damage to the skin carries risks, for example, infection. In attempting to explain this phenomenon, various questions arise. This section will show where a biopsychosocial model can serve as a useful organising role.

5.2   Asking the right questions

Some questions include the following:

- What are the developmental origins of this behaviour, e.g. was there an early experience of trauma?

- What kinds of people display this behaviour? Could there be biological differences between those who do, and do not, exhibit it?

- What are the immediate factors that lead to self-harming? For example, what is the mood state just prior to doing so?

- What are the consequences of self-harming, in terms of both the individual and their social context? Do observable biological changes occur? Could these be characterised as 'reinforcing' (see Chapter 4, Section 3.2)?

Self-reports reveal that self-injury is preceded by strong negative feelings of, for example, self-loathing and self-anger. These are alleviated by self-harming. This supports the belief that the injury represents a form of self-medication (calming), either by intrinsic effects within the body or by recruiting social help, or both. This could constitute reinforcement, tending to increase the strength of the behaviour and the future frequency of exhibiting it.

5.3 Biological insights

Subjective reports suggest that people who self-harm suffer high levels of stress. Could there be an objective measure of this? The sympathetic branch of the ANS is activated at times of challenge (Section 2.8). One consequence of this is increased secretion of sweat on to the skin. There is a technique for measuring this secretion and thereby assessing the sympathetic activation that caused it. Electrodes are attached to the skin to measure its electrical conductance. As the amount of sweat on the skin increases, so does the conductance.

A task was designed to trigger frustration (Nock and Mendes, 2008), and participants with a history of self-harm were compared with controls. Figure 5.32 shows the result: participants with a history of non-suicidal self-injury (NSSI) exhibit a higher change in skin conductance, indicative of a higher sympathetic reaction.

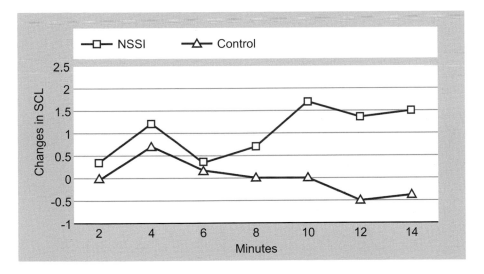

Figure 5.32 Graphs showing changes in skin conductance level over time for people who exhibit self-injury and for controls (NSSI: non-suicidal self-injury; SCL: skin conductance level)

(Source: Nock and Mendes, 2008)

But this is not the only potential biological mechanism underlying self harm. Somewhat surprisingly, a considerable number of the people who self-harm report relatively little pain while doing so (Nock, 2009). As noted earlier, opioids are involved in pleasure and in natural pain relief. This suggests that there is a high level of natural opioids either (a) at a stable elevated level, or (b) triggered at the time of each episode of behaviour. However, studies tend to show relatively low baseline levels of opioids (Bresin and Gordon, 2013), so the evidence points to the second of these.

Some self-harming individuals *crave* the opportunity to perform injury when they are in a strong negative mood. This suggests a similarity with addiction to drugs, such as heroin. Parts of the prefrontal cortex that are activated by physical pain that arises from tissue damage are also active at times of psychological pain. Such regions have a high density of opioid receptors. Hence, a pain-reducing reaction to tissue damage might equally reduce psychological distress (Bresin and Gordon, 2013). There are reports that acupuncture and physical exercise, both of which tend to increase opioid levels, are associated with reductions in self-harm.

In such terms, low levels of opioids are associated with low moods and self-harm is a means of boosting opioid level in the brain and thereby elevating mood. Opioid antagonists have been employed with some success as a therapeutic intervention to try to lower self-harm. However, they are a blunt instrument since, although they might combat self-harm, the cost could be an increase in overall level of negative mood.

Not only humans perform self-harm; some captive rhesus monkeys bite their own bodies and they have been found to have relatively low levels of opioids in their cerebrospinal fluid. Such monkeys bite the area of skin at which acupuncture is effective. This suggests the involvement of opioids in both acupuncture and self-harm. Monkeys show a relatively high heart rate preceding and during an episode of biting but a lowered heart rate immediately afterwards (Marinus et al., 1999). This is compatible with (a) increased negative emotion triggering this behaviour, and (b) released opioids lowering heart rate.

Insight can also be gained into this phenomenon by studying events in the imagination of people who regularly self-harm. Leading up to the imagined event, there is an increase in heart rate, but following it there is a decrease (Haines et al., 1995).

If self-harm triggers the release of opioids, we might expect a lowering of pain only *after* the event. However, the cutting itself is commonly reported as not painful. This might be explained in terms of classical conditioning (see Chapter 4, Section 3.1). The cut would constitute the unconditional stimulus that triggers the unconditional response of opioid release. The unconditional stimulus of the cut is paired with the sight of the cutting instrument and taking it into the hand, which could become a conditional stimulus. Thus the cutting instrument alone may then trigger an opioid response, and reinforce the self-harming behaviour.

For some self-harming individuals, the reinforcement of their behaviour can also come in the form of a more social context. In this case, cutting behaviours allow the sufferer to physically manifest their mental distress, allowing others to see what they are going through. Possible positive reactions to this might involve offers of support and comfort from other people, who might otherwise have been unaware of their mental suffering. Thus the source of reinforcement can most likely be both biological and social.

5.4   Summary

In this section you have learned that self-harm arises at times of particular stress and is characterised by causing deliberate damage to the body. This kind of behaviour appears to trigger the release of opioids which, in turn, brings a mood elevation. However, this effect is short-lived, meaning the behaviour is often repeated. Positive social reactions to this behaviour may also reinforce the self-harm. Thus it can be characterised by a biopsychosocial model.

6   What makes me happy? A brief look on the bright side

6.1   Introduction

Alas, relatively little research has been done on the biological bases of good moods. Even where good moods have been investigated, this is usually in the context of how to avoid or alleviate bad moods. However, the popular literature contains a wealth of information on how to lift moods from bad to neutral or from neutral to good.

Activity 5.3: Mood improvement tips

List what you have encountered in the media that describes how to raise one's spirits.

Your list might well involve aerobic exercise, companionship, prayer, charity work, meditation, yoga, exposure to sunlight, eating chocolate, listening to certain music, sex, rhythmic chanting and humour. We'll explore a few of these in more detail below.

6.2   The pleasures of the brain

One way of understanding the bases of good moods is to look at the brain's activity in a neuroimaging apparatus when a participant is receiving stimulation described as pleasurable. This consists of, for example, giving chocolate or, in the case of one research group in the Netherlands, sexual stimulation (Georgiadis and Kortekaas, 2010). When experiencing pleasure, activation is particularly strong in certain identifiable regions, which the researchers term 'hedonic hotspots'. Figure 5.33 shows a PET scan indicating relatively high activity in a cortical region while someone experiences the pleasure of chocolate. These hotspots could be used as potential targets of therapy in the future in an attempt to tilt the mood of someone suffering from depression in favour of a positive mood. Knowledge of neurochemicals employed there might help the search for chemical therapies.

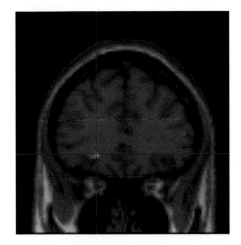

Figure 5.33   PET scan of the brain while someone eats chocolate. An area of the prefrontal cortex is particularly excited. The magnitude of the excitation correlates with the subjective experience of pleasure

(Source: Kringelbach et al., 2003)

6.3   Eating and moods

The potential link between mood and eating is two-way, which complicates matters. Thus, if we find a link between diet and mood, it is not easy to decide whether diet influences mood or mood influences the diet chosen, or both. Another problem is the time scale over which observations are made. One hears a claim of the kind that 'chocolate improves mood'. It might improve mood immediately after ingestion but how long does the effect last? We are better at forming associations between events that are close in time than those that are more remote. People in negative moods tend to eat more sugar and fat-rich snacks (White et al., 2013), presumably as self-medication. Correspondingly, their consumption of fruit and vegetables declines.

Activity 5.4: The influence of diet on mood

List some of the ways that food might alter mood and some of the complications associated with understanding this.

The taste of certain foods could affect our mood but also, after the food has been digested, its chemical ingredients could have effects on the brain. In addition, the cultural connotations of the particular food might affect mood. Fat- and sugar-rich foods could trigger immediate pleasure but a delayed guilt and anxiety linked to weight gain. Fruits and vegetables might give us a glow of eco-friendly self-righteousness!

Chocolate is commonly treated as a substance with a strong ability to trigger pleasure. Figure 5.34 shows its immediate effect on lifting mood, relative to an apple or no food. It can be seen that it also triggers guilt.

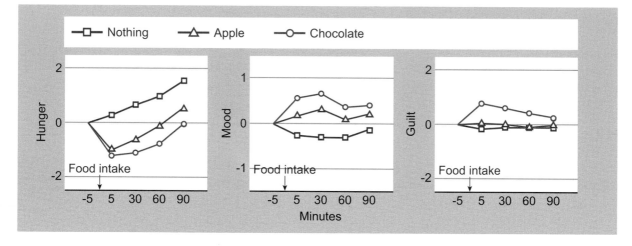

Figure 5.34   The effects of chocolate

Activity 5.5: Taste or consequences?

Take a careful look at Figure 5.34. Is the increase in mood likely to be due to the immediate taste or the consequences for the body following digestion?

The graphs show that the effect is evident within 5 minutes or so. This is too rapid to be mediated by the ingredients acting after digestion.

When so-called 'chocoholics' are in a neutral or positive mood, they crave only chocolate, which points to its sensory properties. People suffering from depression commonly crave chocolate, although it appears to have only short-term effects on mood (Parker et al., 2006). The immediate pleasure that chocolate triggers appears to be due in large part to the release of opioids in the brain that this triggers. Injection of a substance that blocks opioid receptors lowers the intake of sweet foods (Benton and Donohoe, 1999), which supports this claim, as does the finding that when heroin addicts cannot get their drug, they report sweet cravings, suggesting a common mechanism.

In contrast to the short-lived mood effect chocolate has, one study found that eating substantial portions of fruit and vegetables, relative to so-called junk food, had a positive effect on mood during the following day: people reported feeling 'Calmer, happier and more energetic' (White et al., 2013). The researchers suggest two possible processes underlying this. There could be a sociocultural component of feeling worthy for having done the 'healthy thing'. In addition, there could be components within fruit and vegetables that contribute to the effect. One possible candidate is a protein termed 'brain derived neurotrophic factor' (BDNF), which promotes the construction of new neurons and is implicated in mood. (Other possible contributory components include folate and an omega-3 fatty acid.) Those ingesting diets high in fats and sugars and low in fruits and vegetables are deficient in this substance.

6.4   Will exercise make me happy?

Evidence suggests that physical exercise can improve mood, both in people who are depressed or anxious and in those with no psychological distress. However, even designing a good experiment on exercise and mood is difficult.

Activity 5.6: The problem with exercise

What sort of problem is there in forming a control group to investigate whether physical exercise can improve mood, as compared with, say, testing a potential mood-enhancing medicine?

With testing a drug, it is possible to recruit a control group who receive a placebo and compare their reaction with those receiving the drug. Participants would be blind as to what they received. With exercise it is difficult to identify what constitutes the control condition. Obviously it is impossible to 'blind' participants as to their condition.

It appears that when an elevation in mood occurs in association with exercise, there are various psychological components involved. These include gaining mastery over a task, taking time out from otherwise stressful activities, gaining a sense of control over one's well-being and, in some situations, appreciating the countryside and participation in a social activity.

As far as the neurochemical basis of the mood is concerned, a principal focus has been upon elevated secretion of endorphins by the brain (Goldfarb, 2013). Endorphins are a form of opioid and the origin of their name is revealing: an abbreviation of 'endogenous morphine-like substance'. Blocking opioids tends to reduce the intensity of the mood elevation. Alas, measuring endorphin activity presents serious problems. Endorphins are secreted both within the brain and into the blood from the pituitary gland. Measuring the blood levels, though relatively easy, is probably a far from ideal measure of events within the brain. However, neuroimaging enables researchers to examine the level of opioids occupying receptors in the brain following exercise, with confirmation that this is elevated (Boecker et al., 2012). The degree of euphoria felt correlates with the level of opioids released.

Another factor that appears to be implicated is a natural cannabis-like substance released by strenuous exercise (Heyman et al., 2012). This could have immediate and short-lived effects on elevating moods. However, since exercise has a cumulative effect over sessions, there could also be structural changes in the brain and both endorphins and the natural cannabis-like substance are candidates for involvement in this, acting by means of BDNF, the same substance affected by diet, discussed previously.

6.5   Humour

Anecdotal and experimental evidence suggests that humour can elevate moods. There is evidence to suggest that humour triggers an elevation of endorphin levels (Berk and Tan, 2006) with potential effects on mood. Figure 5.35 shows the effects of humour therapy on patients' happiness and pain ratings. Over sessions, as happiness went up, so pain levels came down. This might simply be the effect of lowering pain on elevating mood. As the pain is lifted, so happiness rises. It could also be due to direct effects of humour on both pain and happiness.

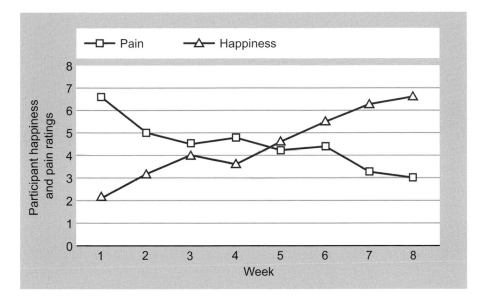

Figure 5.35 Effects of humour on happiness and pain
(Source: Tse et al., 2010)

6.6 Sex

In the popular imagination, sexual behaviour famously can elevate mood. Sex illustrates the general principle that both social factors and biological factors need to be taken into account in understanding sexual desire and pleasure (Toates, 2014). So-called sex hormones sensitise those parts of the brain that underlie sexual desire, making them responsive to social stimuli in the form of attractive others. The brain regions underlying sexual fantasy are sensitised by sex hormones, making sexual fantasies more powerful.

Sex is a good example of the general principle that pleasure is felt when events move in the direction of what is desired (Carver and Scheier, 1990). Of course, goals can conflict and achievement of a sexual goal might bring conflict with another goal, such as to abstain. In this case, an elevated mood might be followed by fear and guilt. In one study, young people were asked to rate their moods prior to and after intercourse (Shrier et al., 2010). Mood increased in the hours prior to intercourse and remained elevated for some hours after. In the wanting phase, an increase in dopamine activity would be expected. Sex hormones sensitise the dopamine-based desire system. Some people take drugs that activate dopamine, such as cocaine and methamphetamine, to increase their level of sexual desire.

Sensory signals from the erogenous zones are not sufficient for pleasure to be experienced. The pleasure also depends, of course, upon the context in which this stimulation arises. If desire is lacking, then the same stimulation can be felt as aversive. So a brain event corresponding to desire integrates the sensory information in the determination of pleasure or aversion.

The activity of the substance termed oxytocin, a neurotransmitter and hormone, increases during sexual behaviour and particularly at orgasm (Carmichael et al., 1994). Opioids are also involved and a combination of these substances appears to confer the pleasures of sexual contact.

6.7   Summary

In this section you have learned that there are hedonic hotspots in the brain that can be identified by neuroimaging. This suggests that various activities could serve to stimulate these areas, resulting in the experience of a positive mood. The mood-elevating effects of chocolate, for example, appear to be due to the release of opioids by the sensory stimulus in the mouth. Exercise appears to involve the release of endorphins, a form of opioid, and humour can also raise mood, possibly via endorphin release.

7   Concluding thoughts

To understand mood, it is necessary to consider biology, the psychology of the individual and the social context. It is pointless to argue whether biology or social context is of greater importance. This is a principle of broad application in psychology and several examples were given to demonstrate it. So, although the 'Crossing boundaries' box in Section 4.7 highlighted a particularly clear application of this principle, the whole chapter involves crossing boundaries.

Depression clearly can often be triggered by complex sociocultural events such as unemployment or divorce. Yet it can also be triggered by hormonal events, exemplified by Cushing's disease. There appears to be a reciprocal relationship between psychological events and hormonal events (e.g. cortisol level). In depression, psychological events can contribute to abnormal cortisol levels, which, in turn, can move brain events out of kilter.

Similarly, understanding post-natal depression involves taking into account both the hormones of the body and such things as lack of social support. Self-injury involves biological factors such as an unusually high activity by the sympathetic division of the nervous system and changes in opioid activity. However, we also need to view it as a desperate cry for help from others.

The role of opioids has been emphasised, both in the positive context of good moods derived from eating chocolate, exercise, humour and sex but also in the relief from bad moods in the case of self-injury. This is not to say that opioids act alone. Other neurochemicals doubtless also play a role in interaction. However, to simplify a hideously complex situation by focusing upon one neurochemical can give valuable insights.

Although rejecting naïve dichotomies of the kind, biology *or* social context being the most important, you might feel that this discussion stimulates a profound ethical issue. In seeking help for people in distress, is it more ethical to address biology or social context? By focusing on biology, are we detracting from the sociocultural and economic causes of distress? My own view is that we should do all we can to address such causes, while acknowledging the biological contribution. Alas, we might be powerless to do anything to alter a person's social world and then biological treatments can be a life-saver.

Further reading

- For the biological psychology of mood:

Ekkekakis, P. (2013) *The Measurement of Affect, Mood and Emotion: A Guide for Health-Behavioral Research*, Cambridge, Cambridge University Press.

- For an account of the biological bases of the various pleasures that we experience:

Kringelbach, M.L. and Berridge K.C. (2010) *Pleasures of the Brain*, Oxford, Oxford University Press.

- For an emphasis upon positive moods:

Nettle, D. (2006) *Happiness: The Science Behind Your Smile*, Oxford, Oxford University Press.

- On the biochemistry of mood:

Stahl, S.M. (2013) *Mood Disorders and Antidepressants: Stahl's Essential Psychopharmacology*, Cambridge, Cambridge University Press.

- For a hand-holding introduction to biological psychology:

Toates, F. (2011) *Biological Psychology*, Harlow, Pearson Education.

- For an account of sexual desire and pleasure written from a biopsychosocial perspective:

Toates, F. (2014) *How Sexual Desire Works: The Enigmatic Urge*, Cambridge, Cambridge University Press.

References

Battes, L.C., Pedersen, S.S., Oemrawsingh, R.M., van Geuns, R.J., Al Amri, I., Regar, E., de Jaegere, P.P.T., Serruys, P. and van Domburg, R.T. (2012) 'Beta blocker therapy is associated with reduced depressive symptoms 12 months post percutaneous coronary intervention', *Journal of Affective Disorders*, vol. 136, pp. 751–7.

Benton, D. and Donohoe, R.T (1999) 'The effects of nutrients on mood', *Public Health Nutrition*, vol. 2, pp. 403–9.

Berk, L.S. and Tan, S.A. (2006) '[beta]-Endorphin and HGH increase are associated with both the anticipation and experience of mirthful laughter', *The FASEB Journal*, vol. 20, A382.

Boecker, H., Tölle, T.R., Valet, M. and Sprenger, T. (2012) 'Effects of aerobic exercise on mood and human opioidergic activation measured by positron emission tomography', in Boecker, H., Hillman, C.H., Scheef, L., and Strüder, H.K. (eds) *Functional Neuroimaging in Exercise and Sports Sciences,* New York, Springer.

Bresin, K. and Gordon, K.H. (2013) 'Endogenous opioids and nonsuicidal self-injury: a mechanism of affect regulation', *Neuroscience and Biobehavioral Reviews*, vol. 37, pp. 374–83.

Carmichael, M.S., Warburton, V.L., Dixen, J. and Davidson, J.M. (1994) 'Relationships among cardiovascular, muscular, and oxytocin responses during human sexual activity', *Archives of Sexual Behavior*, vol. 23, pp. 59–79.

Carver, C.S. and Scheier, M.F. (1990) 'Origin and functions of positive and negative affect: a control-process view', *Psychological Review*, vol. 97, pp. 19–35.

Cozolino, L. (2002) *The Neuroscience of Psychotherapy,* New York, W.W. Norton.

Feelders, R.A., Pulgar, S.J., Kempel, A. and Pereira, A.M. (2012) 'The burden of Cushing's disease: clinical and health-related quality of life aspects', *European Journal of Endocrinology*, vol. 167, pp. 311–26.

Georgiadis, J.R. and Kortekaas, R. (2010) 'The sweetest taboo: functional neurobiology of human sexuality in relation to pleasure', in Kringelbach, M.L., and Berridge, K.C. (eds) *Pleasures of the Brain,* Oxford, Oxford University Press.

Goldfarb, A.H. (2013) 'Exercise and endogenous opiates', in Constantini, N. and Hackney, A.C. (eds) *Endocrinology of Physical Activity and Sport*, 2nd edn, New York, Springer.

Haines, J.W., Williams, C.L., Brain, K.L., and Wilson, G.V. (1995) 'The psychophysiology of self-mutilation', *Journal of Abnormal Psychology*, vol. 104, pp. 471–89.

Chapter 6

How does my brain work?
Neuroscience and plasticity

Jeremy Tree

Contents

1   Introduction

In your study of cognitive processes, you will have encountered a number of specific systems, including attention, language and memory. For the most part, these systems work well, but particular cognitive processes can be impaired when someone has brain damage. In the study of **cognitive neuropsychology**, scientists are interested in understanding the relationship between cognitive impairment and brain injury.

Brain injury can adversely affect cognitive processes in different ways, and can occur for a variety of reasons including **traumatic brain injury** (as a consequence of a blow to the head), **cerebrovascular accident** (as a consequence of blood clot, seen in stroke) or **neurodegenerative disease** (such as Alzheimer's disease). Clinical psychologists can often work with such patients by using testing to understand the nature of the cognitive impairment a particular patient may have, and perhaps assist in the selection of a particular therapeutic intervention to ameliorate their cognitive impairment. This chapter will consider what such neuropsychological patients tell us about the way cognitive function is organised and its relationship to regions of the brain.

Learning outcomes

On completing this chapter you should:

- have an understanding of how cognitive models can inform research on recovery from brain injury or damage

- have an understanding of key psychological theories and research on the effects brain damage has on behaviour and brain plasticity on recovery

- have an understanding of how a cognitive neuropsychological approach can help to investigate and explain specific language impairment following damage to the brain.

Cognitive neuropsychology
A sub-division of cognitive psychology that considers the disruption of cognitive function in the context of brain injury. Its focus is to better understand the manner in which cognitive processes break down and their relationship to neurological structure.

Traumatic brain injury
An injury that occurs as a result of some form of external force on the skull and brain (e.g. a blow to the head for a boxer).

Cerebrovascular accident
Brain damage that occurs as a consequence of a blood clot or rupture of an artery, resulting in lesions to the brain. Such events are also often called a stroke.

Neurodegenerative disease
A generic term for brain-related diseases that lead to cell death and progressive loss of neurons in the brain.

2   Lost for words: anomia

Imagine you are a clinical psychologist and have been referred a patient who has suffered a stroke. We will call the patient JT. (Note, it is a convention for researchers who publish cases to use initials to identify the subjects.) Although JT has recovered reasonably well, he still has a persistent problem retrieving the names of many common items. In everyday speech he is frustrated by knowing the thing he wants to refer to, but being unable to grasp the specific word. For example, when trying to say 'helicopter', he might say: '*It's a whirly thing. Flies around in the sky. Police use them.*' Being unable to produce the correct word, JT is forced to describe the verbal label he is seeking. Clinicians call this a **circumlocution**. The condition that JT is suffering from is called **anomia** (more on this later) and it is often seen in stroke patients who are recovering from language disruption linked to their brain damage. As you can imagine, it is a source of considerable frustration, and in fact mirrors something we are all likely to have experienced in our everyday lives. When you experience a similar sensation, you might say something is 'on the tip of your tongue'.

Here is how the American psychologist William James described this sensation.

> Suppose we try to recall a forgotten name. The state of our consciousness is peculiar. There is a gap therein; but no mere gap. It is a gap that is intensely active. A sort of wraith of the name is in it, beckoning us in a given direction, making us at moments tingle with the sense of our closeness, and then letting us sink back without the longed-for term. If wrong names are produced to us, this singularly definite gap acts immediately so as to negate them. They do not fit into its mould and the gap of one word does not feel like the gap of another, all empty of content as both might seem necessarily to be when described as gaps.
>
> (James, 1890, p. 152)

So what is learned from this description of the process of retrieving the names of things? Well, psychologists might suggest that this process involves at least two stages:

Circumlocution
A verbal description of an object used by someone who is unable to retrieve the correct name of this item.

Anomia
A subtype of aphasia that results in an inability to retrieve the names of everyday items, causing frustration for the individual.

1 a conceptual stage (called 'semantics') where we retrieve the definition of a thing

2 a verbal label stage where we retrieve the word relating to that definition.

This latter stage is called **lexical phonology** because it relates to the speech sound one utters for a given word. As James suggests, when we have a tip-of-the-tongue episode, we have been successful at stage (1) given we can easily describe the word we want, and readily will say we know what it is, but irritatingly can't achieve stage (2). Moreover, if we are given choices of words to assist us (a process called **cueing**), we will readily recognise the word we are seeking. Later on, this chapter will explore further the underpinnings of this process with respect to a cognitive model of naming.

It is also evident that a 'tip-of-the-tongue' episode is essentially similar to what JT is experiencing, but simply more frequent in his case. In other words, performance in a neuropsychological case can be at an extreme of what people without brain damage may experience – that is, they are *quantitatively* rather than *qualitatively* different. This insight is important, because it indicates that we may well be able to learn something about cognitive processing in the brain from studying instances when a given process no longer works properly (as seen in brain damage). This is the motivation that underpins the field of cognitive neuropsychology – which seeks to use the cognitive models of a function suggested in cognitive psychology to better understand the nature of an impairment seen in a neuropsychological case, while also using evidence from such cases to scrutinise the validity of these same cognitive models.

Lexical phonology
The spoken sound relating to a word.

Cueing
The use of information as a means of aiding an individual in producing a correct answer. It is often used in a therapeutic context.

Activity 6.1: Tip of the tongue

Think about when you last had a 'tip-of-the-tongue' episode. What was it like? What kinds of information could you recall specifically and how did it resolve?

You could try to see if you can induce a 'tip-of-the-tongue' episode in a friend or family member. For example, use Google images to look for rare or unusual items, such as a sextant (a navigational instrument), a pagoda (oriental building) or an artichoke (a less common vegetable). Then, without any prompting, show these images to people you know and ask them to name them. What happens when a person recognises an item, but can't name it? Reflect on their responses (and then put them out of their misery!).

2.1   Summary

Brain injury can sometimes result in very specific cognitive impairments that can inform psychologists about the nature of a particular cognitive process.

Functional architecture

The various functional components attributed to a given cognitive process; in short, the various boxes and arrows presented in a cognitive model.

The pattern of impaired performance seen in a brain injury case can effectively lie at the extreme of normal performance. Cognitive models attempt to characterise the **functional architecture** (that is, the various components that are needed for a cognitive process to occur), so that a greater understanding of a system such as language or memory can be achieved. The characteristics of patterns of patient impairment can teach us important lessons about how a normal cognitive process works and the different ways it can break down.

3   Understanding brain damage and cognitive processes: cognitive neuropsychology

In the earlier example of JT, it became apparent that the cognitive processes underpinning naming may well be multifaceted, and that consequential brain damage can disrupt aspects of this process. In your study of cognitive psychology, you will have encountered cognitive models of a particular process, such as ~~memory or attention.~~ Such models usually take the form of 'boxes and arrows', so much so that occasionally supporters of such models are called 'box-ologists'! Figure 6.1 shows a simple two-box cognitive model that would fit the two stages of naming that we inferred earlier from patient JT – namely, a box relating to **semantics** and a box relating to lexical phonology. An arrow links the first to the second (to depict the process of *access* from one to the other).

Semantics
The information that relates to the meaning of a word.

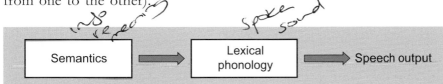

Figure 6.1   A simple model of naming

It is assumed that representations of particular kinds of information are stored in each of the boxes. For example, in the semantics 'box' there would be representations relating to the conceptual or meaning-based information of all the words we know in language (more on this later). Given the main feature of JT's failure to name is that he knows what he wants to say, but can't retrieve the word, using this model we could suggest a hypothesis to explain the nature of his impairment; it is likely due either to a failure of access from semantics to phonology (a problem with the arrow in the model) or some form of disruption to lexical phonology itself (a problem with a box in the model). Already it should be clear that, even with a simple model like this one, describing the cause of a cognitive impairment in this way allows us to construct a hypothesis that relates to damage to a particular component of a cognitive process as an explanation of a given patient's impairment. You will find more detail on this topic later in this chapter.

In sum then, the main purpose of these types of model is twofold:

1 They provide a relatively simple way of outlining the complex component processes that underlie aspects of a particular cognitive system.

2 Once such processes have been outlined in a model, it is assumed that disruption to any particular part will result in clearly predicted outcomes in terms of behavioural impairment.

Importantly, it is also assumed that any two components (such as the two stages of semantics and lexical phonology described above) are functionally independent of each other and therefore can be independently impaired. (There is more on this in the next section.) In other words, conventional models of cognitive function (in the true box-and-arrow tradition) assume that specific cognitive processes (encapsulated within a particular 'box' in the model) fulfil the concept of **modularity** (Fodor, 1983).

3.1   The double dissociation: a powerful tool in cognitive neuropsychology

At this point it is worth pausing to specifically consider one of the major assumptions of the box-and-arrow models mentioned above – the assumption that components of a process can function independently, that is, that damage to one 'box' implies a different pattern of impairment from damage to a different 'box'. This assumption is derived from patterns of impairment seen in neuropsychological patients that are called **dissociations**.

Modularity
This refers to the principle that components of a cognitive system can be independently disrupted as a consequence of brain damage. Modularity assumes that a cognitive 'module' is: (a) functionally autonomous (i.e. each module carries out processing in isolation), (b) domain specific (processes one type of information – i.e. semantics only) and (c) mandatory (i.e. a module operates in an all-or-none fashion).

Dissociations
A pattern of impairment that demonstrates selective disruption to a particular cognitive process with other related cognitive processes remaining intact.

Pause for thought

To understand this term try a thought experiment.

Imagine you had never seen a television before. On observing one for the first time you would notice that this box-like item emits both sounds and images. Now what you don't know is whether a single mechanism (or 'process' if this was cognition) is responsible for both of these outputs, or whether separate mechanisms might be. How could you resolve the answer to this question?

One answer might be obtained by considering what would happen if the television got broken in various ways – clearly, if two separate mechanisms are responsible for the picture and the sound, then you would expect to find hypothetical broken televisions where you had sound but no image and vice versa. These hypothetical patterns would constitute a dissociation.

In the world of cognitive neuropsychology, there are two major types of dissociation. A single dissociation involves the identification of a patient who can do cognitive process A but not B. It is worth noting that a patient may have:

- a *classical dissociation*: the patient is entirely normal at process A and impaired at process B, or

- a *strong single dissociation*: the patient is also impaired (relative to normal) at process A, but the impairment of process B is worse (Shallice, 1988). Note that this pattern *could* imply that A involves a different subsystem from that of B (and therefore potentially different cortical areas of the brain). However, such a pattern of impairment could also simply be due to the fact that in a globally impaired patient, more difficult processes tend to be more likely to be lost, and therefore A may simply be more difficult than B (termed a 'task-resource artefact' (Shallice, 1988)). Alternatively, it may be that the patient used an unusual information-processing strategy when participating in Task B with consequentially poorer performance (a 'task-demand artefact' (Shallice, 1988)).

More compelling evidence is provided by a double dissociation, in which one patient is identified as being impaired at A but not B, whereas another patient is identified as being impaired at B but not A. The identification and interpretation of cases of double dissociation has a long tradition in neuropyschology. For example, Ogle (1867) first reported that patients often had co-occurring deficits of naming in both spoken and written outputs, but some patients showed independent impairments (e.g. spelling was good, spoken naming was bad, or vice versa – a double dissociation). As a result, he concluded that different cognitive processes must underlie speech and writing: '[This] occasional separation … points to the existence of distinct cerebral centres for the faculties concerned in speaking and writing' (Ogle, 1867, p. 100). Clearly, the identification of double dissociations provides evidence that two cognitive processing systems (such as speech versus writing) are functionally independent, and therefore can be selectively impaired.

So it should be apparent that brain damage can provide key evidence that speaks to cognitive models of function in normal populations, and some of the assumptions that underpin these models. It is worth now turning attention to some other assumptions that are key in cognitive neuropsychological research, and that relate to the kinds of evidence being evaluated. In your study of cognitive psychology, you will have encountered examples of experimental studies done in a laboratory, often with a great number of participants. However, in the field of brain damage, the probability of you finding patients with mirror image patterns of impairment (as outlined in the double dissociation above) are quite low. For that reason, a great many studies in the literature use a single case approach. That is, they will describe the pattern of impairment seen in a single patient who has been very thoroughly tested. It is worth considering in detail the assumptions of the case study approach. Suffice to say, though, cognitive psychology has been influenced by some very famous examples of single case studies. For example, case HM (Henry Molaison – Corkin, 2002) taught the field a great deal of useful information about memory impairment in the context of **amnesia** – so the contribution to science of the single case study can be considerable.

Amnesia
Memory impairment that occurs as a consequence of brain damage.

3.2   Case studies: methodological and theoretical assumptions

Earlier we described the patient JT who illustrated a particular condition known as anomia. This single patient gave us clues about how the naming process might be impaired after brain damage, and you might imagine a research study being undertaken with him to further explore the nature of his impairment. The question arises as to how valid it is to draw generalisations from single brain-damaged patients to cognitive processes of the wider general population. Alfonso Caramazza (a famous cognitive neuropsychologist) points out that the case study approach in cognitive neuropsychology is underpinned by three key assumptions outlined below. (These are also outlined in a series of papers: Caramazza, 1986; Caramazza, 1992; Caramazza and McCloskey, 1988).

The first assumption is the 'fractionation hypothesis', under which it is claimed that in some cases brain damage can result in a focal or selective impairment of a particular component of a cognitive process. Note that this echoes the assumptions mentioned earlier in the context of double dissociations. Additionally, it is important to stress that in this case, Caramazza is referring to specific damage to a particular component (or module) in a cognitive model rather than specific regions of the brain. Many traditional cognitive neuropsychologists remain undecided about linking cognitive function to specific brain areas, to the extent that they focus on the behavioural impairment of a patient (what they can and cannot do) rather than the neurological lesion. In other words, models generated from this approach are algorithmic (see Marr, 1982), in the sense that they concentrate on the components of a given functional process independent of its hardware (the brain in this case). In recent years, this distinction may have become somewhat blurred given the rise of functional magnetic resonance imaging (fMRI), but there still remains an open debate about how much (or how little) additional value this neuro-imaging evidence provides for the cognitive neuropsychologist.

An example of a sceptic is Page, who writes:

> All serious cognitive theories acknowledge that cognition is implemented somewhere in the brain. Finding that the brain 'activates' differentially while performing different tasks is therefore gratifying but not surprising. The key problem is that the additional dependent variable that imaging data represents is often one about which cognitive theories make no necessary predictions. It is, therefore, inappropriate to use such data to choose between such theories. Even supposing that fMRI were able to tell us where a particular cognitive process was performed, that would likely tell us little of relevance about *how* it was performed.
>
> (Page, 2006, p. 428)

Page's point is clearly that cognitive psychology has made a great deal of progress over the decades without neuro-imaging evidence, to the extent that many cognitive theories remain mute about specific neuroanatomical details. Given this is the case, neuro-imaging evidence is unlikely to be able to act as a mediator between competing cognitive theories. On balance it seems that neuro-imaging work is clearly going to be a significant activity in the field of cognitive psychology in future, and for that reason may increasingly feature in future cognitive theories, but until we have much more sophisticated ideas of the mapping of cognitive processes to neurological networks, we must be cautious about the evidence neuro-imaging provides. In fact, interpretation of the causal nature of a cognitive function to a particular area of the brain on the basis of lesion location is always problematic because of the issue of **diaschisis**; that is, disruption of a cognitive function by a brain lesion in a particular location may be indirect such that it is actually important connections to the region that are key for the cognitive function that is disrupted (Hillis et al., 2002). In other words, cognitive process X may be disrupted by a patient with a lesion to region Y in the brain. Does this mean process X is undertaken in region Y (the 'box' of a cognitive model), or is region Y a go-between region (an 'arrow' in a cognitive model)? Picking apart these two possibilities can be difficult.

Diaschisis
When functional inactivity in a brain region occurs because of lesions to more distant regions that share neural connections.

The second major assumption Caramazza outlines is the 'transparency assumption', which implies that following brain damage, the cognitive system is not reorganised in some entirely new format. In other words, after brain damage 'resulting behaviour patterns do not represent the creation of new subsystems, rather, they reflect a reorganisation that emphasises intact subsystems' (Saffran et al., 1980, p. 221). This means the pattern of impairment seen in a key case study reflects a cognitive process in which a particular component (X) is damaged – that is to say, all other aspects of the functional architecture remain the same as the general population (i.e. patient impairment equals normal cognitive system *minus* X), rather than some entirely novel overall cognitive system that emerges after brain damage. Clearly, if this assumption is wrong, then attempts to draw inferences about the general (normal) cognitive process on the basis of patient behaviour would be incorrect, because their pattern of performance would reflect a fundamentally different functional architecture. Keep this issue in mind for a later discussion in this chapter, because it is relevant to the issue of neural plasticity (see below) – namely, that brains do 'rewire' to an extent after someone has brain damage. However, this begs the question: what might the implications of this plasticity be to the cognitive process a patient uses to complete a particular task?

Finally, the third major assumption is the 'universality assumption', namely that across individuals the same underlying cognitive processes apply (with the same functional components), such that one can generalise from single cases to the rest of us. In other words, a cognitive process has a universal functional architecture that is true of all human beings, so that when faced with a neuropsychological case there is no reason to believe there was something unusual about them *before* they had their injury. We must assume that **premorbid** patient performance is normal in order to draw any inferences about what impaired performance might imply about a particular cognitive process. It is worth mentioning that if this particular assumption is wrong, then it is not so much a problem for the single case approach as for the entirety of cognitive psychology! On balance, it is fair to say that these three assumptions have not gone unchallenged, and there remains a key debate about whether observed behaviour in a recovering patient reflects functional reorganisation or the processing of the 'normal' cognitive system under some level of disruption.

Premorbid
The ability, behaviour or cognitive function of an individual prior to brain injury or illness.

3.3   Summary

The basic principle of cognitive neuropsychology is to take models of cognition and scrutinise them with respect to the following questions:

- What happens when a cognitive system fails because of brain damage?

- Can this particular cognitive model capture these patterns of impairment?

- Can the components proposed within a particular cognitive model map on to brain regions (lesions locations)?

The pattern of performance from a patient's impaired cognitive profile acts as a means of hypothesis testing – with the hypothesis being: Is the impairment due to disruption to component X in the cognitive model? Answering such a question is useful not just an exercise in science (namely, it shows how good the particular theory might be), but also with respect to understanding the nature of a patient's particular impairment, so that an appropriate therapy can be motivated. Cognitive neuropsychology can provide information that is of use to the experimental psychologist and the clinician alike.

4   The consequences of brain damage: aphasia

Aphasia
A language impairment that occurs as a consequence of brain damage.

Receptive aphasia
A form of language impairment that relates to substantial problems understanding speech, occurring as a result of some form of brain injury.

Expressive aphasia
This is a form of language impairment that relates to substantial problems producing speech, occurring as a result of some form of brain injury.

Broca's aphasia
A form of aphasia that has as a key feature expressive language problems and relates to damage to the left frontal area of the brain.

Wernicke's aphasia
A form of aphasia that has as a key feature receptive language problems and relates to damage to the left temporal lobe of the brain.

Throughout our lives as we engage in conversation with others; the process of speech and comprehension of speech is so effortless we largely take it for granted. But this belies the complexities of the cognitive systems that underpin this activity, which are thrown into stark relief when the process breaks down. **Aphasia** is the term used to describe language impairments that occur as a consequence of brain damage. Patients with brain damage can often present with varying degrees of comprehension (**receptive aphasia**) or speech production (**expressive aphasia**) impairments. Such patterns of impairment are often seen in those who have recovered from a stroke. As early as the mid to late nineteenth century, neuropsychologists have known that some cases can have mainly comprehension problems, while others have mainly production problems. Two famous neuropsychologists of that time, Paul Broca (1865) and Karl Wernicke (1874), separately distinguished 'centres' for comprehension and production aphasic symptoms that implicated specific neuroanatomical regions of the brain.

Cases of **Broca's aphasia** have severe expressive aphasia, which is described as non-fluent because speech output is reduced in phrase length and grammatical complexity, and what speech is generated is clearly extremely effortful on the part of the patient. Despite their severe expressive problems, there is often only mild receptive aphasia, that is to say speech comprehension tends to be relatively normal (Goodglass and Kaplan, 1983). In contrast, cases of **Wernicke's aphasia** have apparent receptive aphasic problems and additionally, although their speech often appears to have a normal rate of production, i.e. it is considered fluent, it often contains 'neologisms' (non-words, such as GWOOL for 'stool' – more on word errors later), so much so that speech is sometimes referred to as 'word salad', given it is hard to understand (Goodglass and Kaplan, 1983).

Pause for thought

You have learned that Wernicke's cases can't understand speech well and their speech contains confused words. Might these two things be connected?

Do you think our capacity to communicate normally is dependent on our understanding of our own speech?

The initial description of these two fundamental 'types' of aphasic cases included the identification of specific areas of the brain that corresponded to each kind of patient. Cases of Broca's aphasia (including Paul Broca's first case '~~Lebourge~~' – also named 'Tan' because that was one of the few words he could say) had damage to the dorso-lateral frontal lobes (see Figure 6.2); and this area has now been linked to speech production (perhaps unsurprisingly called *Broca's area*). In fact, language is a highly 'lateralised' cognitive function, in that it tends to implicate one particular hemisphere over another. In over 90 per cent of right-handed people, and 70–80 per cent of left-handed people, language is left hemisphere dominant (Josse and Tzourio-Mazoyer, 2004) so typically lesions in aphasic cases are in the left hemisphere. In the case of Karl Wernicke's fluent aphasic cases, the brain damage is centred on the superior temporal gyrus (a more posterior part of the brain, see Figure 6.2) and this area has been linked with speech comprehension (called *Wernicke's area*).

'Le Borgne'

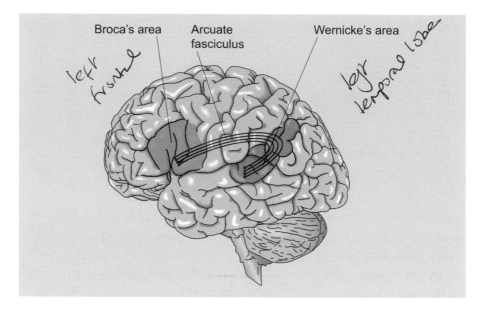

Figure 6.2   Key regions for language processing in the brain

In later work, Lichtheim (1885) provided a model (which was subsequently adopted in a more contemporary account by Geschwind (1965, cited in Catani and Ffychte, 2005)) that made an important prediction on the basis of the impairments of both types of patients. Lichtheim reasoned that Broca's area was the centre for the motor output representations of speech whereas Wernicke's region related to a centre for the input of 'sound images'. In other words, there were two key regions: one implicated in speech output and one in speech input. Now, return to our earlier discussion about box-and-arrow models. Imagine that we might propose a two-box model, each corresponding to these proposed input and output systems. What is missing? The answer is an arrow, i.e. a link between these two systems. The question arises: what might happen if this link were disrupted? Might there be a possible subtype of aphasic condition that would result from a disconnection of these two regions? As it happens, within the brain there are a series of arched fibres (this 'arch' provides the name 'arcuate fasciculus') that connect the Wernicke's (input) and Broca's (output) regions. There is also evidence that suggests damage to these fibres results in a condition in which cases have severely impaired word repetition (a task that involves linking heard spoken input to spoken output). Cases with this condition are called **conduction aphasia** (Dejerine, 1892) and they are argued to be due to a disruption of the flow of information between Wernicke's and Broca's areas (Hickok and Poeppel, 2004). Lichtheim's model is therefore probably one of the

Conduction aphasia
A form of aphasia that has poor word repetition as a key feature.

earliest examples of a cognitive model that echoes those discussed in contemporary cognitive psychology today. It should be clear from this above example that cognitive models and profiles of impairment seen in aphasia can be linked as a means of achieving the larger objective of understanding the language processing system itself. For a more detailed example of this, let's return to the topic of anomia mentioned earlier.

4.1   Testing language impairment by looking at speech errors: anomia

As we saw earlier with the discussion of the case of JT, individuals who have particular problems retrieving object names are classified as anomic. Difficulties in word retrieval are often investigated using a simple confrontation–naming task that involves naming a line drawing or photograph of a common or less common object or animal. When faced with naming a picture, an anomic patient will, on occasion, fail to produce the desired response. So, for example, when shown a duck they might say: '*It swims on the water and goes quack quack*'. (Remember, this is called a circumlocution.) But other aphasic patients will make a number of different kinds of speech errors on a confrontational naming task and these can be sub-classified in different ways – they include semantic errors, when the response is closely related in meaning (knife > 'fork') and phonological errors, when the response is closely related in sound and involves some form of substitution of phonemes (sometimes the substitutions of phonemes can make a word (knife > 'wife') or not (knife > 'nipe')). Earlier you learned about Wernicke's speech containing neologisms (knife > 'glange'), which are an example of a phonological error in which a non-word is produced. Phonological errors can tell us about the structural boundaries of words and clearly indicate that there is a complex speech-planning process that involves structuring the phonological form of a word before utterance.

Research with aphasic patients may focus on different kinds of cognitive psycholinguistic variables to determine whether they predict more or fewer particular types of speech errors. Research might examine the effects of variables such as word length (how many phonemes or syllables a word has), word frequency (how often a word appears in natural language) and age of acquisition (the age at which we learned a word) on naming success. Such work speaks to the wider field of cognitive psychology, because such variables are often utilised to examine non-brain-damaged participant performance (via reaction times) on language tasks. As you will see later in this chapter, such variables can shed light on the nature of representations in the cognitive system (that is to say, what is stored in a 'box' in a cognitive model). You should also bear in mind that later in your studies you will undertake your own cognitive experimental work and you may wish to manipulate such psycholinguistic variables yourself.

4.2 Anomia – the functional components underlying naming

Earlier, in our discussion of anomia, we were introduced to a basic cognitive model (Figure 6.1) that could be used to understand the nature of the processes that may underpin this impairment. At this point, it is worth elaborating on this model further, by broadening it out into a model of object naming – in this case we need to add a new component (box) to the model. Given that a picture is initially visually processed and recognised as a familiar object, we need an object recognition system (see Figure 6.3) that processes the incoming visual information before accessing semantic/conceptual information.

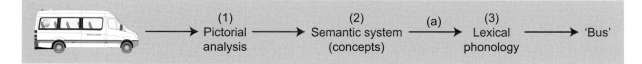

Figure 6.3   An elaborated model of naming

Importantly, the three-box model presented in Figure 6.3 has some important practical implications with respect to understanding why a particular neuropsychological case may be impaired. Again, imagine you are a clinical psychologist, and you have three brain injury patients, all of whom are roughly equal in their inability to do a picture-naming task. Without a cognitive model of this process, we may be fooled into assuming all three patients have the same problem (with consequential implications regarding intervention). But this belies the possibility that the underlying causes for impairment may differ in each individual. The challenge for the clinician is to realise that failure at a picture-naming task may reflect disruption to object recognition rather than name retrieval. Patients with such an impairment are said to have object **agnosia**, and thus their naming failure would reflect a

Agnosia
Impairment of visual object recognition that occurs as a consequence of brain damage.

fundamental problem with making sense of the visual properties of objects in their outside world. (A very famous account of such a case is provided by Oliver Sacks (1985) in his entertaining book *The Man Who Mistook His Wife For a Hat*.)

Remember the case of JT with anomia we discussed earlier? To where in this model might we attribute his impairment? Well, you may recall, he could tell you about an object he couldn't name (so he clearly can't have a problem with the first two steps in the model), and it was suggested he likely had a problem of access from conceptual–semantics to retrieval of the verbal label (lexical phonology). However, it is important to stress that, in principle, an anomic case may be poor at retrieving object names because of:

- a disruption to conceptual semantics (although not true for JT, it could be for others)

- lexical-phonological output, or

- the connections between semantics and phonology.

The challenge for the clinician and researcher is to determine which one may be true of a particular case. Researchers have done just this, and have reported anomic cases consistent with all three of these subtypes:

1 patient JCU – Howard and Orchard-Lisle (1984); patient KE – Hillis et al. (1990)

2 patient MM – Romani et al. (2002)

3 patients GM and JS – Lambon Ralph et al. (2000); patient FAS – McCarthy and Kartsounis (2000).

It should therefore be clear that a cognitive model (like Figure 6.3) can provide finer and finer distinctions about the nature of a particular patient's impairment. In this case, the model suggests that an impairment of picture naming can be attributable to one of the following:

(a) a visual recognition impairment (i.e. visual processing fails to sufficiently help someone recognise an object as a familiar item)

(b) a semantic/conceptual impairment (i.e. knowledge about what an item *is* is disrupted)

(c) a phonological output impairment (i.e. the appropriate name of an object in terms of its speech sound is disrupted)

(d) an access deficit (i.e. a disconnection between (b) and (c) – marked (a) in Figure 6.3).

As a mnemonic, remember that this model comprises the steps: 'seen it before' – 'know what it is' – 'know how to say the name for it' in sequence; moreover, remember that (a) is not a language impairment.

Activity 6.2: Agnosic or anomic?

How might a clinician devise a test to determine whether a patient who fails at a picture-naming test is *agnosic* rather than *anomic*?

The clinician could use an object decision task – a test in which a patient is presented with two pictures: one of a real animal (a zebra), the other of an imaginary animal (a horse with a cow's head). Critically, a patient with agnosia will find such a task hard (because they have a fundamental object recognition impairment), but not so the anomic case.

Upon reflecting on the model in Figure 6.3, you might ask why this model insists on an intervening step of accessing conceptual–semantic information before phonological retrieval. Why not have direct access to the verbal label from object recognition? The motivation for this is that there have been no reported cases of successful picture naming accompanied by an inability to say what the object actually is. In other words, semantic processing appears to be a necessary step in successful picture naming. Clearly, if such a case were reported it would have major implications for the model proposed, and this demonstrates the potential power of the single case study (see Section 3.1); it has the power to falsify a cognitive model or theory, a key element in scientific progress.

4.3   Summary

Language impairment can occur after brain damage (aphasia) and there are different subtypes (Broca's aphasia, Wernicke's aphasia, conduction aphasia). A cognitive model can account for the nature of a particular pattern of impairment seen in a neuropsychological case. Box-and-arrow models can be useful to differentiate patients who may be equivalently impaired on the same task. Just because two neuropsychological cases fail at the same task (e.g. naming) this does not imply the same underlying functional cause. With an appropriately specified cognitive model, researchers and clinicians can become aware of key differentiation across patients.

Our journey into understanding the nature of brain damage and cognitive impairment has largely focused on understanding things in terms of damage to an underlying functional architecture (as outlined in Figure 6.3) in somewhat static terms. However, the brain is a dynamic system (earlier you learned about 'neural plasticity') – which raises the question, what happens in our brains during the recovery process following an event such as a stroke? Might different neural regions of the brain take over the role of regions that were otherwise damaged (otherwise known as 'neural compensation')? This will be the focus of the next section.

5   How is language in the brain organised, and can it be 'reorganised'?

Earlier, you learned that there is a great deal of evidence suggesting for the most part that processes of language function (e.g. speaking, understanding, reading) are strongly lateralised. That is, they are much more dependent on a single hemisphere. In fact, as we saw earlier, left hemisphere lesions are typically implicated in language impairments generally (Harley, 2014). In a small number of cases, though, right hemisphere lesions may implicate a language impairment and this is called *crossed aphasia* (for some left-handed people, language dominance is reversed (Damasio et al., 2004)). Given the clear evidence of language laterality, we might wonder whether the right hemisphere plays a greater role when the left hemisphere is damaged. The motivation for this question is the principle of plasticity – namely, that after injury to the brain different neurological regions may 'take over' or play a greater role in a particular cognitive function than was implicated in the damaged regions.

The idea that the right hemisphere may play a greater role in language processing following left hemisphere damage (the 'lateral shift hypothesis') has a long history. Sir William Gowers (1887) noted that patients with left hemisphere lesions who had recovered their speech lost it again following a second stroke to the right hemisphere. He concluded this was clear evidence of the right hemisphere's role in the initial speech recovery. Henschen (1892) made a similar claim, coined 'Henschen's Axiom' (Kertesz, 1979), and this proposal remains present in the work of contemporary researchers (Basso et al., 1989). In fact, using a process known as the 'Wada' technique (in which one or other brain hemisphere can be selectively anaesthetised), there is additional evidence that aphasic cases use right hemisphere language processes. Kinsbourne (1971) reports three such cases where the subjects all showed some level of speech disruption following instances of their right hemisphere being anaesthetised. This evidence appears to indicate a greater role of the right hemisphere in language processes generally as a consequence of left hemisphere damage, perhaps as a 'neural compensatory system'. That is, that a particular process (in this case speech) can utilise different brain structures depending on where damage has occurred.

Critically, it would appear that the age we are has an important impact on the degree of plasticity or capacity for functional reorganisation across brain regions. Individuals who have hemispherectomies (a surgical procedure that results in removal of most of an entire hemisphere) in *infancy* have the capacity to develop speech and comprehension of speech regardless of which hemisphere is removed (Ogden, 1988). However, if damage to the left hemisphere occurs in adolescence or later, the right hemisphere's ability to subsume a role in speech production decreases dramatically. This is an interesting point, and suggests that the degree of brain plasticity relating to language function reduces as the brain matures (Gott, 1973).

An alternative means of exploring the issue of neural compensation is via measures of neural activation. As we discovered earlier, neural activation can be measured in various ways including functional magnetic resonance imaging (fMRI) or positron emission tomography (PET). Could such procedures speak to the issue of the role of the right hemisphere in recovering aphasic cases? Blasi et al. (2002) argued that if the right hemisphere does indeed take over the processes previously carried out by the left, then neuronal 'activation patterns' in this region should look similar to normal participants in the contra-lateral region (i.e. what was previously seen in one hemisphere switches to the opposite side). There is some evidence that this is indeed the case. Heiss et al. (1999) report a PET study with aphasic cases two and eight weeks post-stroke. Those with left hemisphere damage had a receptive aphasia (see Section 4), but this language impairment improved by eight weeks. What was striking was that this improvement appeared to be accompanied by increasing right hemisphere activation (relating to the equivalent of both Broca's and Wernicke's regions in the left hemisphere). Similarly, case subjects who had speech therapy and recovered the ability to perform a speech repetition task showed fMRI activation of right hemisphere regions, argued to be now compensating for the earlier left hemisphere damage (Abo et al., 2004).

However, not all evidence reported from neuroimaging work suggests that what is occurring in the right hemisphere is necessarily beneficial. Cao et al. (1999) looked at five aphasic cases, five months post-stroke. What they found was a more bilaterally distributed pattern of activation in naming – suggesting there is a partial restitution of the left hemisphere accompanied by activation in the right hemisphere – and the more even the hemispheric distribution, the better the overall naming performance seen in the particular case. Additionally, Leger et al. (2002) reported that right hemisphere activation in speech areas usually active in the contra-lateral regions of the left hemisphere were *unaffected* by the speech therapy – rather, what changed was increased activation in the conventional speech areas of the left hemisphere alongside improved naming. As a consequence, both these studies indicate that although right hemisphere activation clearly increases after left hemisphere damage, the pattern of recovery seems to be linked to re-establishment of the conventional left hemisphere regions.

Finally, Saur et al. (2006) reported a three-stage pattern of re-organisation in their aphasic stroke patients as they passed from the acute (most impaired) to chronic (less impaired) phases. During the former period, left hemisphere language areas showed very low levels of activation, and improved language function was linked to right hemisphere frontal regions that were the neurological equivalents of those in the left (i.e. Broca's area). As patients moved into chronic presentations, language improvement was linked to a steady increase in left hemisphere language areas and a decrease in right hemisphere regions seen active in the acute phase. In sum, there is some debate about whether right hemisphere regions shown to be active in acute cases are genuinely linked to language recovery or in fact demonstrate the 'disinhibition' of neural regions that interfere with language recovery (that is, these regions are normally inhibited during more intact language processing; Abo et al., 2004). Nonetheless, these studies suggest there may well be a complex interaction between recovery of neural regions in the left hemisphere and potential compensatory systems in the right hemisphere during recovery of speech production, but this picture remains unclear and further work is needed. For a recent review of these issues see Meinzer and Breitenstein (2008).

Pause for thought

As neural plasticity can result in the 'reorganisation' of neural functional regions following brain damage, it is worth reflecting on what this might mean about the relative role of the right hemisphere in 'normal' language function (i.e. in those without brain damage). If the right hemisphere is suppressed by the left in this context, the question remains, does the right hemisphere actually play *any* useful role in normal language function, or is it merely providing irrelevant information that must be inhibited? Moreover, if the role of the right hemisphere is largely redundant for normal language function, why did it evolve this way? Think about such questions, which currently remain the challenge for future psychological research.

5.1 Summary

Language function is a strongly lateralised process (that is, it involves much more of the left relative to the right hemisphere of the brain). Given this different distribution of function to neural anatomy, the question arises: what happens when patients have large lesions to the left hemisphere? The answer relates to the lateral shift hypothesis – namely, the possibility that in such situations of brain injury, the right hemisphere may take an increased functional role (a process known as neural compensation). Such dynamic neural reorganisation speaks to a process known as neural plasticity. Cognitive models must therefore address the dynamic nature of the relationship between neural function and cognitive processes, something that is not easily dealt with by the more static and illustrative box-and-arrow models.

In the next section you will learn about 'connectionist computational models' (sometimes called neural networks) that attempt to converge more neurological plausible elements of brain activity with cognitive and computational work.

6   Semantic memory: the organisation of cabbages and things

So far the discussions about cognitive neuropsychology have focused on such issues as: (a) how might a cognitive process be disrupted after brain damage and what cognitive models can account for this impairment, and (b) how might recovery reflect neurological compensatory processes? Now let's turn to the issue of representations in the brain. Figure 6.3 presented a cognitive model of naming and you learned how impairment in a particular case might reflect disruption to a particular module ('box') or access between modules ('arrow'). But there still remains the issue of what damage *within* a module might imply. With respect to the model presented in Figure 6.3, let's focus on the semantic–conceptual system in order to consider this issue. What happens when this particular system is damaged?

6.1   The curious case of SF: a neurodegenerative patient

A new case comes to your hypothetical clinic. SF has semantic dementia, a neurodegenerative condition that appears specifically to target representations in semantic memory, such that the pages in her mental dictionary appear to be erased. 'I can't remember what that word means', she often says. Imagine being in her situation. People are speaking to you in English, but the message of what they are saying just doesn't make sense any more.

Warrington (1975) first described this condition and noted some important characteristics relating to the decline of semantic memory in these cases. The patients didn't simply lose all information about a concept at once; instead they lost fine-grained item-specific information first (e.g. a zebra has stripes), while retaining higher-order semantic information about items (e.g. a zebra is an animal). Keep this in mind as it will be discussed later. Warrington (1975) also proposed that the acquisition of semantic information for children essentially worked under similar principles, namely they learned broad conceptual information (a dog is an animal) before more fine-grained information (the difference between a Labrador and a Collie). Clearly, neuropsychological cases with semantic memory impairment can shed light on this system but, as was evident earlier, interpretation of such evidence depends on having a cognitive model. So what models have been suggested?

6.1.1   A cognitive model of semantic memory

From the example of SF, it is apparent that the consequences of semantic memory decline can be severely disabling to language comprehension and expression. The store of all our semantic knowledge (or 'mental lexicon') is vast, with it being predicted that most adults have learned the meanings of some 50,000 words during the course of their lives. But how are representations in this system organised? Collins and Quillian (1969) were among the first to suggest a cognitive model. This model proposes that word meanings are represented in a semantic network, with each word (e.g. BIRD) consisting of conceptual 'nodes' (e.g. has wings, can fly, etc.) that are connected to each other such that activation of a single node passes activation on to other interconnected nodes (see Figure 6.4). This early account was hierarchical in that concepts were arranged with a more general label (or 'superordinate' label – ANIMAL) at the top of a pyramid of nodes of information, while more specific labels (or 'subordinate' information – CANARY) sits at the bottom.

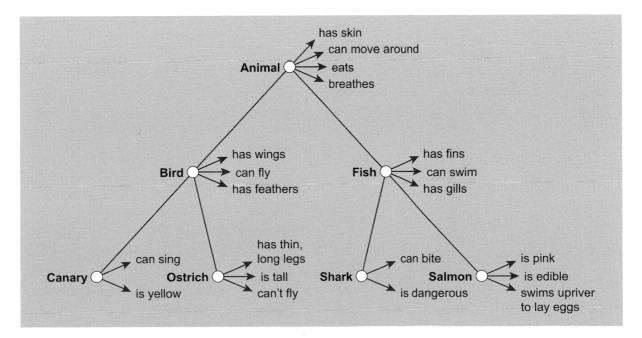

Figure 6.4   The Collins and Quillian model of semantic memory

Collins and Loftus (1975) revised this model by including the principle of 'spreading activation', such that connections between nodes in the model vary both in activation strength and relative distance; this made the model much more than a simple hierarchy and introduced important principles that were the precursor to current connectionist computational models (more on these later). Although this initial model has been highly influential on subsequent research it still raises several unanswered questions, such as: how many features are needed to appropriately represent a particular word, and which features should be considered critical? Some items are more prototypical examples of a semantic category (e.g. for the category BIRD, SPARROW would be considered a more prototypical example than PENGUIN). Does such an issue have an impact on the way such items are stored? Although you could further cloud the issue of prototypicality by pointing out that it could be considered to be culturally and/or geographically influenced (i.e. you might think differently about birds if you live in the desert rather than the Arctic) and thus personal familiarity is likely to be key. (Keep this in mind for later.)

Activity 6.3: Objects and categories

Think of a category of object (e.g. bird, vegetable, musical instrument) and write down five examples from this category you judge to be very typical or representative, and five examples from this category you judge to be very atypical or unrepresentative. Try to do it reasonably quickly. (Don't over-think things.)

Now look at the ten items you have written down. Why do you think you made the choices you did? What features of these items made them more or less representative? What do you think that says about the manner in which the category you selected is organised?

If you can find a couple of willing friends or family members, ask them to do the same task. Compare your answers. Did they choose the same items for typicality? Perhaps their answers differed much more from you on the less representative items. Why do you think that might be? What kinds of factors in personal experience might drive differences in the choices people make?

One of the earliest reported and potentially most important psycholinguistic variables considered to underpin representations in semantic memory is known as the 'imageability' or 'concreteness effect' (Katz and Goodglass, 1990). Cases with disruption of semantic memory are typically far superior at accessing conceptual information specific to words that are highly imageable or concrete (i.e. relate to tangible objects in the outside world – like chairs and tables) compared with their abilities with low imageability or abstract words (i.e. words like justice and peace). A computationally implemented model of semantic memory has since provided an account of how imageability may play a part in the representations of semantic memory – see Box 6.1 for more information on this illustrative study.

Box 6.1   Crossing boundaries: computational models and the brain

So far cognitive models have been discussed in terms of schematic box-and-arrow accounts. However, in recent decades researchers have used computationally implemented models to simulate performance in normal and abnormal populations. They typically consist of artificial neural networks of representational nodes, where information passes across the network via the principle of 'spreading activation'. For our purposes, given that we are focused on semantic memory, the key issue to bear in mind is that a given representation relating to a concept (e.g. DOG – and its related features) comprises an activation pattern across a number of distributed nodes within the network, which are interconnected by links of varying activation strength. It should be clear that the inspiration for such models is the brain itself; consider the nodes to be interconnected neurons and the links between them to be synapses. The fact that a computational model is implemented into a simulation gives it an important additional advantage over and above classical box-and-arrow models.

First, you can test hypotheses about your model by deleting elements of the implemented architecture (an artificial lesion) to simulate impaired performance. A key study that followed this process was a model devised by Plaut and Shallice (1993), which attempted to capture the impact of the imageability variable by having concrete words contain more semantic features (or nodes) and therefore richer overall conceptual representations. They demonstrated that after the model was randomly lesioned, semantic representations specific to abstract words were more vulnerable to disruption and therefore the damaged model was more likely to exhibit poorer performance with such items. (This is a pattern we

---

have seen is present in patients.) An additional characteristic of this model was that it demonstrated 'graceful degradation' – that is, as damage increased so performance dropped, but semantic impairment was not an all-or-nothing pattern (as seen in the patient description earlier). In other words, progressive impairment in the model somewhat mirrored semantic decline in patients. This example serves to demonstrate that computationally implemented models can fulfil an interesting role; namely, they can simulate performance in brain-injured cases.

A second advantage of these models is that they can potentially capture the learning process. In other words, the system itself can develop in ways that attempt to simulate human cognitive development. In fact it was for this reason that the Plaut and Shallice model was criticised; their connectionist model seemed to learn in an unrealistic way compared with normal human cognition. Early connectionist models acquired new representations in a very slow manner, whereas children are evidently able to acquire information about items very rapidly (sometimes on the basis of one or two exposures (Bloom, 2000)). As a result, McClelland et al., (1995) proposed an alternative model known as the 'complementary learning systems theory', under which it is proposed that semantic information can be obtained by two complementary processes: (a) a slow-learning semantic system (similar to the type of model above), and (b) a fast learning system that operates by rapidly generating connections within this system. These 'newly formed' semantic memories can be reconstructed by the fast learning system and critically act as a 'teacher' (a learning model) for the slow-learning (more permanent) semantic system distributed in the neocortex.

As you will recall, SF had a condition called semantic dementia. What areas of her brain appeared to be affected? Early accounts of semantic dementia (Hodges et al., 1992) reported atrophy to be concentrated (focal) on the temporal lobes (in particular the anterior – nearer the front – part of this region, see Figure 6.5) of both hemispheres (bilaterally).

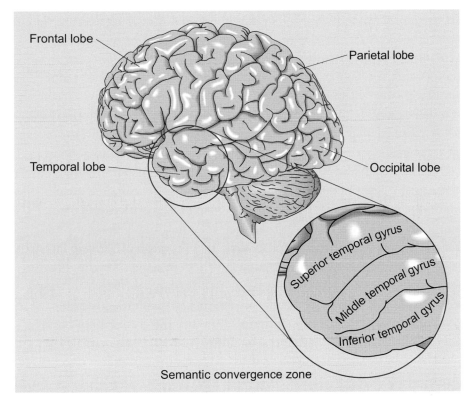

Figure 6.5   A brain with the temporal lobe components labelled

In recent years, it has been argued that the temporal lobes of the brain play a critical role in the representation and retrieval of semantic information. This proposal is consistent with the fact that the anterior part of the inferior temporal gyrus is considered to be the terminus of the ventral visual processing stream (the 'what' visual pathway), the middle temporal gyrus is considered to integrate input from visual and auditory processing streams, and the superior temporal gyrus is important for speech and auditory perception (as you saw in the earlier discussion of Wernicke's aphasia).

The exact role of the anterior temporal lobe in semantic memory has been suggested to be a convergence process – that is, specific semantic information (e.g. that a duck quacks, a banana is yellow, etc.) is likely distributed around the brain. The anterior temporal lobe aggregates this information to assist in choosing the desired target concept. In other words, the anterior temporal lobe does not actually encode semantic representations themselves, but instead serves as a relay station of some kind (Meyer and Damasio, 2009) by acting as a repository of addresses or 'tags' for conceptual representations (consistent with a connectionist computational model of semantics, mentioned earlier). In a more contemporary connectionist model of semantic memory, Rogers et al. (2004) suggest that the anterior temporal lobes have a key role in resolving the degree of semantic similarity between objects independent of surface similarities (more on this later). Under this proposal, damage to the anterior temporal lobe leads to an inability to activate the fine-grained item-specific properties of concepts stored elsewhere (although 'general' properties remain largely intact). As you may recall, this is the kind of pattern that Warrington described with respect to her semantic-impaired case mentioned earlier. Such patients don't lose all semantic information about an item (e.g. zebra), in that they may recall it is living or an animal (i.e. general information). What they have greater difficulty with is discriminating between an item and others in a similar category (e.g. a zebra versus a horse). In other words, damage to the temporal lobes seen in semantic dementia results in a difficulty aggregating semantic information sufficiently to know the difference between a zebra and a horse, but sufficient to know a zebra is an animal – a pattern seen in the case described by Warrington earlier.

So far, then, you have learned about representations in semantic memory with respect to a psycholinguisitc variable (imageability) and how connectionist computational models can capture this variable in their accounts. You have also learned that the anterior temporal lobe has a key role in mediating streams of semantic information, particularly when it relates to fine-grained category member discriminations. But are large-scale category distinctions (such as living versus non-living) seen in the pattern of impairment reported in neuropsychological cases? Let us turn to this topic now.

6.1.2   Category-specific deficits in semantic memory

In some cases patients can present with what is claimed to be a very specific semantic memory impairment, in that their comprehension or semantic processing of a particular category of items (e.g. living things) is impaired relative to other categories of items (e.g. non-living things). This has led to several researchers claiming that semantic–conceptual knowledge exhibits **category specificity**. Patients who were survivors of a viral condition known as **herpes simplex encephalitis** were among the first to be reported exhibiting category-specific semantic deficits. For example, JBR and SBY (Warrington and Shallice, 1984) were reported to have a severe impairment in naming and identifying

Category specificity
A pattern of semantic memory impairment in which patients appear to have greater difficulties with a particular category of items (e.g. animals) than others.

Herpes simplex encephalitis
A rare viral disorder that results in inflammation of the brain and consequential brain damage.

living items relative to substantially superior performance with non-living items. Several other cases were subsequently reported with this dissociation (e.g. Silveri and Gainotti, 1988) as well as cases with the reverse dissociation (i.e. poor performance on non-living items – YOT, Warrington and McCarthy, 1987; see also Hillis and Caramazza, 1991; Sacchett and Humphreys, 1992), although it must be stressed that accuracy differences across categories are often relative rather than absolute. Neuro-imaging studies have also provided similar findings with neural regions implicating specific categories of items (Humphreys and Forde, 2001; Martin et al., 2000 for reviews).

However, in order for others to have any confidence in this apparent dissociation, it is critical that the stimuli used in testing are equivalent in all ways other than category membership (i.e. are sufficiently controlled for all other 'confounding variables'). As we have already seen, certain key variables (like imageability) have been linked to semantic memory, so tests must ensure that item sets are suitably matched. Among the first to criticise the existence of category-specific impairments were Sartori and Job (1988), who claimed that a living/non-living distinction may arise due to a failure to suitably match items for differences in visual complexity. Their case (Michaelangelo) was better at naming inanimate objects relative to animals, fruits and vegetables. However, he was very poor at object decision (i.e. is this picture a 'real' item or 'unreal' item?) with both animals and inanimate items. (You may recall that this kind of test was mentioned in Section 6.3 when you were introduced to agnosia with respect to a model of naming impairments.) As a consequence, Sartori and Job (1988) suggested their case's poor performance might be confounded by an underlying agnosia, such that his apparent category-specific deficits may not implicate a deficit of semantic memory at all. In other words, category-specific deficits may well arise owing to a pre-semantic impairment involving components of the visual analysis system (the first box in the model of naming, presented in Figure 6.3). This illustrative example demonstrates again why it is important to consider alternative possibilities for explaining the pattern of performance seen in a neuropsychological case.

A second raft of criticism was provided by Funnell and Sheridan (1992) and Stewart et al. (1992), who pointed out that previous studies reporting a living/non-living dissociation did match testing stimuli for name frequency, but not for an additional variable considered to be vital in psycholinguistic research: familiarity (an issue touched on earlier on the question of typicality). It was shown that apparent category-specific impairments demonstrated by their cases disappeared when this and other cognitive variables were sufficiently matched across living and non-living category stimuli. These authors argued that previously reported category-specific impairments might merely be the result of insufficiently stringent selection of experimental stimuli. Unfortunately, the notion of personal familiarity is very difficult to quantify, since it is clearly dependent on the types of things individuals are exposed to, interested in, etc. Curiously, familiarity (based on personal experience) may even differ across gender lines; females tend to be better at naming living things while males are better with non-living things (McKenna and Parry, 1994), and when Albanese et al. (2000) reviewed cases with greater living or non-living impairments they found that typically cases with greater impairment of animals versus fruits were female, whereas cases of the reverse were male!

In summary, Funnell and colleagues make a number of important points about interpreting the consequences of patterns of impairment seen in neuropsychological patients – and the issue of confounding variables is just as important in cognitive psychology in general. However, later research studies (see below) continued to report the presence of category-specific impairments after having controlled for such issues – and as such this particular pattern is felt to need a cognitive account.

6.1.3   Explanations for category-specific semantic memory impairments

Warrington and Shallice (1984) first explained the apparent dissociation in their patients as reflecting the fact there was an important sensory versus functional knowledge representational dichotomy in the acquisition of new semantic knowledge (called the sensory functional theory (SFT)). Armed with this distinction, they further suggested that biological animate/living categories are learned primarily through sensory/perceptual characteristics (e.g. a zebra is different from a horse because of its black and white stripes), whereas inanimate/non-living categories focus on functional knowledge (e.g. our ability to identify a hammer draws on knowing what it is for). Thus patients who demonstrate poor performance on animals relative to tools or vice versa reflect specific impairments to either sensory/perceptual or functional semantic knowledge structures. Farah and McClelland (1991) adopted the functional versus sensory dichotomy in their construction of a connectionist model of semantic memory. Each item (be it living or non-living, for example) comprised a number of both functional and sensory properties (or nodes) that underpinned the representations specific to that item (for more on such distributed semantic representations, see 6.1.2). However, Farah and McClelland hypothesised that it was the *relative* proportion of functional or sensory properties specific to each item that determined the important differences across semantic categories (i.e. the differences between biological or artificial things). In other words, the semantic representation for a living thing comprised more sensory components than functional components (and vice versa for non-living things). After constructing their computational model, Farah and McClelland lesioned the model by targeting disruption to either functional or sensory units within the model. In so doing, they reported selective impairments specific to living or non-living items in their simulations. This was compelling evidence that category-specific impairments could be demonstrated by damage to a semantic memory system that did not actually organise itself categorically. Rather, such categorical impairments could emerge owing to high levels of damage to a particular type of information (sensory or functional) stored in semantic representations.

However, the SFT position has not been without its critics. Caramazza and Mahon (2006) point out that there have been reports that living versus non-living category-specific disorders may be divisible into further subtypes – for example, cases may be impaired for living animate things versus living inanimate things, or vice versa. This fact is potentially problematic for the SFT. Given it suggests all living things fall under the same semantic subsystem, how can further dissociations be explained? At the same time, Caramazza and Shelton (1998) criticised the fact that Farah and McClelland gathered information about functional information (linked to tools) for their model, by asking participants 'what things are for'. This overlooks the possibility of other kinds of 'functional'-based information (such as biological functional information – an animal has lungs that help it breathe and eyes that help it see, etc.). A more complete account of semantic memory must consider that functional information can vary in important ways. Moreover, patient-based evidence has also been presented that is somewhat problematic for the SFT's proposals. Several cases have been reported with specific impairments in retrieving perceptual-based semantic knowledge relative to functional-based semantic knowledge, but despite this showed *no* category-specific impairment for living things (Coltheart et al., 1998; Lambon Ralph et al., 1998a, 1998b). As a result, Caramazza and Mahon (2006) proposed a domain-specific hypothesis of semantic organisation that proposes that the semantic system consists of four main object domains: living animate; living inanimate; conspecifics (faces); and tools. They also suggest that the important category distinction between living and non-living things is dependent on evolutionally motivated innate neural mechanisms

Although the above accounts have assumed that category-specific performance likely reflects differences in item-based information, it is also possible that differential performance may reflect something about the process involved in identifying stimuli from different categories. For example, the process of deciding on a particular type of animal may be complicated by the fact that animals tend to share a number of features (i.e. many have four legs, two eyes, etc. (Moss et al., 1998)) and this might underpin poor performance. Rogers et al. (2005) report a neuro-imaging study that involved normal participants categorising photographs of animals or vehicles. What they found was different activation patterns depending on whether the category judgment related to a *superordinate* level of specificity (CATEGORY – CAR or DOG) compared with a *subordinate* level of specificity (e.g. AUDI or POODLE). When judgements were of the former type, different activation patterns were seen across semantic category (i.e. artificial versus animal), but not so in the latter case. The authors argue this reflects the fact that the latter shared neural regions involved in processes that have to make more fine-grained distinctions between items that are both visually and semantically similar. This proposal essentially echoes the issue raised earlier regarding the anterior temporal lobes and 'convergence zones' – namely, that semantic memory must include not just representations but also processes that operate *on* those representations (i.e. select from critical information). For our purposes, it seems that semantic memory can contain complex and varied representations and for that reason a model of this system must not just reflect this reality, but also because of these complexities an account of selection processes relating to conceptual selection must also be provided.

6.2   Summary

This section has discussed the issues relating to cognitive representations, the information that may be stored in a 'box' or module of a cognitive model. Understanding how a very complex representational system like semantic memory is organised remains a key challenge for psychologists. One intriguing pattern of impairment reported in semantic deficit patients is a disproportionate loss of a specific semantic category relative to others (category specificity). Such evidence has led to the construction of cognitive theories of semantic memory and its organisation. Some of these theories are based on more contemporary computationally implemented cognitive models (connectionist models) that allow for patterns of cognitive impairment to be simulated (a convergent field called connectionist cognitive neuropsychology). Such models have various advantages that go beyond more static classical box and arrow models of cognitive processes. In future, such models can enable researchers also to further explore the relationship between representational organisation (e.g. how we order the information we know about different kinds of animals) and the processes that act upon such representations (i.e. how we search through this information to retrieve the sought-for target).

7   Concluding thoughts

In this chapter you have learned about the field of cognitive neuropsychology, which involves the study of the characteristics of cognitive impairments seen in brain injury patients in order to better understand a given cognitive process. Such work can inform the development of a cognitive model (and its functional architecture) and guide potential remediation via appropriate cognitive therapy. In the presentation of patient evidence, you learned about double dissociation, a powerful tool in the interpretation of such evidence. The discovery of double dissociations enables those who propose cognitive models to determine the sub-processes that may act independently of one another (and thus can be selectively impaired). You also learned that interpreting patient-based evidence (as with the normal population) can be fraught with difficulties because of confounding variables. Confounding variables are potentially important differences between conditions of testing that have been overlooked, and which may actually be driving the findings that are obtained (such as category-specific patterns of semantic impairment). Always bear such things in mind when you decide to undertake your own research in future.

Later in the chapter you learned about the key issue of neural plasticity, which relates to the principle that the mappings of cognitive function to neural regions of the brain may be dynamic, and therefore neural organisation can change after brain damage. In the examples given, you learned about the lateral shift hypothesis (that is, the right hemisphere may take a greater role in language following left hemisphere damage as part of a compensatory system). Clearly, cognitive models need to be able to capture some of these dynamic qualities that the human brain possesses. More contemporary cognitive models (called connectionist models) involve creating computational simulations of neural networks that can attempt to address this issue. Such models have the advantage that once they are set up, researchers can disrupt the network by introducing disruption in order to determine if the damaged system can simulate performance in brain-injured cases. Additionally, such models can attempt to address how we learn (or, in the case of patients, how they relearn) information we subsequently store in our brains. With respect to this learned and stored information, in the final sections of the chapter you read about the issue of cognitive representations (i.e. the things stored in modules of a cognitive model) – in particular, semantic memory representations.

Semantic memory is clearly vital for human experience because it contains the sum of all the things we have learned during our lives, and understanding how this vast repository of information is organised is a key challenge for psychologists. It is the convergence of work from neuropsychology, neuroscience and computational modelling that holds the best hope for our progress in further understanding the nature of semantic memory organisation, as well as wider issues concerning the relationship between brain and behaviour.

Further reading

- This a very clear and easy introduction to the larger field of cognitive neuroscience, covering key methodological approaches in the field (particularly chapter 10):

Ward, J. (2010) *The Student's Guide to Cognitive Neuroscience*, Hove, Psychology Press.

- A classic book describing case studies of patients with fascinating impairments as a consequence of brain damage – both entertaining and sometimes sad, this book has remained an inspiration to a number of students past and present:

Sacks, O. (1985) *The Man Who Mistook His Wife For a Hat*, London, Duckworth/New York, Summit Books.

- A well-written, clear, concise and approachable textbook covering a number of the issues raised in this chapter in greater detail (particularly chapter 6):

Stirling, J.D. and Elliott, R. (2008) *Introducing Neuropsychology*, 2nd edn, Hove, Psychology Press.

References

Abo, M., Senoo, A., Watanabe, S., Miyano, S., Doseki, K., Sasaki, N., Kobayashi, K., Kikuchi, Y. and Yonemoto, K. (2004) 'Language-related brain function during word repetition in post-stroke aphasics', *Neuroreport*, vol. 15, pp. 1891–4.

Albanese, E. Capitani, E., Barbarotto, R. and Laiacona, M. (2000) 'Semantic category dissociations, familiarity and gender', *Cortex*, vol. 36, pp. 733–46.

Basso, A., Gardelli, M., Grassi, M.P. and Mariotti, M. (1989) 'The role of the right hemisphere in recovery from aphasia. Two case studies', *Cortex*, vol. 25 no. 4, pp. 555–66.

Blasi, V., Young, A.C., Tansy, A.P., Petersen, S.E., Snyder, A.Z. and Corbetta, M. (2002) 'Word retrieval learning modulates right frontal cortex in patients with left frontal damage', *Neuron*, vol. 36, pp. 159–70.

Bloom, P. (2000) *How Children Learn the Meanings of Words*, Cambridge, MA, MIT Press.

Broca, P. (1865) cited in Tesak, J. and Code, C. (2008) *Milestones in the History of Aphasia*, Hove, Psychology Press.

Cao, Y., Vikingstad, B.S., Paige-George, K., Johnson, A.F. and Welch, M.A. (1999) 'Cortical language activation in stroke patients recovering from aphasia with functional MRI', *Stroke*, vol. 30, pp. 2331–40.

Caramazza, A. (1986) 'On drawing inferences about the structure of normal cognitive systems from the analysis of patterns of impaired performance: the case for single patient studies', *Brain and Cognition*, vol. 5, pp. 41–66.

Caramazza, A. (1992) 'Is cognitive neuropsychology possible?', *Journal of Cognitive Neuroscience*, vol. 4, pp. 80–95.

Caramazza, A. and McCloskey, M. (1988), 'The case for single-patient studies', *Cognitive Neuropsychology*, vol. 5, pp. 517–27.

Caramazza, A. and Mahon, B.Z. (2006) 'The organisation of conceptual knowledge in the brain: the future's past and some future directions', *Cognitive Neuropsychology*, vol. 23, no. 1, pp. 13–38.

Caramazza, A. and Shelton, J.R. (1998) 'Domain-specific knowledge systems in the brain: the animate-inanimate distinction', *Journal of Cognitive Neuroscience*, vol. 10, pp. 1–34.

Catani, M. and Ffytche, D.H. (2005) 'The rises and falls of disconnection syndromes', *Brain*, vol. 128, no. 10, pp. 2224–39.

Collins, A.M. and Loftus, E.F. (1975) 'A spreading activation theory of semantic processing', *Psychological Review*, vol. 82, no. 6, pp. 407–28.

Collins, A.M. and Quillian, M.R. (1969) 'Retrieval time from semantic memory', *Journal of Verbal Learning and Verbal Behaviour*, vol. 8, no. 2, pp. 240–7.

Coltheart, M., Inglis, L., Cupples, L., Michie, P., Bates, A. and Budd, B. (1998) 'A semantic subsystem specific to the storage of information about visual attributes of animate and inanimate objects', *Neurocase*, vol. 4, pp. 353–70.

Corkin, S. (2002). 'What's new with the amnesic patient H.M.?', *Nature Reviews Neuroscience*, vol. 3, no. 2, pp. 153–60.

Damasio, H., Tranela, D., Grabowskia, T., Adolphsa, A. and Damasio A. (2004) 'Neural systems behind word and concept retrieval', *Cognition*, vol. 92, pp. 179–229.

Dejerine, J. (1892) cited in Tesak, J. and Code, C. (2008) *Milestones in the History of Aphasia*, Hove, Psychology Press.

Farah, M.J. and McClelland, J.L. (1991) 'A computational model of semantic memory impairment: modality-specificity and emergent category-specificity', *Journal of Experimental Psychology: General,* vol. 120, pp. 339–57.

Fodor, J.A. (1983) *Modularity of Mind: An Essay on Faculty Psychology,* Cambridge, MA, MIT Press.

Funnell, E. and Sheridan, J. (1992) 'Categories of knowledge? Unfamiliar aspects of living and non-living things', *Cognitive Neuropsychology*, vol. 9, pp. 135–54.

Geschwind, N. (1965) cited in Catani, M. and Ffytche, D.H. (2005) 'The rises and falls of disconnection syndromes', *Brain*, vol. 128, no. 10, pp. 2224–39.

Goodglass, H. and Kaplan, E. (1983) *The Assessment of Aphasia and Related Disorders*, 2nd edn, Philadelphia, PA, Lea & Febiger.

Gott, P. (1973) 'Language after dominant hemispherectomy', *Journal of Neurosurgical Psychiatry*, vol. 36, no. 6, pp. 1882–8.

Gowers, W. (1887) cited in Tesak, J. and Code, C. (2008) *Milestones in the History of Aphasia*, Hove, Psychology Press.

Harley, T.A. (2014) *The Psychology of Language: From Data to Theory*, 4th edn, Hove, Psychology Press.

Heiss, W.D., Kessler, J., Thiel, A., Ghaemi, M. and Karbe, H. (1999) 'Differential capacity of left and right hemispheric areas for compensation of poststroke aphasia', *Annals of Neurology*, vol. 45, pp. 430–8.

Hickok, G. and Poeppel, D. (2004) 'Dorsal and ventral streams: a framework for understanding aspects of the functional anatomy of language', *Cognition*, vol. 92, no. 1–2, pp. 67–99.

Hillis, A.E. and Caramazza, A. (1991) 'Category-specific naming and comprehension impairment: a double dissociation', *Brain*, vol. 114, pp. 2081–94.

Hillis, A.E., Rapp, B.C., Romani, C. and Caramazza, A. (1990) 'Selective impairment of semantics in lexical processing', *Cognitive Neuropsychology*, vol. 7, pp. 191–243.

Hillis, A.E., Wityk, R.J., Barker, P.B., Beauchamp, N.J., Gailloud, P., Murphy, K., Cooper, O. and Metter, E.J. (2002) 'Subcortical aphasia and neglect in acute stroke: the role of cortical hypoperfusion', *Brain*, vol. 125, pp. 1094–104.

Hodges, J.R., Patterson, K., Oxbury, S. and Funnell, E. (1992) 'Semantic dementia – progressive fluent aphasia with temporal lobe atrophy', *Brain*, vol. 115, pp. 1783–806.

Howard, D. and Orchard-Lisle, V.M. (1984) 'On the origin of semantic errors in naming; evidence from the case of a global aphasic', *Cognitive Neuropsychology*, vol. 1, no. 2, pp. 163–90.

Humphreys, G.W. and Forde, E.M.E. (2001) 'Category specificity in mind and brain?' *Behavioral and Brain Sciences*, vol. 24, no. 3, pp. 497–504.

James, W. (1890) 'The stream of thought' (Chapter XI) in *The Principles of Psychology*, Volume 1, London, Macmillan. Available online at https://archive.org/details/principlesofpsyc01jameuoft (Accessed 5 November 2014).

Josse, G. and Tzourio-Mazover, N. (2004) 'Hemispheric specialization for language', *Brain Research Reviews*, vol. 44, no. 1, pp. 1–12.

Katz, R.B. and Goodglass, H. (1990) 'Deep dysphasia: analysis of a rare form of repetition disorder', *Brain and Language*, vol. 39, no. 1, pp. 153–85.

Kertesz, A. (1979) 'Visual agnosia: the dual deficit of perception and recognition' *Cortex*, vol. 15, no. 3, pp. 403–19.

Kinsbourne, M. (1971) 'The minor cerebral hemisphere as a source of aphasic speech', *Archives of Neurology,* vol. 25, pp. 302–6.

Lambon Ralph, M.A., Graham, H.K., Ellis, A. and Hodges, J. (1998a) 'Naming in semantic dementia – what matters?' *Neuropsychologia*, vol. 36, no. 8, pp. 775–84.

Lambon Ralph, M.A., Howard, D., Nightingale, G. and Ellis, A.W. (1998b) 'Are living and non-living category-specific deficits casually linked to impaired perceptual or associative knowledge? Evidence from a category-specific double dissociation', *Neurocase*, vol. 4, pp. 4–5.

Lambon Ralph, M.A., Sage, K.E. and Roberts, J. (2000) 'Classical anomia: a neuropsychological perspective on speech production', *Neuropsychologia*, vol. 38, no. 2, pp. 186–202.

Leger, A., Demonet, J. F., Ruff, S., Aithamon, B., Touyeras, B., Puel, M., Boulanouar, K. and Cardebat, D. (2002) 'Neural substrates of spoken language rehabilitation in an aphasic patient: an fMRI study', *Neuroimage*, vol. 17, no. 1, pp. 174–83.

Lichtheim, L. (1885) cited in Tesak, J. and Code, C. (2008) *Milestones in the History of Aphasia*, Hove, Psychology Press.

Marr, D. (1982) *Vision: A Computational Investigation into the Human Representation and Processing of Visual Information*, New York, Freeman.

Martin, A., Ungerleider, L.G. and Haxby, J.V. (2000) 'Category-specificity and the brain: the sensory–motor model of semantic representations of objects', in Gazzaniga, M.S. (ed.) *The New Cognitive Neurosciences*, 2nd edn, Cambridge, MA, MIT Press, pp. 1023–36.

McCarthy, R.A. and Kartsounis, L.D. (2000) 'Wobbly words: Refractory anomia with preserved semantics', *Neurocase*, vol. 6, pp. 487–97.

McClelland, J.L., McNaughton, B.L. and O'Reilly, R.C. (1995) 'Why there are complementary learning systems in the hippocampus and neocortex: insights from the successes and failures of connectionist models of learning and memory', *Psychological Review*, vol. 102, pp. 419–57.

McKenna, P. and Parry, R. (1994) 'Category-specificity in the naming of natural and man-made objects: normative data from adults and children', *Neuropsychological Rehabilitation*, vol. 4, pp. 255–81.

Meinzer, M. and Breitenstein, B. (2008) 'Functional imaging of treatment-induced recovery in chronic aphasia', *Aphasiology*, vol. 22, pp. 1251–68.

Meyer, K., and Damasio, A. (2009) 'Convergence and divergence in a neural architecture for recognition and memory', *Trends in Neurosciences*, vol. 32, no. 7, pp. 376–82.

Moss, H.E., Tyler, L.K., Durrant-Peatfield, M. and Bunn, E.M. (1998) '"Two eyes of a see through": impaired and intact semantic knowledge in a case of selective deficit for living things', *Neurocase*, vol. 4, pp. 291–310.

Ogden, J.A. (1988) 'Language and memory functions after long recovery periods in left-hemispherectomised subjects', *Neuropsychologia*, vol. 26, no. 5, pp. 654–9.

Ogle, W. (1867), cited in Tesak, J. and Code, C. (2008), *Milestones in the History of Aphasia*, Hove, Psychology Press.

Page, M.P.A. (2006) 'What can't functional neuroimaging tell the cognitive psychologist?' *Cortex*, vol. 42, no. 3, pp. 428–33.

Plaut, D.C. and Shallice, T. (1993) 'Deep dyslexia: a case study of connectionist neuropsychology', *Cognitive Neuropsychology*, vol. 10, pp. 377–500.

Rogers, T.T., Hocking, J., Mechelli, A., Patterson, K. and Price, C. (2005) 'Fusiform activation to animals is driven by the process, not the stimulus', *Journal of Cognitive Neuroscience*, vol. 17, no. 3, pp. 434–45.

Rogers, T.T., Lambon Ralph, M.A., Garrard, P., Bozeat, S., McClelland, J.L., Hodges, J.R. and Patterson, K. (2004) 'The structure and deterioration of semantic memory: a neuropsychological and computational investigation', *Psychological Review*, vol. 111, no. 1, pp. 205–35.

Romani, C., Olson, A., Semenza, C. and, Grana A. (2002) 'Phonological errors in two aphasic patients: a phonological vs. an articulatory locus of impairment', *Cortex,* vol. 38, pp. 541–67.

Sacchett, C. and Humphreys, G.W. (1992) 'Calling a squirrel a squirrel but scissors a knife: a category-specific deficit in identifying inanimate objects', *Cognitive Neuropsychology*, vol. 9, pp. 73–86.

Sacks, O. (1985) *The Man Who Mistook His Wife For a Hat*, London, Duckworth/New York, Summit Books.

Saffran, E.M., Schwartz, M.F. and Marin, O.S. (1980) 'The word order problem in agrammatism. I. Comprehension', *Brain and Language*, vol. 10, pp. 249–62.

Sartori, G. and Job, R. (1988) 'The oyster with four legs: a neuropsychological study on the interaction of visual and semantic information', *Cognitive Neuropsychology*, vol. 5, pp. 105–32.

Saur, D., Lange, R., Baumgaertner, A., Schraknepper, V., Willmes, K., Rijntjes, M., and Weiller, C. (2006) 'Dynamics of language reorganization after stroke', *Brain*, vol. 129, no. 6, pp. 1371–84.

Shallice, T. (1988) *From Neuropsychology to Mental Structure,* Cambridge, Cambridge University Press.

Silveri, M.C. and Gainotti, G. (1988) 'Interaction between vision and language in category-specific semantic impairment', *Cognitive Neuropsychology*, vol. 5, pp. 677–709.

Stewart, F., Parkin, A. and Hunkin, N. (1992) 'Naming impairments following recovery from herpes simplex encephalitis: category-specific?', *Quarterly Journal of Experimental Psychology*, vol. 44, pp. 261–84.

Warrington, E.K. (1975) 'The selective impairment of semantic memory', *Quarterly Journal Experimental Psychology*, vol. 27, pp. 635–57.

Warrington, E.K. and McCarthy, R.A. (1987) 'Categories of knowledge: further fractionations and an attempted integration', *Brain*, vol. 110, no. 5, pp. 1273–96.

Warrington, E.K. and Shallice, T. (1984) 'Category specific semantic impairments', *Brain*, vol. 107, no. 3, pp. 829–54.

Wernicke, K. (1874), cited in Tesak, J. and Code, C. (2008) *Milestones in the History of Aphasia*, Hove, Psychology Press.

Glossary

Achromatic sensitivity

The sensitivity of some photoreceptive cells to overall levels of illumination (i.e. dark/light) and contrast rather than colour.

Action potential

A spike of electrical change that forms the means of communication in neurons. Neurons transmit information by the frequency of action potentials that occur.

Adventitious reinforcement

Unintentional strengthening of a response by its coincidence with a positive event.

Agnosia

Impairment of visual object recognition that occurs as a consequence of brain damage.

Amnesia

Memory impairment that occurs as a consequence of brain damage.

Amodal completion

The perceptual experience of a whole object, despite parts of the object being hidden from view.

Anomia

A subtype of aphasia that results in an inability to retrieve the names of everyday items, causing frustration for the individual.

Antagonists

A type of chemical that occupies the receptors for a particular neurotransmitter but that is chemically inert and therefore blocks the action of the natural substance.

Aphasia

A language impairment that occurs as a consequence of brain damage.

Associative learning

Learning about the relationship between or among stimuli.

Attention

A cognitive process involving the selection of information for further processing, such as the extraction of meaning.

Automaticity

A mode of information processing in which processing of incoming stimuli and selection of an appropriate response seem to occur in the absence of conscious awareness.

Autonomic nervous system (ANS)

The part of the nervous system responsible for controlling the internal activity of the body, e.g. heart rate and digestion.

Binocular rivalry

The perceptual experience that arises when completely different images are seen by the left and right eye. Rivalry can produce a range of unusual perceptual experiences, including seeing part of the right eye's image and part of the left eye's image.

Biopsychosocial model

A model that recognises the importance of biology, psychology and social factors in the determination of mental states and behaviour. It incorporates interactions between these component factors.

Blindsight

The neurological phenomenon of having damage to areas of the brain that give rise to conscious visual experience. In blindsight patients can still locate features of the environment using a non-conscious visual route in the brain.

Blind spot

An area on the retina in each eye where the optic nerve is formed and where there are no photoreceptive cells to signal information in the visual field.

Blocking

A situation in which prior learning about one stimulus reduces learning about another stimulus.

Bottleneck in processing

A restriction in the speed or amount of information that can be processed, arising from a limitation in the capacity of our information-processing systems.

Bottom-up processing

Within the field of perception this view emphasises the importance and the role of information in the environment and its influence on our perceptual experience.

Broca's aphasia

A form of aphasia that has as a key feature expressive language problems and relates to damage to the left frontal area of the brain.

Category specificity

A pattern of semantic memory impairment in which patients appear to have greater difficulties with a particular category of items (e.g. animals) than others.

Cells

The basic building block of the body. The body is composed of billions of different cells, serving various functions. The primary interest here is in a type of cell known as neurons.

Central nervous system (CNS)

The brain and spinal cord.

Cerebellum

('Little brain' in Latin.) Two small hemispheres located beneath the cortical hemispheres, at the back of the head; the cerebellum plays an important role in directing movements and balance. Recent research shows it is also implicated in executive control, spatial cognition and emotional processing.

Cerebrovascular accident

Brain damage that occurs as a consequence of a blood clot or rupture of an artery, resulting in lesions to the brain. Such events are also often called a stroke.

Change blindness

The inability to notice changes in a visual scene.

Choice blindness

The inability to notice when a less-preferred choice is presented as a replacement for the choice one has already made.

Circumlocution

A verbal description of an object used by someone who is unable to retrieve the correct name of this item.

Classical conditioning

Conditioning in which a stimulus acquires the capacity to trigger a response by virtue of its pairing with an unconditional stimulus.

Cognitive neuropsychology

A sub-division of cognitive psychology that considers the disruption of cognitive function in the context of brain injury. Its focus is to better understand the manner in which cognitive processes break down and their relationship to neurological structure.

Cognitive workload

The amount of mental activity or effort that is required at a given time.

Conditional response (CR)

The behaviour evoked by a conditional stimulus as a result of that stimulus predicting an unconditioned stimulus.

Conditional stimulus (CS)

A stimulus that evokes a response after being paired with an unconditional stimulus via conditioning. For example, the sound of a bell will evoke a salivation response in hungry dogs after being paired with the presentation of food.

Conduction aphasia

A form of aphasia that has poor word repetition as a key feature.

Cones

A class of photoreceptive cell that is sensitive to colour. There are three types of cone cell, sensitive to long, medium and short wavelengths of light.

Conscious perception

The subjective experience and awareness of perceiving something.

Cortex

('Bark' in Latin.) In psychology and neuropsychology, usually shorthand for 'cerebral cortex', the outer layer of the cerebral hemispheres of the brain. It consists of 'grey matter' (principally neurons, q.v.).

Cortical magnification

The process by which some parts of the visual field (e.g. the fovea) take up a disproportionate amount of the occipital cortex to reflect the density of cells in that area and to maintain a high degree of sensitivity.

Cueing

The use of information as a means of aiding an individual in producing a correct answer. It is often used in a therapeutic context.

Cultural ratchet

The accumulation of modifications to learned actions that emerge because of uniquely human processes (such as teaching, social learning and normativity) that underlie the establishment and maintenance of social groups.

Cultural tool

A means of achieving something that is passed on by cultural transmission (for example, a hammer is a physical cultural tool). Language is a psychological cultural tool: what we say and how we say it depends on how we interpret the words, which, in turn, reflect our culture.

Cultural transmission

A learned behaviour or tradition that is passed on through the generations.

Diaschisis

When functional inactivity in a brain region occurs because of lesions to more distant regions that share neural connections.

Dichotic listening task

An experimental procedure in which two different messages are presented simultaneously, one to each ear. Normally the participant is asked to show that they are attending to one of them by repeating ('shadowing') it.

Discrimination

Learning to respond in the presence of one event (e.g. a green light) but not in the presence of another (e.g. a red light).

Dissociations

A pattern of impairment that demonstrates selective disruption to a particular cognitive process with other related cognitive processes remaining intact.

Dorsal stream

Also known as the dorsal pathway, this stream of processing ascends from the occipital cortex to the parietal cortex and is involved in spatial awareness and action. It is often referred to as the 'where' or 'how' pathway because of its functions.

Early selection

Stimuli are selected early on for processing, at the expense of competing stimuli, which receive little further processing.

Ecological theory of perception

Gibson's theory of perception which emphasises the direct and important link between actions and perception, with a strong emphasis on information revealed by optic flow.

Emulation

Learning by copying the product or outcome of a behaviour.

Endogenous factors

Factors within the body or mind, rather than external factors. For example, lost and thirsty in a desert, our internal state would direct our attention towards any potential sources of water.

Executive control

The overall management of cognitive resources, including the ability to regulate and monitor how information is being processed.

Executive function

Our ability to plan, organise and coordinate our activities in a coherent and adaptable way.

Exogenous factors

External factors or events in our environment, rather than internal thoughts or feelings. For example, a sudden loud noise is an exogenous factor that automatically grabs our attention.

Expressive aphasia

This is a form of language impairment that relates to substantial problems producing speech, occurring as a result of some form of brain injury.

Filter models of attention

Theoretical models that propose we actively select only a limited amount of information to attend to, either at an early or a late stage in the sequence of information processing.

Fixation

Brief or sustained pause in eye movements, normally to scrutinise an object or event and bring it into focus.

Focusing power

The ability of the cornea and lens of the eye to either diverge or converge incoming light to focus it on the retina.

Fovea

A small area in the centre of the retina that provides high acuity and colour vision.

Functional architecture

The various functional components attributed to a given cognitive process; in short, the various boxes and arrows presented in a cognitive model.

Functional magnetic resonance imaging (fMRI)

A neuroimaging technique that measures brain activity by detecting changes in blood oxygen levels.

Galvanic skin response (GSR)

A measure of the change in electrical resistance of the skin, often used as a measure of autonomic reaction and arousal.

Generalisation

Responding in the presence of a stimulus that is similar to the trained stimulus.

Grand illusion

The suggestion that our lived perceptual experience is fundamentally different from what is actually being accomplished by our sensory systems.

Herpes simplex encephalitis

A rare viral disorder that results in inflammation of the brain and consequential brain damage.

Hormone

A chemical that is released into a blood vessel. It is then transported in the blood to a site where it occupies receptors and thereby effects action.

Hyperopia

Or long-sightedness, where the image viewed is focused behind the retina (rather than on it), meaning that you can see objects in the far distance, but not those near to you.

Hypothesis theory

Richard Gregory's development of the idea of indirect perception, which emphasises the role that hypotheses play in the perceptual experience we end up having. In many ways this is a more detailed version of the idea of unconscious inferences.

Imitation

Learning by copying a behaviour.

Implicit perception

Cognitive processing that the individual is largely unaware of. Although we are unaware of what we are processing, it can nevertheless have an influence on our behaviour.

Inattentional blindness

The inability to notice events in a visual scene due to attention being applied elsewhere or due to current cognitive resources being exhausted.

Indirect perception

The idea that perception is not a direct mapping of experience to the information in the environment, but rather that additional cognitive processes influence our perception.

Information-processing systems

The cognitive systems responsible for manipulating information in all its aspects, i.e. receiving, selecting, storing, integrating and using information. Psychologists produce models of these systems that are based on behavioural and neuroanatomical/neurophysiological data. Information-processing models often rely heavily on analogies to computer information-processing systems.

Instrumental conditioning

A form of conditioning in which the outcome depends upon the action of the animal, as exemplified by obtaining food on turning a latch or negotiating a maze.

Interthinking

When people think together, ideas emerge that wouldn't emerge by individual effort. Littleton and Mercer suggest that exploratory talk facilitates interthinking.

Late selection

Stimuli are selected for full attention after some processing of competing stimuli has occurred.

Lateral geniculate nucleus

These thalamic structures are the main relay points between the retina and the occipital cortex.

Learning

A change, or potential change, in behaviour that occurs as a result of experience.

Lexical phonology

The spoken sound relating to a word.

Magnetic resonance imaging (MRI)

A form of neuroimaging that examines either the structure of the brain or both the structure and activity of the different brain regions.

McGurk effect

A multisensory distortion of reality when what one hears is incongruent with the lip movements one sees. The resulting perception is often a fusion of what is heard and seen.

Mediation

In the sociocultural perspective, tools and technologies affect how we interact in the physical and social environments; and learning emerges from interactions with others and the tools they use.

Modal completion

The sensory–perceptual experience of parts of an object that do not exist, yet can be inferred from parts that are visibly present.

Modularity

This refers to the principle that components of a cognitive system can be independently disrupted as a consequence of brain damage.
Modularity assumes that a cognitive 'module' is:
(a) functionally autonomous (i.e. each module carries out processing in isolation),
(b) domain specific (processes one type of information – i.e. semantics only) and
(c) mandatory (i.e. a module operates in an all-or-none fashion).

Multi-modal perception

Perceptual experiences that are derived from more than a single sensory modality.

Myopia

Or short-sightedness, where the image viewed is focused in front of the retina (rather than on it), meaning that you can see objects in the near distance, but not those far away.

Negative reinforcement

The process of removing something as a consequence of a particular behaviour, which increases the frequency of showing that behaviour.

Neurodegenerative disease

A generic term for brain-related diseases that lead to cell death and progressive loss of neurons in the brain.

Neuroimaging

A generic term referring to techniques for visualising brain activity ('functional' imaging, e.g. PET, SPECT, MEG and fMRI) or brain structure ('structural' imaging, e.g. CT and MRI).

Neuron

A type of cell that is specialised for the transmission and processing of information within the nervous system.

Neurotransmitter

A chemical stored at the terminal of a neuron and which is released by the arrival of an action potential. It occupies receptors on a neighbouring cell.

Occipital cortex

The most posterior part of the brain whose role is to process visual information received from the retina. Information is analysed in terms of several features (e.g. colour, motion, orientation, etc.). Information is then relayed to higher centres via the dorsal and ventral streams.

Optic array

The light experienced by the eyes as it is structured by the surfaces and textures in the environment.

Optic flow

The ordered change in patterns of light which results from movement within an environment.

Parietal cortex

This area of the brain, just above the occipital cortex, has a major role in integrating information from different senses and also in spatial mapping and bodily sensation.

Partial reinforcement

Responses that are reinforced only occasionally.

Perception–action model

A theoretical and biological model that views the dorsal and ventral streams as having defined and independent roles in action and perception respectively.

Perceptual learning

The enhancement of learning about a stimulus by exposure to that stimulus.

Perceptual load

The amount of perceptual operations required by a target: the greater the number of items in a visual display, the higher the perceptual load.

Phenomenology

The way things appear or are experienced subjectively.

Photoreceptors

A class of sensory neuron that responds (i.e. is sensitive) to light. In the eye there are cone (colour-sensitive) and rod (contrast-sensitive) photoreceptive cells.

Positive reinforcement

The process of giving something as a consequence of a particular behaviour, which increases the frequency of showing that behaviour.

Positron emission tomography (PET)

A neuroimaging technique for examining the activity of different parts of the brain.

Post-natal depression

Depression experienced by a percentage of women following birth. It is also known as post-natal illness or post-partum depression.

Premorbid

The ability, behaviour or cognitive function of an individual prior to brain injury or illness.

Presbyopia

A condition that normally occurs with age where the lens stiffens, losing its elasticity, changing its focusing power and making near objects difficult to bring into focus.

Primary visual cortex

Also called V1, the most posterior part of the occipital cortex, where inputs from the lateral geniculate nucleus first arrive. Further processing is then carried out within the occipital cortex before being transferred to the dorsal and ventral streams.

Psychological refractory period (PRP)

The delay in responding to the second of two stimuli presented very close together in time, assumed to occur because information-processing systems are still preoccupied with processing the first stimulus.

Punishment

An event that follows a response and that leads to a decrease in the frequency of that response.

Receptive aphasia

A form of language impairment that relates to substantial problems understanding speech, occurring as a result of some form of brain injury.

Receptor

The structure on a cell that may be occupied by a chemical, either neurotransmitter or hormone.

Retina

The light-sensitive layer of cells at the back of the eye. Photoreceptors here convert light into neural responses to be passed to the brain via the optic nerve.

Reuptake

The process by which a neurotransmitter released from a neuron is taken back into that neuron.

Rods

A class of photoreceptive cell that signals the luminance differences across the retina and does not code for colour.

Saccade

A short and rapid eye movement which shifts one's fixation from one visual location to another.

Saccadic suppression

The reduction of input from the eyes to the brain during an eye movement. Suppression is thought to assist with our ability to focus on specific objects and also to prevent the experience of blurred vision due to eye movement.

Selective attention

Focusing on specific elements of a stimulus or task. Looking for your friend at a railway station, ignoring all other faces, would be an example of selective attention.

Semantics

The information that relates to the meaning of a word.

Sensory adaptation

The process by which a neuron stops signalling a constant input when that input stops changing.

Sensory neuron

The class of neuron that serves the role of detecting sensory information, e.g. light or pressure on the skin.

Short-term memory

A mechanism for the brief storage (in the order of a few seconds) of information to assist current thinking and awareness.

Sideways rules

An important part of Gregory's hypothesis theory, which apply basic forms of organisation and order to the raw input received through the eyes.

Situational awareness

An individual's understanding and perception of their environment, and their position in that environment both in the present and the near future.

Social learning

A theory of learning based on observing and imitating the behaviours of others.

Sociocultural theory

A theory that stresses that learning involves the use of tools and artefacts and is embedded within the context of interpersonal relationships, which in turn are embedded in social and cultural systems.

Spinal cord

A column within the backbone consisting of neurons, as well as glial cells.

Structural invariant

A central principle of Gregory's theory which emphasises the lawful (i.e. invariant) relationships that occur between our actions (including movement) and the resulting changes in our perceptual experience.

Synapse

The junction between a neuron and another cell, either another neuron or a muscle cell.

Temporal cortex

A complex structure situated at the side of the brain and responsible for object recognition, face processing, emotion, memory and language comprehension.

Thalamus

The key relay station for incoming (i.e. afferent) sensory information to the cerebral cortex and also for outgoing (efferent) motor information to the body.

Top-down processing

Within the field of perception this view emphasises the importance and the role of internal representations and intentions upon our perceptual experience.

Traumatic brain injury

An injury that occurs as a result of some form of external force on the skull and brain (e.g. a blow to the head for a boxer).

Troxler effect

A visual illusion where an unchanging stimulus that is stable on the retina fades from perceptual experience. The effect is largely thought to be due to the fact the most sensory neurons adapt to an unchanging stimulus and cease sending a signal, known as sensory adaptation.

Unconditional response (UR)

The unlearned reflexive behaviour evoked by a stimulus, for example salivation in response to the presence of food in the mouth.

Unconditional stimulus (US)

A stimulus that evokes a response without any conditioning taking place; for example, the smell of food will evoke a salivation response in hungry dogs.

Unconscious inferences

The idea that some conclusions about our experience of the world can be made without us necessarily being aware of them.

Ventral stream

Also known as the ventral pathway, this stream of processing descends from the occipital cortex to the inferior temporal cortex and is involved in objects recognition. It is often referred to as the 'what' pathway owing to its primary function.

Visual buffer

A short-lived mechanism for the storage of visual information for later processing.

Visual field

Also known as the field of view, this is all the light in the environment currently available directly to the eye.

Wernicke's aphasia

A form of aphasia that has as a key feature receptive language problems and relates to damage to the left temporal lobe of the brain.

Working memory

A flexible memory system comprising three components: a supervisory system (the central executive) and two temporary memory systems, the phonological loop and the visuospatial sketchpad. These are specialised for retaining verbal material and visual/spatial material respectively.

Zone of proximal development (ZPD)

The difference between what the child can do with and without the aid of others; this aid comprises encouragement, demonstrations, suggestions and general nudging rather than overt instruction and is often referred to as 'scaffolding'.

Acknowledgements

Grateful acknowledgement is made to the following sources:

Every effort has been made to contact copyright holders. If any have been inadvertently overlooked the publishers will be pleased to make the necessary arrangements at the first opportunity.

Cover
Copyright © Majcot/Dreamstime.com

Figures
Figure 1.1: Copyright © Simon Davies; Figure 1.3: Arnold, D. (2003) 'Latency differences and the flask-lag effect', *Vision Research*, vol. 43, Elsevier Science; Figure 1.5: Copyright © Mysid, This file is licensed under the Creative Commons Attribution Licence http://creativecommons.org/licenses/by/3.0/; Figure 1.7a: Copyright © Brian Ventrudo; Figure 1.7b: Copyright © Rags Gardner; Figure 1.9: adapted from Hubel, D. (1988) *Eye, Brain and Vision*, Scientific American Library; Figure 1.10: Crick, F. and Koch, C. (1992) 'Visual image in mind and brain', *Scientific American*, vol. 267, no. 3; Figure 1.11: 'Central Processing, Anatomy & Physiology', Openstax.CNX, This file is licensed under the Creative Commons Attribution Licence http://creativecommons.org/licenses/by/4.0; Figure 1.12b: Copyright © Animated Healthcare Ltd/Science Photo Library; Figure 1.13: Copyright © Heini Schneebelie/Science Photo Library; Figure 1.14: Gregory, R. L. (1997) 'Knowledge in perception and illusion', Phil Trans, Royal Society of London, B, vol. 352, no. 1358; Figure 1.15b: Copyright © James Dean/Mighty Optical Illusions www.moillusions.com/video-ames-window-optical-illusion; Figure 1.18: Courtesy of Division of Rare and Manuscript Collections, Cornell University Library; Figure 1.19: Courtesy of Johannes Zanker; Figure 1.20: Gibson, J. J. (1979) *Ecological Approach to Visual Perception*, Psychology Press; Figure 1.21: Vallortigara, G. et al. (2005) 'Visually inexperienced chicks exhibit spontaneous preference for biological motion patterns', *PLOS Biology*, vol. 3 no. 7; Figure 1.22: 53937, Petkova, V. I. (2011) 'The perspective matters! Multisensory integration in ego-centric reference frames determines full-body ownership', *Frontiers in Psychology*, vol. 2; Figure 1.23: Hunter, J. P. (2003) 'The effect of tactile and visual sensory inputs on phantom limb awareness', *Brain*, vol. 126, no. 3 Copyright © Guarantors of *Brain*, by permission of Oxford University Press; Figure 2.4: Copyright © Valerie Lo, This

file is licensed under the Creative Commons Attribution Licence http://creativecommons.org/licenses/by/3.0/; Figure 2.5: adapted from Shallice, T. and Burgess, P. W. (1991) 'Deficits in strategy application following frontal lobe damage in man', *Brain*, vol. 114, Oxford University Press; Figure 2.6: Wickens, C. D. (2002) 'Multiple resources and performance prediction', Theoretical Issues in Ergonomics Science, vol. 3, Taylor & Francis Ltd; Figure 2.9: Pashler, H. (1998) *The Psychology of Attention*, The MIT Press; Figure 2.10: Copyright © Monika Wisniewska/Shutterstock; Figure 3.1: Courtesy of Stuart Anstis; Figure 3.2: Copyright © Colin Palmer Photography/ Alamy; Figures 3.3 and 3.4: Copyright © Ronald A Rensink; Figure 3.5: Courtesy of Kevin O'Regan; Figures 3.6 and 3.8: figures provided by Daniel Simons; Figure 3.7: Simons, D. J. (2007) 'Inattentional Blindness' Scholapedia, This file is licensed under the Creative Commons Attribution-Non-commercial Licence http:// creativecommons.org/licenses/by-nc/3.0/; Figure 3.9: Most, S. B. (2001) 'How not to be seen: The contribution of similarity and selective ignoring to sustained inattentional blindness', *Psychological Science*, vol. 12, Sage Publications; Figure 3.12: Copyright © Mark Hanlon; Figure 3.13: Jones, B.C., Jones, B.T., Blundell, L. and Bruce, G. (2002) 'Social users of alcohol and cannabis who detect substance-related changes in a change blindness paradigm report higher levels of use than those detecting substance neutral changes', Psychopharmacology , vol. 165, Springer; Figure 4.1: Gibson, J. J. and Gibson, E. J. (1955) 'Perceptual learning: Differentiation or enrichment?', *Psychological Review*, vol. 62, no. 1, American Psychological Association; Figure 4.2: Gibson, E. J. and Walk, R. D. (1956) 'The effect of prolonged exposure to visually presented patterns on learning to discriminate them', Journal of Comparative and Psychological Psychology, vol. 49, American Psychological Association; Figure 4.4: Copyright © Blickwinkel/Alamy; Figure 4.6 left: Copyright © 3Dalia/ Shutterstock; Figure 4.6 right: Copyright © Twee Art/Getty Images; Figure 4.7 left: Copyright © Charles Masters/Shutterstock; Figure 4.7 right: Copyright © TruSelf Sporting Club; Figure 4.8: Thornton, A. and Clutton-Brock, T. (2011) 'Social learning and the development of individual and group behaviour in mammal societies', Philosophical Transactions of The Royal Society B, vol. 366, The Royal Society; Figure 4.9: Whiten, A. et al. (2009) 'Emulation, imitation, over-imitation and the scope of culture for child and chimpanzee', Philosophical Transactions of The Royal Society B, vol. 364, The Royal Society; Figure 4.10b: Jensen, P. S. (1975) Den Gronlandske Kayak og

Den Redskaber, Nyt Nordisk Forlag Arnold Busch; Figure 4.10c: Copyright © Harvey GoldenFigure 4.10d: Copyright © Wili Hybrid, This file is licensed under the Creative Commons Attribution Licence http://creativecommons.org/licenses/by/2.0/; Figure 4.10e: Copyright © John Petersen; Figure 4.11: 56360: Copyright © Katherine McAuliffe; Figure 5.6: from Elements4Health, www.elements4health. com; Figures 5.11, 5.15, 5.19, 5.20, 5.21, and 5.23: adapted from Toates, F. (2011) *Biological Psychology*, Pearson; Figure 5.16: Horne, J. (1988) *Why We Sleep: The functions of sleep in humans and other mammals*, Oxford University Press; Figure 5.17: Silbersweig, D. A. et al. (1995) 'A functional neuroanatomy of hallucinations in schizophrenia', *Nature* vol. 378, Macmillan Publishers Ltd; Figure 5.24: adapted from Kalat, J. W. (1998) 'The sympathetic nervous system and parsympathetic nervous system', *Biological Psychology*, 6th edition, Brooks/Cole Publishing Company; Figure 5.32: Nock, M. K. and Mendes, W. B. (2008) 'Physiological arousal, distress tolerance, and social problem-solving deficits among adolescent self-injurers', *Journal of Consulting and Clinical Psychology*, vol. 76, American Psychological Association; Figure 5.33: Kringelbach, M. (2003) 'Activation of the human orbitofrontal cortex toa liquid feed stimulus is correlated with its subjective pleasantness', Cerebral Cortex, vol. 13, by kind permission of Morten Kringelbach; Figure 5.34: Macht, M. and Dettmer, D. (2006) 'Everyday mood and emotions after eating a chocolate bar or an apple', *Appetite*, vol. 46, Elsevier Science; Figure 5.35: Tse, M. M. Y. et al. (2010) 'Humor therapy: relieving chronic pain and enhancing happiness for older adults', *Journal of Aging Research*, 2010, Hindawi Publishing Corporation http://www.ncbi.nlm.nih.gov/pmc/articles/PMC2989702/; Figure 6.4: Collins, A. M. and Collins, R. M. (1969) 'Retrieval time from semantic memory', *Journal of Verbal Learning and Verbal Behaviour*, vol. 8, Academic Press.

Index